Klaus Wolfsperger · Annette Miehle-Wolfsperger

Tenerife

**88 selected walks along the coasts
and in the mountains on the 'Island of the Blest'**

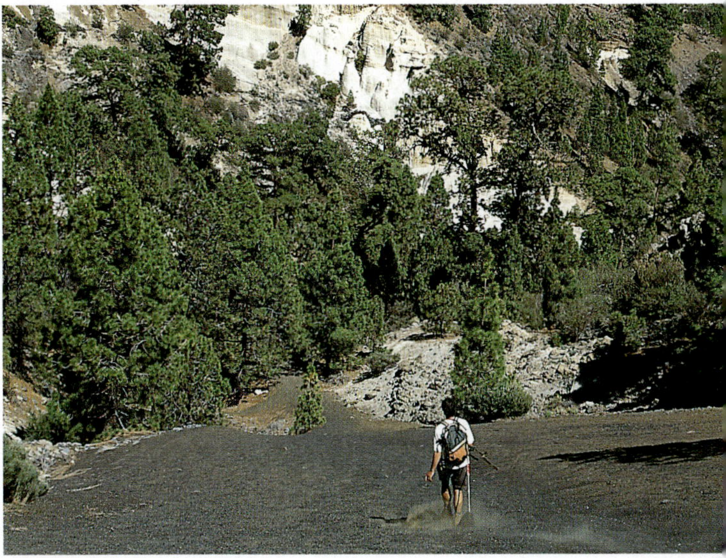

PREFACE

Tenerife can be described as the most diverse walking paradise of the Canary Islands – not only on account of Pico del Teide, at 3718m, the highest peak in the Canary Islands and, in fact, the whole of Spain, but also because the island comprises a variety of landscapes. The extremely barren, almost desert-like South boasts a number of splendid walking routes along the coast as well as at the foot of the Cumbre. In the fertile North, the countryside is dominated by agriculture: lush gardens, banana plantations, fabulous steep coastlines, friendly villages and towns characterise this picturesque region. On the northern side of the Anaga and Teno mountains you will still find a good deal of laurel forests while the slopes of the Cumbre Dorsal and the areas around the caldera are covered with extensive pine woods. However, the scenic highpoint is, without a doubt, the Lunar Landscape of the Cañadas del Teide National Park.

This guide offers walkers a wide variety of interesting walks. Always within sight of the vast, deep blue ocean, the walks range from leisurely paths to steep and precipitous coastlines, from tranquil mountain rambles to panoramic summit climbs – trails through enchanting, primeval laurisilva forests are included, as are the sometimes stone-paved caminos which formed the main linking routes between the villages in days gone by. Many of the routes are also excellent choices for less experienced walkers. Veteran mountain walkers, who do not shy away from 'extreme walks' and enjoy a shot of adventure and excitement, will also find a rich selection of routes: daring cliff walks, spectacular gorge walks and lengthy mountain treks, whose highlights are definitely the classic peaks of the national parks. Despite the variety of walks, this guide still leaves mountain enthusiasts enough space for their own discoveries.

This current edition has been thoroughly updated and extended by three walks (special thanks to the many friendly letters received). However, due to the construction of new roads, alterations to waymarking, restoration of the trail network and, not least, the constant changes made by natural elements, there will always be modifications. This also applies to the fierce forest fire in August 2023 that ravaged the Cumbre Dorsal and its magnificent pine forests – here you have to reckon with road closures and/or be prepared to face challenging hindrances (Walks 5–11, 77). We encourage you to inform the publisher of any corrections or additions that you may have encountered.

We wish you a pleasant and eventful holiday on the 'Island of the Blest'.

January 2024　　　　　　　　　　　　　　　　Klaus and Annette Wolfsperger

The dramatic Masca Gorge is at the very top of the island walker's wish list.

CONTENTS

Preface...3
   Symbols..6
Top Walks on Tenerife..8
General information...10
   Walking Grades..10
   GPS tracks and coordinates of the starting points...................12
Walking on Tenerife...15
   Leisure activities on Tenerife......................................17
Information and adresses..18
   Timetable for the most important bus routes.........................20

The North 24

TOP	**1**	4.40 hrs	Camino de Las Lecheras – from La Laguna to Santa Cruz . 26
	2	4.00 hrs	From Puerto de la Cruz to the Vista Paraíso café 30
	3	1.40 hrs	From Puerto de la Cruz to the Mirador de San Pedro 33
	4	2.00 hrs	From La Caldera to Aguamansa 36
	5	2.10 hrs	Barranco Madre del Agua 38
	6	4.00 hrs	Órganos high mountain trail 40
	7	2.00 hrs	Choza Chimoche, 1425m 44
	8	5.00 hrs	Montaña del Limón, 2106m. 46
TOP	**9**	4.10 hrs	Candelaria trail I: Aguamansa – La Crucita, 2061m 49
TOP	**10**	7.00 hrs	Candelaria trail II: Arafo – La Crucita, 2061m 52
TOP	**11**	5.25 hrs	Ventanas de Güímar 56
	12	2.00 hrs	Malpaís de Güímar. 60
	13	3.45 hrs	From Araya to Risco de la Vera 62
	14	6.40 hrs	From Realejo Alto to Chanajiga 65
	15	6.30 hrs	From the Chanajiga picnic area to Fortaleza 68
	16	2.40 hrs	From Barranco de Ruíz to San Juan de La Rambla 72
	17	2.30 hrs	From Garachico to San Juan del Reparo 76
	18	3.50 hrs	From Arenas Negras to Chinyero 78
	19	2.00 hrs	Montaña de la Botija, 2122m; Montaña Samara, 1936m .. 80

The Teno mountains and the South......................................82

	20	5.15 hrs	From Los Silos to Erjos 84
	21	3.45 hrs	Cruz de Gala, 1347m 88
	22	3.30 hrs	From Buenavista to Masca via El Palmar. 90
TOP	**23**	3.40 hrs	From El Palmar to Teno Alto. 94
TOP	**24**	4.00 hrs	Risco alpine path – from Buenavista to Teno Alto 97
	25	4.15 hrs	From Teno Alto to Punta de Teno 100
	26	2.20 hrs	Abache alpine path 102
	27	4.00 hrs	Guergue alpine path 104
TOP	**28**	5.45 hrs	Masca Gorge 108
	29	3.00 hrs	From Santiago del Teide to Masca. 112

#	Time	Route	Page
30	3.45 hrs	From Tamaimo to Santiago del Teide	115
31	3.10 hrs	Ruta del Almendro: Arguayo – Santiago del Teide	118
32	2.30 hrs	From Tamaimo onto Guama	121
33	6.20 hrs	Barranco Seco – from El Molledo to Playa Seco	124
34	5.00 hrs	From Tamaimo to Los Gigantes	128
35	2.10 hrs	From Guía de Isora to Chirche	132
36	2.45 hrs	From La Caleta to Playa Paraíso	134
37	1.45 hrs	From La Quinta to Boca del Paso	136
38	5.45 hrs	From Arona via Ifonche to Adeje	138
39	1.20 hrs	Ifonche short circular walk	143
40	3.45 hrs	Roque de los Brezos, 1108m	145
41	3.15 hrs	Conde, 1001m	147
42	5.20 hrs	From Vilaflor to Arona	150
43	4.00 hrs	From Los Cristianos to Las Galletas	154
44	2.00 hrs	From Costa del Silencio to Los Abrigos	157
45	2.15 hrs	From El Médano onto Montaña Roja	160
46	3.45 hrs	From San Miguel to Aldea Blanca	162
47	7.00 hrs	From Cruz de Tea to the Paisaje Lunar	166
48	2.40 hrs	Camino de Las Vegas	170
49	7.50 hrs	From Arico to El Contador	173
50	1.30 hrs	Arco de Tajao	178
51	2.00 hrs	Barranco de la Linde and Arco del Jurado	180

The Anaga mountains ... 182

#	Time	Route	Page
52	3.35 hrs	From Tegueste onto the Mesa de Tejina and to Bajamar	184
53	5.05 hrs	From Bajamar via Moquinal to Punta del Hidalgo	187
54	5.30 hrs	From Punta del Hidalgo to Batán de Abajo	190
55	3.20 hrs	Punta del Hidalgo – Chinamada – Las Carboneras	194
56	5.30 hrs	From Cruz del Carmen to Chinamada	197
57	2.40 hrs	From Pico del Inglés to Santa Cruz	200
58	4.25 hrs	From Valleseco over the Pico del Inglés to Taborno	203
59	3.15 hrs	Canal de Chabuco – from Valle Grande to La Galería	206
60	2.30 hrs	Roque de Taborno	210
61	4.30 hrs	From Taborno to the Playa de Tamadite	212
62	4.20 hrs	From Afur to Taganana	215
63	5.15 hrs	From the Casa Carlos to Afur	218
64	3.30 hrs	Vueltas de Taganana: Casa Forestal – Taganana	222
65	3.30 hrs	From the Casa Forestal de Anaga to Valle Brosque	224
66	5.25 hrs	From the Casa Forestal to Roque de las Bodegas	226
67	2.15 hrs	From Benijo to El Draguillo	230
68	2.10 hrs	Chinobre circular walk	232
69	2.20 hrs	Montaña Tafada, 593m	234
70	5.30 hrs	Grand Faro de Anaga circular walk	236
71	4.45 hrs	From Lomo de Las Bodegas to Playa de Anosma	240
72	6.00 hrs	From Lomo de Las Bodegas to Playa de Ijuana	242

73	4.30 hrs	From Igueste to Las Casillas	244
74	2.30 hrs	Barranco de Igueste	248
75	5.30 hrs	From Igueste to Playa de Antequera	250

The Cañadas del Teide 254
76	3.10 hrs	Fortaleza, 2159m	256
77	2.15 hrs	Volcán de Fasnia	258
78	3.30 hrs	Arenas Negras and Alto de Guamaso	260
79	4.30 hrs	Siete Cañadas – from the Parador Nacional to El Portillo	262
80	1.15 hrs	Roques de García	266
TOP 81	4.20 hrs	From Parador Nacional onto Guajara, 2718m	268
82	4.20 hrs	Paisaje Lunar	271
83	7.30 hrs	From Vilaflor onto Guajara, 2718m	274
84	2.55 hrs	Sombrero de Chasna, 2405m	277
85	5.30 hrs	Huevos del Teide and Montaña Blanca, 2748m	280
TOP 86	7.00 hrs	Pico del Teide, 3718m	283
87	4.30 hrs	From Teide via Pico Viejo, 3135m, to the Parador	288
88	6.15 hrs	From the Mirador de Chío onto Pico Viejo, 3135m	291

Index 296

SYMBOLS

Symbols in the tour headings
- accessible by bus
- places to eat along the way
- suitable for children

Symbols for height profiles
- village with bar/restaurant
- staffed hut/inn
- mountain hut/shelter
- visitor centre
- bus stop
- cable car station
- cable car ride
- summit, peak/shrine, cross
- pass, col/threshing circle
- church, chapel, monastery
- cave
- picnic site/viewpoint
- lighthouse
- bridge/gate
- tunnel/mill
- turn-off/rock arch
- remarkable tree
- boat mooring
- water tunnel/waterfall
- spring/reservoir
- swimming opportunity

Trail in the marvellous 'palm barranco' of San Andrés.

TOP WALKS ON TENERIFE

Pico del Teide
In every sense, the highpoint of Tenerife *(Walk 86, can be combined with Pico Viejo, Walk 87; 7–8 hrs).*

Guajara
Most beautiful panoramic summit on the rim of the caldera *(Walk 81; 4.20 hrs).*

Masca Gorge
An absolute must: the most famous gorge on the Canary Islands *(Walk 28; 5.45 hrs).*

Ventanas de Güímar
Spectacular canal route through the sheer rock face *(Walk 11; 5.25 hrs).*

From Tamaimo to Los Gigantes
Solitary titillating walk through the Gigantes sheer rock face *(Walk 34; 5 hrs).*

Grand Faro de Anaga walk
Fabulous circular walk at the north-eastern tip *(Walk 70; 5.30 hrs).*

From Las Carboneras to Taganana
Impressive walk across the Playa de Tamadite *(Walks 60, 61 and 62; 5 hrs).*

Candelaria trail
Traversing the Cumbre Dorsal *(Walks 9 and 10; 5.15 hrs).*

Chinobre circular walk
Atmospheric ridge walk through the laurisilva forest *(Walk 68; 2.10 hrs).*

From Punta del Hidalgo to Batán
Circular walk to the idyllic mountain valleys of Bejía and Batán *(Walk 54; 5.30 hrs).*

From Buenavista to Masca
Along the spectacular Risco path to Teno Alto, then over the Tabaiba pass to Masca *(Walks 24, 23, 22; 5 hrs).*

From La Laguna to Santa Cruz
Along the 'Milkmaids Trail' from the old capital to the new *(Walk 1; 4.40 hrs).*

GENERAL INFORMATION

Grade
Most of the walks follow distinct paths and trails. However, this should not detract from the fact that some walks demand good physical fitness, sure-footedness, a head for heights and orientation skills. Bear in mind that the difficulties can be greatly increased by inclement weather. To judge the difficulty of the suggested walks more easily, the route numbers are colour-coded as follows:

WALKING GRADES

■ = Easy
These walks follow paths which are generally wide, only moderately steep and thus relatively harmless, even in poor weather. They may also be undertaken by children and older people without any great danger.

■ = Moderate
These paths are often narrow and short stretches can be somewhat preciptious. For these reasons, these walks should only be undertaken by the sure-footed, experienced hiker. Some stretches could demand an extraordinary challenge to your orientation skills.

■ = Difficult
These walks are frequently narrow and steep. In places, they can be extremely exposed and/or are at risk from landslides. At times, the use of your hands will be required. Such routes should only be undertaken by surefooted, physically fit and experienced mountain hikers who have a head for heights and well-developed orientation skills.

Dangers
Most walks follow well-maintained, distinct trails. The text makes reference to hazards such as extreme exposure or demanding route finding. Thick fog, caused by trade wind clouds, can be expected on mountain slopes and ridges, especially from midday onwards. The clouds do not usually disperse again until the evening and can pose considerable orientation problems for mountain walkers. In addition, extremely strong and gusty winds often develop on the mountain ridges. After heavy rainfall it is wise to avoid *barrancos* and mountain slopes where there is a risk of landslides.

Best season
Tenerife is an all-year round walkers' destination, however in the winter months (November to April) the weather is not quite as stable as in the summer, and snowfall in elevations of 1500m as well as heavy rain

Typical ancient cobbled trail (Camino Real) near Arico.

showers are not uncommon. In the summer, on the other hand, extreme heat (above all, during periods of calima = Sahara wind) can be a problem, especially in the mid-elevations.

Equipment
Sturdy shoes with non-slip soles, durable trousers, sunscreen and possibly a sun hat, protective gear for the wind, rain and cold, as well as provisions and sufficient beverages are required for most of the walks.

Walking times
The times given are pure walking times and do not include rests!

Height difference
The figures are always calculated from the cumulative height differences.

Some walks – like the splendid descent here to the Playa de Ijuana – demand absolute sure-footedness and a complete lack of vertigo. These should only be undertaken by experienced mountain walkers.

From the Mirador de Humboldt, you can enjoy a fantastic view over the Orotava Valley.

Food and accommodation
With the exception of the Refugio de Altavista, the Albergue de Bolico (Las Portelas) and the Albergue Montes de Anaga (El Bailadero) there are no huts. A distinctive feature are the chozas – shelters with tables and benches.

Access
Most of the walks are accessible by public transport but sometimes a private vehicle is indispensable. A timetable for the main bus routes can be found on page 20, however, it is best to acquire an up-to-date timetable (at the local bus depots, at tourist offices or in the internet).

Emergency
The general emergency number (fire brigade, police, paramedics) is 112.

GPS TRACKS AND COORDINATES OF THE STARTING POINTS

On gps.rother.de, GPS tracks and coordinates of the starting points are available for free download which can be accessed by scanning this QR code.
8th edition, password: **480908snc**
The GPS tracks can be imported into the **Rother App**. The app tells you exactly where you are and where you are going when you are on the move. You can find instructions on **rother.de/gps**
As possible changes and errors can never be ruled out completely, we advise you to never entirely rely on GPS data for orientation, but to assess the conditions on the ground.

Maps
We recommend the walking map by Freytag & Berndt to a scale of 1:50,000. The superlative and current 4-map set (to a scale of 1:25,000) from Editorial Alpina covers the island's important walking regions (Teide, Anaga, Teno).

Waymarking and trail network (Red de Senderos de Tenerife):
Tenerife's walking trails are waymarked according to the norm of the European Walking Association (ERA):
GR (Sendero de Gran Recorrido): these long distance trails are waymarked in *white/red*. The GR 131 (Camino Natural Anaga-Chasna, 84km, La Esperanza – Arona) has already been inaugurated, the GR 133 (Camino de los Altos y Medianías, 188km, round walk from Candelaria) was planned.
PR (Sendero de Pequeño Recorrido): these less-demanding, generally full day walks are waymarked in *white/yellow*.
SL (Senderos Locales): these local walks, 10km maximum in length, are waymarked in *white/green*.

	right way	wrong way	change in direction
GR	white/red	X	⌐
PR	white/yellow	X	⌐
SL	white/green	X	⌐

Nature and the environment
Please respect all plants and animals, never leave any litter behind (also no toilet paper or tissues – please dispose of these, for example, by putting them in a plastic bag for later discarding in a bin), do not throw away cigarette stubs, do not make campfires – wildfires are not uncommon on Tenerife. Beware: In summer, due to an acute danger of forest fire, it is possible that walking trails (sometimes even all of them), can be closed.

Winter Wonderland on the Cumbre.

Taking care of the environment ...

When we are out hiking, we also leave an ecological footprint, however, being in harmony with the environment is not that difficult!

PREPARATION AND GETTING THERE
- Before you go, find out what you can do to protect the nature and the environment in the hiking area you are visiting.
- Wherever possible, use public transport such as busses and trains as well as hiking busses.
- If you travel by car, share the ride with others.
- If it's a long drive to the starting point, plan multi-day trips or find a local guesthouse from where you can do several walks.
- Try to limit air travel as much as possible and offset it by contributing to climate protection projects.

CLOTHING AND EQUIPMENT
- Buy environmentally friendly and fair-trade outdoor gear and use your clothes as long as possible.
- You can also buy second hand equipment or use rental gear.
- Fix broken things rather than buying new equipment.

FOOD
- Make sure you buy organic food as well as regional and seasonal products.
- Stay in huts and guesthouses that offer local products.
- Bring your own water bottle and sandwich box instead of buying disposable bottles or food that is wrapped in plastic.

ACCOMMODATION
- Book your accommodation directly with the locals, so they can benefit.
- Save electricity and water in huts and other places you stay in.

WHEN WALKING
- Use designated trails and avoid shortcuts.
- Respect closed trails and conservation areas.
- Don't pick flowers or take plants home with you.
- Respect forest fire warnings.
- Take your rubbish with you and dispose of it at home.
- If possible, avoid going to the toilet in the open.
- Avoid noise.
- Put your dog on a leash.

WALKING ON TENERIFE

The most varied of the Canary Islands
Just like all the other islands in the Canary Archipelago, Tenerife is of volcanic origin. In terms of its area (2057km^2) as well as its elevation (3718m), Tenerife surpasses all the other islands by far – the landscape is accordingly diverse, ranging from the desert-like and dry South to the damp North with its lush forests in middle elevations and the sub-alpine high mountain region around Pico del Teide.

The heart of the island is Pico del Teide with its dramatic caldera that has a diameter of about 16km. It constitutes the youngest part of the island which, millions of years ago, started out as three islands – Anaga, Teno and Adeje. With the upsurge of the Cumbre Dorsal and the caldera, they were subsequently joined to become one island.

Flora and Fauna
Tenerife consists of several completely different zones of vegetation depending on the altitude as well as the climatic conditions. The flora is accordingly diverse and includes countless endemics (plants found exclusively on the island). In the coastal regions several modest desert plants thrive: dragon trees and palm trees are common here, however, succulents

The pride of the Tinerfeños: red and blue bugloss on Teide (Echium).

Shelter (choza) in the Orotava Valley.

predominate the landscape (spurge and cacti) and, of course, bananas are one of the most important economic products of the island; plantations of these cultivated plants, intensively irrigated and subsidised by the State as well as the EU, cover vast areas of the coastal regions up to an elevation of about 300m.

About 20% of the island is covered by forest: the dense, jungle-like laurel forest (laurisilva forest), with the exception of a few remnants in the Anaga and Teno mountains, has been almost completely destroyed – most of the rest grows on the damp northern and eastern slopes and in gorges. Above the laurel forest is the fayal-brezal zone (tree heathers and wax-myrtles) and the sparse pine forests on the western and southern slopes. The Canary pine (Pinus canariensis) is extremely fire resistant and can survive even the most severe forest fire.

In elevations above 2000m the broom-like laburnum bushes, bearing yellow blossoms in early summer, and the white-blossoming Teide gorse dominate the landscape. A special feature of the Cañadas is the lavishly blooming, up to 2m high giant Tenerife bugloss (also called Tajinaste, found at elevations of 2800m) and the Teide violet which can be found up to 3000m.

The only mammals encountered in the mountains with any regularity are rabbits and rats. Mouflon are also very common in the Teide National Park – but these maned, wild sheep are seldom seen (in contrast to the feral goats found in Anaga and elsewhere).

National Park (Parque Nacional de las Cañadas del Teide)

The Parque Nacional de las Cañadas del Teide was established in 1954 and it was named a World Heritage Site in 2007. It basically includes the entire crater area and, with 18,990 hectares and a circumference of approximately 75km, is one of the largest national parks in Spain.

It is divided into several zones of conservation. In general, all plants and animals, and also the bizarre rock formations, are protected. Furthermore, wandering off the official walking paths and camping in the wild are prohibited. A brochure from the state-run National Park Commission provides detailed information regarding the conservation regulations. There are small exhibitions at the Visitor Centres at El Portillo and Parador (Cañada Blanca) about the history and geology of the Caldera and Teide; on request, visitors may participate in guided walks.

LEISURE ACTIVITIES ON TENERIFE

Animal parks
The Loro Parque in Puerto de la Cruz has the largest collection of parrots in the world – in addition, orcas, dolphins, sea lions, crocodiles, penguins, monkeys and a shark tunnel; also the Parque Las Aguilas at Las Américas.

Botanical gardens
Jardín Botánico, Puerto de la Cruz (luxuriant tropical and subtropical flora). Bananera El Guanche, Puerto de la Cruz (banana cultivation). Jardines del Atlántico near Buzanada, Valle de San Lorenzo (cross-section of Canary Island plants). Cactus park at Los Cristianos (large collection of cacti).

Canyoning
The deep-cut, mostly dry *barrancos* offer adventurous gorge trips, amongst others, Barranco del Infierno, del Río, the gorges on the steep coast of Gigantes (Barranco del Carrizal, etc.) and in the Anaga mountains.

Caves
There are numerous caves – the most famous, the Cueva del Viento near Icod, is open to visitors (www.cuevadelviento.net).

Climbing
There are several good crags for climbing on the island: Catedral and Cañada del Capricho in the Cañadas, Arico (3km towads the Contador valley), Las Vegas (near Granadilla), Guía de Isora (2.5km towards Adeje, then left to Acojeja), Tabares (near Santa Cruz), Mesa de Tejina, Playa de San Marcos.

Donkey and dromedary safaris
The donkey (Arafo, Buzanada, Santiago del Teide) and dromedary safaris (El Tanque, Las Galletas) are very popular.

Forest Adventure Park
High ropes course with spectacular zip-lines in Las Lagunetas, at Km 16 on the TF-24 La Esperanza – Teide (www.forestalpark.com/tenerife).

Golf
Several golf courses, eg. at Las Galletas, Tacoronte and Buenavista.

Mountain biking
The island offers ideal conditions for both leisurely and adventurous trips, especially around Teide National Park.

Museums
Museo Arqueólogico in Santa Cruz (valuable collection of remains of Guanche culture artefacts). Pirámides de Güímar Ethnographic Park (step pyramids).

Teide cable car
The cable car (2356–3555m) is one of the attractions of the Cañadas; service discontinued in storms/snow/ice.

Water parks
Lago Martiánez in Puerto de la Cruz is the island's largest seawater swimming pool. Another large one is the seawater swimming pool in Santa Cruz. In addition, Siam Park and Aguapark Octopus in Las Américas.

Whale-watching
There are many excursion boats in the south of the island (Los Cristianos, Playa de San Juán, Los Gigantes) especially dolphin and whale-watching trips.

INFORMATION AND ADRESSES

Getting there
Flights are available to Tenerife from all the major airports in Great Britain and Europe. There are ferry and flight connections to the Spanish mainland and to all of the Canary Islands.

Information
Tourist information: Oficina de Turismo de Tenerife, Plaza de España, E-38003 Santa Cruz de Tenerife, tel. +34 922 281 287, webtenerife.com.

Camping
There are campgrounds, e.g., at Guía de Isora, Las Galletas, El Médano, Tajao/Abades, Mesa del Mar and Punta del Hidalgo (campsites run by the *Cabildo*: centralreservas.tenerife.es/?a=5). Wild camping is not permitted.

Theft
The crime rate is relatively high, therefore never leave valuables unattended in the car or anywhere else.

Climate
Tenerife is characterised by a subtropical climate with slight temperature

CLIMATE TABLE FOR PUERTO DE LA CRUZ														
		Jan	Feb	Mar	Apr	May	June	July	Aug	Sep	Oct	Nov	Dec	Ø
Maximum temperature	°C	19	19	20	21	22	23	24	26	26	24	22	20	22
Minimum temperature	°C	13	13	14	14	16	18	19	20	20	18	17	14	16
Water temperature	°C	19	19	19	19	20	20	22	23	22	22	21	20	20
Hours of sun/day	h	5	6	7	8	9	10	11	10	8	6	6	5	7
Days of rain/month		10	7	8	4	3	2	1	1	3	5	7	9	5

Almond blossom time (January, February) is for many the most beautiful time of year.

fluctuations. The weather is determined by the trade winds which bring warm, moist air masses from the north-east that collect in the mountains and often cover large areas of the island, especially in the north, in a thick blanket of clouds.

Taxi
There's a taxi rank in almost all of the larger settlements – otherwise, you can usually phone for a taxi from a local bar.

Telephone
The dialling code for Spain/Tenerife is 0034/922. The dialling code for Great Britain from the Canary Islands is 0044, for the USA 001.

Walking organisations and guides
There are several walking organisations (ask in the hotels).

TIMETABLE FOR THE MOST IMPORTANT BUS ROUTES

100   **Puerto de la Cruz**   **– Santa Cruz**   (Direct bus)
No intermediate bus stops Puerto de la Cruz – Santa Cruz
Mon-Fri 6.15, 6.50, 9.30, 10.00, 13.50, 15.15   7.00, 7.40, 9.10, 10.25, 11.10, 16.15, 18.30

102   **Puerto de la Cruz**   **– Santa Cruz**   (via La Laguna)
Bus 103 (no intermediate stops) Puerto de la Cruz – La Laguna – Santa Cruz
daily   6.05–20.10 every 30 mins   6.25–20.35 every 30 mins

343   **Puerto de la Cruz**   **– Los Cristianos**   (EXPRESS bus)
Mon-Fri 6.00, 10.15, 14.45, 18.00   9.30, 12.45, 17.30, 21.30
Sat/Sun 6.00, 9.20, 13.40, 16.50   9.00, 12.05, 16.20, 19.20

325   **Puerto de la Cruz**   **– Los Gigantes**   (via Icod de los Vinos)
daily   5.45, 9.00, 10.35, 15.50, 18.45   8.15, 11.00, 12.35, 18.30, 20.45
Sat/Sun 6.20, 10.45, 15.00   8.30, 12.35, 17.30

363   **Puerto de la Cruz**   **– Buenavista del Norte**
(via Realejo Bajo–San Juan de la Rambla–Icod–Garachico–Los Silos)
daily   6.10–21.30 every 30–40 mins   6.00–20.00 every 30–40 mins

345   **Puerto de la Cruz**   **– La Caldera**
(via El Botánico–La Orotava–Aguamansa, * only to/from Aguamansa)
daily   *6.45, *7.45, 8.45– 16.45 every hr,   *6.45, *7.45, *8.45, 9.45–17.45 every hr,
*17.45, *19.45, *20.45, *22.10   *18.45, *19.45, *20.45, *21.45

348   **Puerto de la Cruz**   **– Las Cañadas (Parador Nacional)**
(via El Botánico–La Orotava–Aguamansa–El Portillo–Teléferico)
daily   9.30   16.00

360   **Icod de los Vinos**   **– Puerto de Erjos**
(via El Amparo–La Vega–La Montañeta–San José de Los Llanos)
daily   7.15, 9.30, 11.40, 14.40, 18.30   7.50, 10.10, 12.20, 15.45, 19.10

460   **Icod de los Vinos**   **– Las Américas**
(via El Tanque–Erjos–Santiago del Teide–Tamaimo–Chío–Guía de Isora)
daily   5.45, 7.35, 10.00, 11.50, 14.00, 16.10, 18.15,   5.45, 7.45, 9.50, 11.55, 14.10, 16.00, 18.25, 20.00
20.15

355   **Buenavista del Norte**   **– Santiago del Teide**
(via El Palmar–Las Portelas–Masca, * Linie 365 only to/from Masca)
daily   *6.20, 9.35, 12.00, *14.20, 15.45, 17.55   *6.50, 11.00, 13.05, *14.50, 15.05, 17.00, 19.30

366   **Buenavista del Norte**   **– Las Portelas**   (via El Palmar)
Mon-Fri 5.25, 7.35, 8.20, 15.10, 20.20   5.40, 7.55, 8.40, 15.35, 20.35

473   **Los Cristianos**   **– Los Gigantes**
(via Las Américas–Adeje–Armeñime–San Juan–Alcalá–Puerto Santiago)
daily   5.20–20.05 every 30–45 mins   6.20–21.55 every 30–45 mins

480   **Los Cristianos**   **– Arona**
Mon-Fri 7.30, 8.45, 9.30, 10.15, 11.30, 13.00, 14.35,   5.30, 7.15, 8.00, 8.40, 9.15, 10.45, 12.00, 13.55, 15.05,
15.45, 16.55, 18.25, 19.35, 20.40   16.15, 17.25, 18.55, 20.05
Sat/Sun 7.30, 9.00, 10.00, 13.05, 14.00, 15.00, 16.00,   5.30, 8.00, 9.30, 10.30, 13.30, 14.25, 15.25, 16.25, 19.30
19.05, 20.00

482	**Los Cristianos**	**– Vilaflor**	**(via Arona, La Escalona)**

Mon–Fri 5.55, 8.05, 11.00, 14.05, 15.25, 17.35, 21.10   6.30, 9.30, 12.10, 15.20, 16.25, 19.05, 21.50
Sat/Sun 5.50, 11.00, 17.25   6.35, 12.00, 18.10

342	**Las Américas**	**– Las Cañadas (El Portillo)**	

(via Los Cristianos–Arona–La Escalona–Vilaflor–Parador Nacional–Teleférico)
daily 9.15 (9.30 Los Cristianos)   15.15 (15.40 Teleférico, 16.00 Parador)

341	**Parador (Roques de García)**	**– El Portillo**	

daily 11.05, 12.00, 13.00, 14.00, 16.00   10.45, 12.00, 12.50, 14.40, 15.15

111	**Las Américas**	**– Santa Cruz**	

(EXPRESS bus via Los Cristianos–Aeropuerto Sur)
daily 5.55–21.25 every 30 mins   5.55–21.25 every 30 mins

946	**Santa Cruz**	**– Taganana (– Almáciga)**	

(via San Andrés–Kreuzung El Bailadero) (Almáciga 10 mins earlier)
Mon–Fri 5.10, 5.50, 6.55, 10.30, 13.10, 14.25, 17.15, 19.35   6.00, 6.50, 7.55, 11.40, 14.20, 15.40, 18.20, 20.35
Sat/Sun 6.45, 9.10, 11.40, 14.15, 17.05, 19.55   7.55, 10.15, 12.45, 15.30, 18.10, 21.00

947	**Santa Cruz**	**– Chamorga**	**(via El Bailadero)**

Mon–Fri 5.10, 15.00, 18.00   6.20, 16.30, 19.25
Sat/Sun 7.00, 10.15, 15.00, 18.25   8.20, 11.45, 16.30, 19.55

945	**Santa Cruz**	**– Igueste**	**(via San Andrés–Teresitas)**

Mon–Fri 5.15, 7.30, 9.30, 11.35, 14.10, 16.10, 18.15   6.40, 8.10, 10.25, 12.20, 15.10–21.10 every 2 hrs
Sat/Sun 6.40, 8.40, 10.40, 12.30–20.30 every 2 hrs   7.30–21.30 every 2 hrs

050	**La Laguna**	**– Punta del Hidalgo**	

(via Tegueste–Tejina–Bajamar)
daily 6.00–20.30 every 30 mins, 22.05   6.25–21.55 every 30 mins

273	**La Laguna**	**– Pico del Inglés**	**(via Cruz del Carmen)**

Sat/Sun 9.25, 11.00   9.50, 11.25

274	**La Laguna**	**– El Batán**	**(via Cruce El Moquinal)**

Mon–Fri 7.30, 9.05 (Sat/Sun), 14.15 (Sat/Sun), 15.05, 18.00 6.45, 8.15, 9.50 (Sat/Sun), 15.00 (Sat/Sun), 15.50, 18.45

275	**La Laguna**	**– Taborno (*Las Carboneras 15 mins earlier)**	

Mon–Fri 5.25, 6.50, 9.35, 13.15, 15.25, 18.50   7.35, 10.20, *14.15, *16.20, *19.50
Sat/Sun 7.25, 12.00, 16.05   8.10, *13.00, *17.00

076	**La Laguna**	**– Afur**	**(via Las Canteras–C.d. Carmen)**

daily 7.00, 13.30, 16.05, 19.00 (Mon–Fri)   6.00 (Mon–Fri), 8.00, 14.35, 17.30, 20.00 (Mon–Fri)

077	**La Laguna**	**– El Bailadero**	**(via Cruz del Carmen)**

daily 10.25, 18.00 (Sat/Sun)   11.40, 19.15 (Sat/Sun)

Tip: if you are making many trips by bus/tram, you could consider the Ten+ or TenMas ticket.
The TITSA timetable is available at the local bus depots or at tourist offices, tel. +34 922 53 13 00, titsa.com
Timetable for the Tranvía (tram) Santa Cruz – La Laguna at metrotenerife.com
Beware: Dogs are not permitted in the busses or trams.

The North
Garden landscape at the foot of the Cumbre

The northern part of the island is the garden of Tenerife: banana plantations along the coasts and quaint villages characterise this traditionally agricultural region on both sides of the Cumbre Dorsal and at the northern foot of Teide.

Visitors travelling on the motorway from La Laguna heading to the northern side of the Cumbre and down to the almost 10km wide Orotava Valley will be immediately struck by the sprawling countryside, gently sloping down to the sea and dominated by Teide, which is sometimes snow-covered in winter. Puerto de la Cruz is the tourist centre of the region. This fashionable seaside resort, probably the island's most beautifully situated, offers the holiday-maker ideal conditions for a voyage of contrasts on the island: a varied choice of tourist activities, beautiful gardens, majestic cliffs with picturesque beaches and excellent connections by public transport. Many walkers favour Puerto due to its proximity to the forests of the upper Orotava Valley. Those preferring more diverse walking routes choose the higher elevations of the Cumbre Dorsal at the foot of Teide, following beautiful walking trails that start from the Orotava Valley. The southern side of the Cumbre Dorsal, especially the Güímar Valley, likewise bordered by two massive rock faces, has also been opened up and developed with a few excellent walking routes.

The Milenario dragon tree in Icod de los Vinos – the oldest dragon tree on the island.

To the west of the Orotava Valley in the higher elevations, there are extensive pine forests which give way abruptly to the black sand and lava terrain at the foot of Teide and Pico Viejo – an almost endless walking region, still widely undiscovered.

The beaches also leave nothing to be desired – especially Camello beach near Mesa del Mar, Jardín beach and Bollullo bay near Puerto de la Cruz, Socorro beach near La Rambla and San Marcos beach near Icod de los Vinos. Be aware that all beaches have one thing in common – an exceptionally dangerous surf, especially in winter.

STARTING POINTS FOR WALKS

La Orotava–El Portillo road

This road which leads through the rural Orotava Valley and then from Aguamansa through the sprawling pine forest on to El Portillo (the north-eastern entrance to the Parque Nacional de las Cañadas del Teide) is an ideal starting point for walks in the upper Orotava Valley. Some of the car parks for walkers located along the way are Aguamansa (environment centre and forestry house, km 15), turn-off to La Caldera Zona recreativa (picnic area with barbecue sites, km 16), Choza Bermeja (Km 21), Choza Wildpret (Km 23.5), Choza Bethencourt (Km 25.9) and Choza Sventenius (Km 29.2).

Cumbre Dorsal high ridge road

The ridge road TF-24 connecting La Laguna with La Esperanza, Izaña and El Portillo not only boasts numerous *miradores*, offering wonderful downward views of the northern and eastern coasts, but also starting points for lovely walking excursions through the Esperanza forest (e.g. from Las Lagunetas to Gaitero, 1¾ hrs) and into the Güímar and upper Orotava Valleys.

Further ideal starting points are, amongst others, the picnic sites of Chanajiga (near Las Llanadas), La Corona (near Icod el Alto), El Lagar (near La Guancha) and Las Arenas Negras (near La Montañeta).

TOP 1

Camino de Las Lecheras – from La Laguna to Santa Cruz

↗ 290m | ↘ 840m | 16.4km
4.40 hrs

Along the 'Milkmaids Trail' from the sometime capital to the modern one – sightseeing included

What a walk! No, not because of the landscape, which is rather less than spectacular since the route runs often over tarmac and is only pretty along some sections – but nevertheless, this ancient connecting route between the island's two most important cities exudes an extraordinary charm. Is this because of its history? Up until the 1960s, the trail was used by milkmaids (lecheras) that plied the toilsome trail to carry cow's milk from the dairy farms in the countryside to La Laguna and to Santa Cruz. In any case, the trail has a lot to offer: after a stroll through the lovely old town of La Laguna, it continues over green hills to the Valle Jiménez and then along the mighty Barranco de Santos to descend to Santa Cruz. Afterwards, a special treat can be enjoyed with the return trip, using the tram that runs to La Laguna.

The prelude: view taking in Las Mercedes and La Laguna with Teide in the background. Page left: the Camino de Las Lecheras begins at La Laguna's Church of the Immaculate Conception (left) and ends at the Church of the Immaculate Conception in Santa Cruz (right).

Starting point: Plaza de la Concepción (parish church) in La Laguna, 555m. A good 5 mins on foot from the bus station (via Calle San Antonio). If you approach by car, it is best to park in one of the large car parks at the Plaza del Adelantado at the eastern city limits (near the TF-13).
Destination: Tranvía tram stop 'Fundacion' (line 1) at the Plaza de la Iglesia in Santa Cruz (the return to La Laguna, terminus La Trinidad, takes a good ½ hr and, from there, a good 10 mins on foot to the bus station or a good 5 mins to the Plaza del Adelantado).
Grade: mostly an easy walk along trails and roads. *White/yellow* waymarked although the stretch of trail from Degollada de los Horneros to Valle Jiménez is not marked. A fair head for heights is demanded between El Roque and Cueva Roja even though the trail is sufficiently broad and well-secured.
Refreshment: bar/restaurant Casa Horacio in Valle Jiménez, bar/restaurants in La Laguna and Santa Cruz.
Alternative: you could begin or end the walk in Valle Jiménez (bus lines 228, 912).

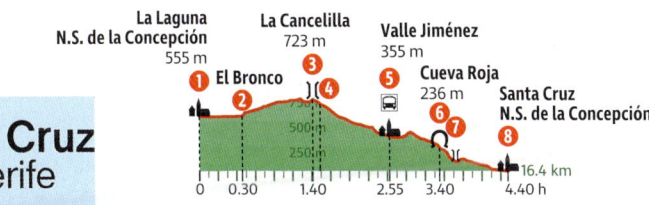

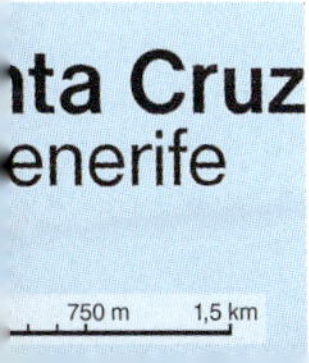

Backwards view from El Roque taking in the Hilario valley and towards Valle Jiménez.

From the bell tower of the church **Nuestra Señora de la Concepción** ❶ follow the Calle Obispo Rey Redondo (boasting lovely mansions) in a southeasterly direction. 400m further on, pass the cathedral with its mighty dome. 200m after that, turn left onto the Calle Viana (the Calle Obispo Rey Redondo continues to the nearby Plaza del Adelantado where the town hall is located) – this street is also pedestrianised and leads past the convent of Santa Catalina de Siena to reach the spacious Plaza del Cristo with indoor market. Cross over the square by bearing somewhat to the right and then follow the street (Camino La Rúa) keeping in the same direction as before (*white/yellow* waymarked). 350m on, the street hooks right, following the course of the stream. Afterwards, at the junction, turn left and then take the underpass below the ring road TF-13. Just after the underpass, bear right and then left, ascending along the Camino El Bronco ❷. The road ascends steeply for a short stretch and then bears left to continue parallel to the ridge whilst presenting a view of the valley between La Laguna and Las Mercedes lying below. A good half hour later (now on a track) reach a fork near a walled-in property – here, turn diagonally right to ascend along the right-hand side of the ridgeline. Near a goat pen, the farm road becomes a path; continue along it to a trail of stone plates – take this trail to the right, passing a little cistern, then turn left onto the trail leading to the other side of the valley. The trail now crosses over the next ridge by passing through a breach in the rock with a gate, **La Cancelilla** ❸. Now along a marvellous high mountain trail, pass the Cuevas de Hilario whilst descending to the **Degollada de los Horneros** ❹ (gate). From here, enjoy a lovely view taking in the Barranco de Carmona all the way to Santa Cruz.

Unfortunately, the trail through the Barranco de Camona is closed, so we must turn left past the gate onto a farm road descending through the Hilario valley (it would be nicer to take the path that turns left before the gate but this is often very muddy and slippery). The farm road is sometimes paved in concrete or tarmac and passes scattered farm-

Starting at El Roque, we have Santa Cruz constantly in view.

steads. Past a junction, catch a lovely view of the Tahodio reservoir. In Lomo de Las Casillas the farm road merges with the TF-111. Turn left to continue. At the height 150m on, to the right of the little bus shelter (lines 228/912) meet a farm road that forks away. 30m along this road a camino (Camino Pedegrales) forks away to the right and, some minutes later, merges into a road. In **Valle Jiménez**, opposite the bar/restaurant Casa Horacio ❺ this road joins the TF-111 (bus stop for line 228).

Still before reaching the TF-111, turn left onto a narrow road (*Camino Real El Toscal*) that continues the descent in the Hilario Valley. Soon change over to the left side of the valley. Now the road ascends steeply whilst opening a lovely view to reach **El Roque**, with a viewpoint that is just perfect for a long break. The following stretch, high above the clamorous capital, is most certainly the cherry on the cake for this walk – it traverses a steep slope, sometimes secured with railings and cable. Directly next to the immense **Cueva Roja** ❻ it merges into a road. We continue the ascent on the opposite side (now waymarked *white/yellow*). Past a *mirador*, the road becomes a stepped trail that descends whilst opening a spectacular view of Santa Cruz. At the end of the steps, meet up with the Ctra. los Campitos (right) and at the following junction, continue straight on via the stepped trail. At the next fork, bear left (Calle Tamarcos), then right (Calle Los Santos) and descend along the **Barranco de Santos** ❼ (bridge, Camino la Ermita). Now cross over a major road and afterwards turn left onto the Calle Banahoare to climb down to the next bridge. Here, turn right to descend steps to the Avenida Barranco Molina and then follow the *barranco* to continue the descent. Follow the waymarking to cross over to the other side of the road. Subsequently, we pass the Ramblas, the city's promenade. At Clavijo Park the waymarkers lead to the right-hand side of the street, afterwards keep to the right along the edge of the *barranco*. Now, it is not much further to the bell tower of the church **Nuestra Señora de la Concepción** ❽, the tram stop is located directly behind it (direction is to La Trinidad/La Laguna).

2 From Puerto de la Cruz to the Vista Paraíso café

↗ 560m | ↘ 560m | 13.1km
4.00 hrs

Stroll along the steep coast on the Camino de la Costa

The well-maintained, mostly paved Camino de la Costa is one of the most popular walking routes in Puerto – leading from the Mirador de la Paz along a charming panoramic promenade to Hotel Semiramis and from there through banana plantations to what is probably the most beautiful beach in the north of the island, Playa del Bollullo. Due to the dangerous undercurrents and a powerful surf, the fine sandy beach is only suitable for swimming during calm seas. From here we recommend ascending to one of the most famous panoramic spots in Tenerife, the Vista Paraíso café – although the ascent requires surefootedness and good hiking boots on a sometimes rather steep and slippery path.

Starting point: Puerto de la Cruz, 15m, Playa de Martiánez at the eastern end of the shoreline promenade.
Grade: easy walk on broad trails and roads – only the ascent to the Vista Paraíso café follows a steep and narrow path (unpleasantly rough at the outset).
Refreshment: bar/restaurant Bollullo, café/restaurant San Diego (closed on Wednesdays), Café Vista Paraíso (closed on Mondays), bars and restaurants in Cuesta de la Villa.

Bollullo beach is one of the finest sandy bays on the island. Nevertheless, you can expect huge waves in the winter months.

From **Martiánez beach** ❶ walk up the palm-lined avenue Avenida Aguilar y Quesada between the San Felipe and Atlantis hotels. Past the Martiánez shopping centre (on your left, 5 mins) – at the Plaza Viera y Clavijo square (planted with palm trees) – turn left up the steps of the Camino las Cabras which connects the old town with the districts of La Paz and El Botánico. A few minutes later it merges with a wider promenade (Camino San Amaro); continue the ascent to the left. Benches on this pretty stepped footpath repeatedly offer the walker nice spots for a break. 5 minutes later, meet up with a road and turn left towards the **Mirador de la Paz** ❷.
Enjoying a tremendous view down to Puerto de la Cruz and Martiánez beach, now continue above the steep coastline along the balcony-like Camino de la Costa, passing several cafés and blocks of apartments. At the Semiramis hotel (a total of half an hour) the camino merges into the Calle Leopoldo Cólogan Zulueta; turn left here to follow the route. The Camino de La Costa continues straight on. Soon leave the last villas and holiday complexes behind (bear left at a fork). At first the wide footpath

passes above the eastbound arterial road leading out of town but soon passes under it to the left through a tunnel. You are now surrounded by banana plantations. About 10 mins after the tunnel, cross the Barranco de la Arena to reach a narrow road on the other side of the *barranco* and continue straight on along this (to the right at the edge of the *barranco* – the trail leading to the Vista Paraíso café). After just a few minutes, at the **Bollullo restaurant** ❸, a trail branches off to the left, leading high above the **Playa del Bollullo** ❹ along the steep coastline – at the eastern end of the beautiful sandy bay a set of broad steps leads down to the beach where you will also find a snack bar. Incidentally, above the cliffs, a path continues that leads for a short stretch to the right of a wall (to the left of the wall, the terrain has fallen away) and, a good 5 minutes later, turns right through a little *barranco* to ascend to the road in El Rincón (a possible short-cut to the Vista Paraíso café).

Back at the edge of Barranco de la Arena, walk uphill along the narrow road keeping left. Not quite 15 mins later, pass the San Diego café/restaurant in the hamlet of **El Rincón** ❺. To the right, along the wide tarmac road, it is possible to ascend to La Orotava, but we continue straight on between the banana and avocado plantations. 15 mins after that, the road ends at a gate (possible descent on the left along a camino to the beautiful, although tiny, strip of beach at the Playa del Ancón, ¼ hr; then continue straight ahead through a vineyard and then along a steep slope (the first stretch somewhat buried in debris but no serious hindrance) climbing steeply to Santa Úrsula, ½ hr; here, keep bearing right along the streets and, in 10 mins, reach the bus stop by the motorway exit La Orotava; see below). Directly in front of the gate, a trail leads on the right between walls up to the Vista Paraíso café. It ascends steeply for a few minutes and then takes a short turn to the right to join the previous main trail. Sometimes stone-paved, this trail continues a zigzag ascent steeply up to the left. After a few steps, the trail eventually joins a road in a villa complex that brings you left to the traditional **Café Vista Paraíso** ❻ (150m). Delicious cakes and a magnificent view of Puerto de la Cruz and the Orotava Valley from the terrace more than make up for the strenuous ascent.

If you do not wish to return the same way to Puerto, you can continue the ascent along the wide trail diagonally across from the café. This soon merges with a road that leads along the northbound motorway. Head along the road to the left, then to the right over the bridge (motorway exit La Orotava) to Cuesta de la Villa. On the main road there is a bus stop immediately to the right (10 mins from the Vista Paraíso café; No 101 bus to La Orotava and, from there, with bus 253, return to Puerto de la Cruz).

↗ 360m | ↘ 320m | 5.4km

1.40 hrs
🚌 🍴 🚻

From Puerto de la Cruz to the Mirador de San Pedro 3

Popular coastal walk with a possible extension

The two coastal walking trails that set off from Puerto de la Cruz are amongst the most popular walks on Tenerife. Since they are both short-distance, the walks offer hardly more than a good ramble. However, plans have been made, for the foreseeable future, to extend the western stretch to continue on as far as San Juan de La Rambla.

Starting point: Loro Parque in Punta Brava, at the western city limits of Puerto de la Cruz, 15m. Bus stop for the 381 and the Loro-Parque open-air shuttle 'train'. Alternatively, the Hotel Maritim.
Destination: Mirador de San Pedro, 130m, busstop for the 330, 363.
Grade: easy walk on leisurely caminos and roads.
Refreshment: bar/restaurants in Punta Brava, La Romántica II and at the Mirador de San Pedro (closed on Mondays).
Alternative: from the Mirador de San Pedro to the Playa del Socorro and to San Juan de La Rambla: 30m before the bar/restaurant, the coastal trail continues on the right past the chapel. After a few minutes, it joins a road that leads downhill left and then after 25m turns right through banana plantations to the Playa del Socorro ('Help Beach', bar; 20 mins) — a paradise for surfers; ordinary swimmers, on the other hand, need to take care. The continuation of the trail to San Juan can only be recommended to hardened hikers (only at low tide and when the sea is calm): follow the coarse pebble beach practically without a path (very strenuous) and, after 25 mins, pass below a few derelict houses (El Terrero). A good 10 mins later you reach an enormous boulder about 10m high (El Roquillo) — go left here steeply uphill to a stone wall to meet a well-maintained trail that ascends to a house. Past the houses, the trail descends into the Barranco de Ruíz and ascends steeply on the other side to a house. Now continue along a marvellous coastal promenade through La Rambla (a good hour from the Playa del Socorro; after a few minutes you can go up left to the TF-5 near the Barranco de Ruíz picnic site, bus stop). 20 mins later, along the coastal trail, reach the village of Las Aguas (bar/restaurants, swimming pool). From here climb up the access road to the TF-5 main road in San Juan de La Rambla (¼ hr; bus stop, the *plaza* is on the right along the village road).

From the main entrance of the **Loro Parque** ① follow the main road in a westerly direction and, just under 10 mins later, after the first high-rise building on the right (**Hotel Maritim**; ②), turn right onto a road. The coastal trail starts at the end of this road and then immediately forks: straight ahead is the former path (now closed but possible to undertake at your own risk). Head left up the broad cobbled path. A few minutes later, turn right to join the Calle El Cedro at the first houses. Follow this straight ahead to the **Mirador de Los Roques** ③ (beautiful view over rock islands to the Hotel Maritim), where the former path joins the road.

Now we have entered **La Romántica II villa estate**. Cross over the estate by continuing straight ahead along the road. After some minutes the road veers to the left and 100m after that the signposted coastal trail turns off on the right (after 50m camino). Later on it passes below **La Romántica I** villa estate and then crosses the Barranco El Patronato over a bridge. Immediately afterwards ignore trails ④ turning off right to the derelict Casa Hamilton (formerly a water-pumping house) and to the Playa de La Fajana. Now bear left up along the broad concrete track. After 5 mins keep right at the barrier and shortly afterwards the trail narrows again and descends steeply down into the Barranco del Agua, which you again cross on a bridge. Immediately afterwards at the fork stay on the main trail straight ahead (a trail turns off right to the stony Playa de La Fajana where there's a waterworks, 10 mins). 100m later the trail divides again: if you want to continue along the direct way to the Mirador de San Pedro carry straight on. Otherwise turn off right and soon afterwards pass above the Fort San Fernando (on the right there are detours to the fort and to a tunnel) and walk more or less on the level over to a beautiful old manor house, **La Casona** ⑤. From here ascend along the broad paved trail up to the main road,

Casa Hamilton (above left), La Casona (below left) and Rambla del Castro (above).

the TF-5 Puerto de la Cruz – Icod de los Vinos (a good 10 mins). 200m on the left, on San Vicente's village limits, there's a bus stop, on the right, the **Mirador de San Pedro** ❻ with a chapel and a bar/restaurant.
If you want to extend the walk you can continue further along the coastal trail to Playa del Socorro and to San Juan de La Rambla (see Alternative).

↗ 210m | ↘ 360m | 6.4km

4 From La Caldera to Aguamansa

2.00 hrs

🚌 ✕ 👥

Popular circular walk in the pine forests of the upper Orotova Valley

This short circular walk through the splendid pine forests in the upper Orotava Valley is definitely a must for every holidaymaker to Tenerife. The trail leads from the La Caldera picnic grounds, nestled in a natural crater, past the Órganos rock formations and then down to Aguamansa. The environment centre there is worth a visit.

Location: Aguamansa, 1000m.
Starting point: Zona recreativa La Caldera, 1192m (picnic area, bus terminus for the 345, 346).
Destination: Aguamansa, 1043m (bus stop for the 345, 346).
Grade: mostly leisurely walk on forest tracks and roads.
Refreshment: bar/restaurant at the Zona recreativa La Caldera (closed in 2023), bar/restaurants in Aguamansa.
Alternative: from the bus stop in Aguamansa walk back to La Caldera picnic area (about 25 mins): continue ascending for 50m along the main road and then turn right onto the narrow road that ascends along the fence of the environment centre. Just before the road ends in front of a gate, a camino turns off to the left. 5 mins later, the camino merges with the *GR 131* (*white/red/green*, here continue straight ahead). Soon after, the trail crosses a track – via a tunnel, go under the main road and then ascend in 10 mins to the La Caldera picnic area.
Linking tip: with Walk 5.

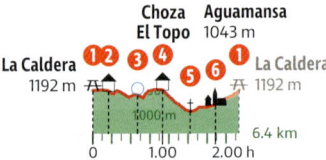

From the bus terminus at **La Caldera** picnic area ❶ follow the road left past the restaurant and, 2 minutes later, turn left onto a wide forest road (signpost to 'Los Órganos'). After 10 minutes, pass the **Choza Pedro Gil** ❷ (shelter; water tap; the Camino de Candelaria branches off to the right), 5 minutes later, continue below the Órganos rock formations – erosion has virtually sculptured 'organ pipes' out of this enormous basalt rock

Along the return route to Aguamansa, pass by fields and orchards.

face. Enjoying the partial shade cast by massive pines, the wide track now leads through the Barranco Madre del Agua where, after a good half an hour, you pass a large waterworks ❸. 5 minutes later, ignore a forest track branching off to the left. From time to time you are able to catch some views of Teide and the Orotava Valley – you can make out Puerto de la Cruz on the coast, and when visibility permits, even see La Palma in the distance. After a total of one hour, reach the **Choza El Topo** shelter ❹.

Here a trail branches off to the left, descending in zigzags through the pine and scrub wood. After a good 5 minutes, the trail forks – go straight on (right) continuing downhill. Just under 10 minutes later, reach a trail junction and descend the steep forest road to the left. A few minutes later, the forest road merges into a narrow road ending here. Now continue the descent along this road down through fields.

At the fork 5 minutes later (shrine ❺) bear left uphill (to the right leads to La Florida); a few minutes later, at the next junction, turn right. The narrow road then crosses two *barrancos* (in the second one, you could turn left onto the *white/yellow* marked PR TF 35 to ascend to the Casa Forestal/environment centre) and finally merges with the steep village street of **Aguamansa** ❻ onto which you turn left and ascend to the bus stop on the main road (200m further up, the Casa Forestal environment centre).

(Return to the La Caldera picnic area in 25 mins see Alternative.)

↗ 320m | ↘ 320m | 6.9km

5 Barranco Madre del Agua

2.10 hrs

🚌 👣

Circular walk on ancient water channel trails

This route through the impressive Barranco Madre del Agua which had almost faded into obscurity, was restored in 2009 and is a reminder of the history of irrigation in the upper Orotava Valley.

Location: Aguamansa, 1000m.
Starting point: Zona recreativa La Caldera, 1192m (picnic area, bus terminus for the 345, 346).
Grade: gentle forest track walk at the start, then frequently along steep forest trails.
Refreshment: bar/restaurant at La Caldera picnic area (closed in 2023).

Linking tip: with Walks 4 and 6.

From the car park with the bus terminus at **La Caldera** picnic area ❶ follow the road to the left (PR TF 35/GR 131) running past the restaurant and after 2 minutes turn left onto the broad forest road (amongst others, signpost to 'Los Órganos'). Keep always straight on along this road past the **Choza Pedro Gil** ❷ (just under 10 minutes) and the Los Órganos rocks. After a good half an hour, ignore the PR TF 35.2 forking off to the right (this is your return route later on). 2 minutes later, the forest road passes a large **waterworks** ❸ (Casa del Agua) in the Barranco Madre del Agua.

Next to this building, a camino turns off right (PR TF 35.2, *white/yellow*, Ruta del Agua) which becomes steep only a few minutes later and ascends, sometimes climbing steps, at the edge of the impressive deep-cut **Barranco Madre del Agua**. It runs along beside an old water canal and, after a quarter of an hour, meets a broad camino (coming up from a forest road) which you now continue to follow uphill. 5 minutes later, the trail forks – left goes through the bottom of the *barranco* to a ravine with a derelict stone house. After this short detour, continue right and, at the next fork after 10m, keep straight on ❹ (a very steep zigzag path turns off left to the Órganos high mountain trail; 20 minutes.

The trail now runs gently up and down across the slope and, after

Aqueduct and water distributor (below) at the side of the path.

10 minutes, passes a galería (access trail on the left in a small *barranco*). Then a disused water canal joins the edge of the trail. The camino now descends and passes a water distributor. A good 5 minutes afterwards, pass another distributor and a few minutes after that, ignore a path branching off to the left. Another 5 minutes later, the trail forks (right goes into a *barranco* to reach a small bridge with a water canal).

A few minutes later, the camino meets the forest road from the start of the walk (2 minutes on the right leads to the **waterworks** ❸). Go left along this road to return to **La Caldera** picnic area ❶ in a half an hour.

↗ 550m | ↘ 550m | 11.1km
4.00 hrs

6 Órganos high mountain trail

Spectacular circular walk around the 'organ pipes'

This untamed and idyllic mountain trail offers a diversity of alpine delights, sometimes even truly spectacular: the walk above the famous Los Órganos ('organ pipes') traverses right through the heart of an area characterised by gorges and crags. Time after time amazing breath-taking views open up of the Orotava Valley and Teide.

Location: Aguamansa, 1000m.
Starting point: Zona recreativa La Caldera, 1192m (picnic area, bus terminus for the 345, 346).
Grade: at first a leisurely walk on a forest track, then on a trail, sometimes steep, in places rather narrow and precipitous (sporadically secured). Attempt only in stable weather, never after heavy rainfall (danger of rockfall and slipped away sections!).
Refreshment: bar/restaurant La Caldera (closed in 2023).
Linking tip: with Walk 5.

Cumbre Dorsal with the 'organ pipes' as seen from Aguamansa.

Starting at the car park and bus terminus at **La Caldera** picnic area ❶ follow the road to the left (PR TF 35/GR 131) running past the restaurant and 2 minutes later, bear left onto the wide forest road (amongst others, signpost to 'Los Órganos'). Follow this road straight on, passing **Choza Pedro Gil** ❷ (not quite 10 mins; do not turn right; water tap) and the Órganos rocks.

After a good half hour, pass a large waterworks in the Barranco Madre del Agua ❸. 5 minutes later, 10m past a forest track that turns off left towards Aguamansa, take a sharp right onto the *white/red* marked Camino El Topo ❹ (GR 131; alternatively, continue on the forest track: after a good 15 minutes, next to Choza El Topo, turn right onto the ascending forest road; some minutes later, ignore

a left turn; 5 minutes after that, on the first left bend, ignore the forest path turning right). Your trail ascends in zigzags along a ridge at the edge of the Barranco Madre del Agua and after just less than a quarter of an hour meets the forest road coming from Choza El Topo. On the left hand bend 10m later (a forest track turns off here to the right), the route continues along the trail to the right.

A good quarter of an hour later, the trail touches the forest road again at a left hand bend and, not quite 10 minutes later, runs along a flat ridge nearby. After a few minutes the gradient noticeably increases – the trail now runs, in places steeply, up along the mountain ridge and after a good 15 mins reaches a **viewpoint** ❺ (Portillo de El Topo, 1565m) on a rocky promontory with a view of Teide and the Orotava Valley.

10m on (sign), our trail meets up with the junction of the Órganos high mountain trail; follow this to the right (to the left, a delightful detour is possible along the *white/red* marked GR 131 to Lomo de la Resbala, a good 1½ hrs there and back). This splendid trail with velvety-soft pine needles (although at the outset somewhat overgrown) leads almost on the level towards Teide. After a short zigzag descent into the Barranco Madre del Agua (20 mins) there's another leisurely section of the route where a trail joins from the right ❻ (15 mins; see Walk 5). 10 mins later, the prominent Roque Guanchijo comes into view. The trail descends once more in zigzags and passes a craggy viewpoint (5 mins). Now cross over the **Barranco de las Aguas** ❼ (a good 5 mins) – the path here is somewhat precipitous, especially along one section where it runs across a rock ledge skirting around a sheer rock face (safety railings). Immediately afterwards, a rocky ridge is reached (with viewpoint, 10 mins). A good 10 mins later, pass what is perhaps the

Some sections of the alpine trail are rather vertiginous but secured with wire cables.

The most beautiful viewpoint on the walk – a narrow rocky ridge with a view of Teide.

finest viewpoint on the walk: a narrow, vertiginous overlook from a projecting rock ❽. A half an hour later, after a last stretch of steep up-and-down walking leading out of a *barranco*, reach the **Camino de Candelaria** ❾ and descend along this to the right. A few minutes later a trail turns off left; descend here to the right. 10 mins later cross over a forest track and continue the descent along the trail which, another 10 mins later, near **Choza Pedro Gil** ❷ joins the forest road that you walked along on your approach. Take this to the left and return to **La Caldera** picnic area ❶ in 10 minutes.

7 Choza Chimoche, 1425m

↗ 380m | ↘ 260m | 6.4km
2.00 hrs

Stroll in the upper Orotava Valley

The densely forested upper Orotava Valley is one of the island's regions most abundant in water. During an expedition through the formidable valley at the foot of the Cumbre Dorsal, you will meet up, again and again, with Galerías (water tunnels) penetrating deep into the mountain, pipelines and heaps of rubble.

Starting point: Casa Forestal/environment centre, 1075m (on the hairpin bend above Aguamansa, bus stop for the 345, 346).
Destination: Zona recreativa La Caldera, 1192m (bus terminus for the 345, 346).
Grade: mostly leisurely walk on forest tracks and trails.
Refreshment: bar/restaurant at La Caldera picnic area (closed in 2023), several bar/restaurants in Aguamansa.
Linking tip: with Walks 4–9.

Behind the bus stop shelter, diagonally opposite from the gate of the **Casa Forestal/environment centre** ❶, find the PR TF 35 (*white/yellow*; sign). The trail leads pleasantly along the slope above the main road and then, 3 minutes later, turns right onto a camino. A quarter of an hour later, cross over the access road for the La Caldera picnic grounds. Now the trail ascends somewhat more steeply and in 10 minutes reaches **La Caldera** ❷ (barbecue pits and a children's playground on the crater floor).

Walk along the road to the right around the picnic area. After a few minutes, at the highest point of the road, a slightly ascending forest road branches off to the right (signpost 'Chimoche'). After 200m, it passes a campsite and then continues, at first on the level, afterwards gently ascending. You can soon see the Órganos rocks on your left. About 25 mins after the picnic area, reach a major junction; turn right here continuing along the forest road. A good 5 mins later, pass the **Galería Chimoche** ❸ – the entrance to the tunnel is closed off with a grill and is located in the valley basin on the right behind the buildings. The track now leads a bit steeper uphill. After 15 minutes it reaches the little shelter of **Choza Chimoche** ❹ – here, a forestry road forks left to the Camino de Candelaria and to the right, you could head to Choza Bermeja (½ hr); a trail continues upwards to Montaña del Limón (see Walk 8).

Now turn back to the major junction (20 mins). Turn right onto the gently descending forest road. 5 mins later, the Camino de Candelaria crosses

Choza Chimoche.

the forest road (Pedro Gil, a viewpoint 100m further on); turn left onto it and descend further via zigzags. 10 minutes later, after passing the Tres Cruzes (three crosses), next to the **Choza Pedro Gil** ❺, the trail merges into a track which leads left in 10 minutes to the **La Caldera** picnic area ❷. If you wish to return to Aguamansa, follow the track for just 5 minutes to a bridge. 50m after the bridge, a wide trail branches off to the right and leads straight on, following bends leading downward to the Casa Forestal ❶ (15 minutes).

The spoil heap from the Galería Chimoche is situated directly on the trail.

↗ 940m | ↘ 940m | 14.5km

8 Montaña del Limón, 2106m

5.00 hrs

Long, but varied forest walk with summit joy

The cinder cones of Montaña del Limón rise up at the foot of the Cumbre Dorsal from the forest of the upper Orotava Valley, often shrouded in trade wind clouds, and are among the most beautiful panoramic viewpoints in northern Tenerife.

Location: Aguamansa, 1000m.
Starting point: Zona recreativa La Caldera, 1192m (picnic area, bus terminus for the 345, 346).
Grade: sometimes a steep walk along forest tracks and trails. The last part of the ascent lacks a distinct path (possible route-finding problems in poor visibility).
Refreshment: bar/restaurant at La Caldera picnic area (closed in 2023).

From the bus stop at **La Caldera** picnic area ❶ follow the road to the right and after 150m turn onto the first forest track branching off to the right (sign: 'Camino de los Guanches'). 200m further on, the forest track swerves to the left – at this point the old camino continues straight ahead. At first, the ascent is easy, then it climbs more steeply across the densely wooded slope. 10 mins later, bear diagonally left at the fork. A few minutes after that, the camino crosses over a large water conduit to the left. About 20 mins later, there's a fork in the trail – turn left here towards the slope (do not go uphill on the right) and after 5 mins, meet a forest road ❷. Follow this road for 10m to the right and then take a sharp left along a distinct trail, stone-flanked on both sides (sign: 'Montaña Limon'). The undulating trail leads above the forest road through a pine wood and forks after a good 5 mins ❸ (35m after a pile of stones, almost 2 metres high, to the right and above the trail). The main trail leads straight ahead down to the nearby **Choza Chimoche** (your return route later on)

The observatories of Izaña can be found above Montaña del Limón.

– but turn sharply right onto the distinct trail (subsequently, *white/yellow* marked) which soon becomes a wide, steep forest track. After a good 10 mins, a camino, waymarked with cairns, turns left away from the left branch of the forest track and continues uphill at the edge of the sheer-sided Barranco de Pedro Gil and, after 5 mins, meets the forest track again. A good 5 mins later, at the **Pasada del Fraile** stone column ❹ (barrier), cross a forest road. A quarter of an hour later, leave the forest track on a right hand bend along a trail going straight ahead (left). [If you want to avoid this unclear stretch, you could ascend the forest track straight on via the Cuevitas de Limón (5 mins, left uphill) as far as the Cumbrita Fría stone column (35 mins). Here, a wide trail of coarse sand branches off to the left up to Montaña del Limón (½ hr); see the return route.]

The sometimes rather indistinct path, marked only sporadically with cairns, crosses an intersecting trail 5 minutes on. You now need to keep a close eye on the continuing path (and look out for the cairns) – 10 mins later, it runs for 5 minutes along the edge of the colourful Barranco de Pedro Gil, to which it leads back again after another 5 minutes ❺ (the *barranco* drops away steeply here so do not go too close to the edge!). A fabulous stretch of trail! Soon afterwards the observatories of Izaña emerge ahead. The pine forest now thins out and you reach a plateau covered with gorse. The indistinct path crosses this plateau keeping left and in 10 minutes reaches a

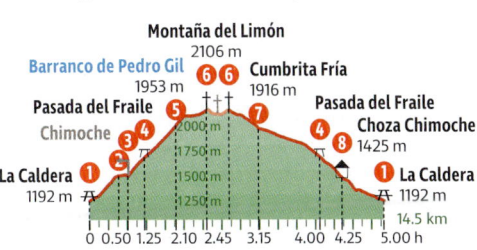

Teide with new snow on the summit – seen from Montaña del Limón summit.

roadway which ends in the high valley. Leave the roadway on the left and walk straight on up through the sandy ravine onto a wide, dark sandy col, 2064m (a good 5 mins). Here you meet a distinct intersecting trail (No 34; a possible ascent left to the TF-24 near Izaña) from which a path leads up on the right over a broad scree-covered ridge to the nearby summit of **Montaña del Limón** ❻ (a good 5 minutes). From the summit of the main peak, enjoy a wonderful view of Teide and the Cumbre Dorsal with the observatories of Izaña. The secondary peak to the north (10 minutes) provides a superb view down into the Orotava Valley.

After a rest, go back to the flat col and follow the intersecting trail there (trail No 34) to the right. 5 minutes later, it zigzags down through a pine forest and, a quarter of an hour later, meets a forest road at the **Cumbrita Fría** stone column ❼. Walk along this road leisurely downhill to the right. 20 minutes later, ignore a forest track branching off left on a right hand bend. 10 minutes later, on the following left hand bend, a broad forest track turns off to the right next to the Cuevitas de Limón stone column and leads gently downhill at first, but soon gets steeper and rougher. After a quarter of an hour, pass the **Pasada del Fraile** stone column ❹ and 20 minutes later meet up again with the intersecting trail ❸ met during the approach; turn right and descend in 3 minutes to a forest road which leads to the **Choza Chimoche** shelter ❽. Keep right here and turn immediately left along the forest road (PR TF 35 cuts away to the right).

After a few minutes, before a sharp left hand bend, a distinct trail turns off straight ahead which is edged with a line of stones while running parallel to the forest road and, after 10 minutes, meets it again. Turn left here, always following the straight forest road, and return to **La Caldera** picnic area ❶ (20 minutes).

↗ 910m | ↘ 910m | 8.9km

4.10 hrs

Candelaria trail I: Aguamansa – La Crucita, 2061m

TOP 9

Ascent from the upper Orotava Valley to the Cumbre Dorsal

The Candelaria trail is an old pilgrim route which connects Aguamansa with Candelaria – every year on August 14, countless Tinerfeños (inhabitants of Tenerife) make a pilgrimage here for the festival of the archipelago's patron saint. The beauty of the upper Orotava Valley is revealed in all its splendour: through the vast pine forests above Aguamansa and across volcanic slopes shimmering in every shade of red, the trail ascends to the ridgeline of the Cumbre Dorsal which offers a spectacular view of the Orotava Valley in the west and the Güímar Valley in the east. If you wish, you can walk the entire length of the Candelaria trail to Arafo or even as far as Candelaria.

Location: Aguamansa, 1000m.
Starting point: Casa Forestal/environment centre, 1075m (on the hairpin bend above Aguamansa, bus stop for the 345, 346).
Grade: strenuous walk on a sometimes steep, eroded trail.
Refreshment: bar/restaurants in Aguamansa.
Alternative: descent from the Mirador La Crucita to Arafo (just under 3 hrs, see Walk 10): a track forks off to the right from the *mirador*, then 200m further on, a camino forks off to the left. The camino crosses over the track several times and then joins it not far past the Montaña de las Arenas (barrier), only to leave it again on the left 100m on. Just below the former Refugio de Las Arenas, the path joins up with a camino coming from there. Continuing straight on (at the fork 100m before a water canal, also straight on) reach a tarmac road (¾ hr) then bear left at a fork descending steeply to reach Arafo (½ hr; the bus stop for the 121 is to the right in the Avenida Reyes de España). If you wish to continue on to Candelaria, walk past the *plaza* with the church on the left, then descend straight ahead (also straight on at the roundabout on the main road below the town centre). 1km on, turn left into the *barranco*. Immediately afterwards, turn right onto a narrow road. Continue straight ahead, passing fincas, finally along a stretch of roadway to reach the TF-247. Turn left and in the following left-hand bend, turn right onto a roadway, then bear left at the two forks (*yellow arrow*). At a major junction 600m on (C/Guarrajo), the *yellow arrow* points straight ahead – here it is better to turn diagonally right onto the Camino La Caseta (a short stetch of gravel). At the end of the C/Icerse turn left, cross the motorway bridge, turn left, then take the next road on the right down to the basilica of Candelaria.

Wall of lava beside the trail.

At the hairpin bend at the **Casa Forestal** ❶ the signposted Camino de Candelaria begins, ascending in a leisurely fashion through a wood of heather trees and pines. After a good 5 minutes, the camino merges with a forest track that leads left to a forestry house. Walk on the left past the house and immediately afterwards continue uphill to the right along the camino. Directly afterwards you cross a forest track (on the right is the Galería de la Puente). Now either continue straight ahead ascending along the forest track or – much nicer – after 10m, fork to the left onto a trail flanked by stones that ascends over a ridge skirting the Barranco de Los Llanos, with a sublime view of the Órganos rocks. Not quite 10 minutes later, the two trails come together again and merge with a forestry road coming from La Caldera picnic area. Follow this 20m to the left, then, to the right of **Choza Pedro Gil** ❷ (water tap), change over to the old camino (signpost 'Camino de Candelaria'). The steep zigzag trail passes Tres Cruzes (three crosses) and then, after a quarter of an hour, crosses over a forest road (Pedro Gil) – the ascent continues steeply keeping to the left. After another 15 minutes, the Órganos high mountain trail merges from the left ❸ (see Walk 6, to the right, a trail forks off to Choza Chimoche).

The camino continues a steep zigzag ascent. Half an hour later, the pine forest begins to thin out, opening up a view of the Orotava Valley

View of the Orotava Valley from the trail.

and the coast. Pass a wall of lava, now walking across colourful, mostly dark-red volcanic terrain. After another half an hour – traversing in a north-easterly direction – climb over a lava wall ❹. Unfortunately, the traverse soon comes to an end, then the ascent becomes steep again as it crosses a craggy outcrop up to the ridgeline road of the Cumbre Dorsal which you reach 30m before the **Mirador de La Crucita** ❺ (halfway along this stretch a path forks left away from the road and ascends in 10 mins to the highest point of **Montaña de La Crucita** ❻).

View of Teide from the Cumbre Dorsal by Montaña de la Crucita.

TOP 10

Candelaria trail II: Arafo – La Crucita, 2061m

↗ 1570m | ↘ 1570m | 16.7km
7.00 hrs

Fabulous walk passing through vineyards, verdant forests of pine and chestnut trees and a unforgettable mountain landscape – one of the best walks on the island!

Due to its diverse scenery the strenuous ascent from Arafo to Montaña de la Crucita is one of the most beautiful routes on Tenerife. Especially impressive in the higher stretches is the unique setting of black sand and dark-red lava slopes with pine woods shimmering bright green and rocky mountains reaching up into the sky.

Starting point: church square in the centre of Arafo, 470m (bus stop for the 121).
Grade: strenuous, extremely varied day walk along a camino, steep in places.
Refreshment: you will find bars and restaurants in Arafo
Alternatives: an ascent of Montaña de las Arenas from the track by the barrier (just under ¼ hr one way, no paths; excellent 360° view). Descent from La Crucita to Aguamansa (see Walk 9).

The village square of **Arafo** ❶ is situated directly above the church and, in the middle of it, there's a kiosk. Walk past the kiosk and continue straight on up the Calle La Libertad which, at a little square (Plazoleta del Llano) 400m on, becomes the Calle de Eduardo Curbelo Fariña. Now, the road gradually gets steeper. Soon, pass an old *gofio* mill and leave the last houses of Arafo behind. Ignore all the roads that branch off. A good quarter of an hour later (1.2km; large water tank on the right) turn left and then immediately (15m on) turn right again to ascend steeply through terraced vineyards, orchards and potato fields. 20 minutes later, the narrow road ends at a gate (if you want to approach by car, park before the road narrows as it leads straight ahead). At the gate, the camino ❷ begins on the right. It immediately runs between two little waterworks and a water

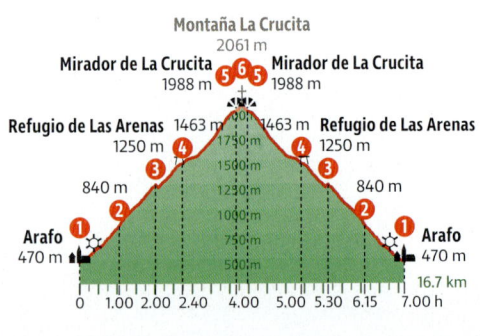

A uniquely beautiful backdrop – view across the high valley with the black cinder cone of Monatañ de las Arenas down to the coast at Güímar.

canal joins here at the edge of the trail. The stone-paved trail now enters an open pine wood and, not quite 10 minutes later, veers left away from the water canal to begin a zigzag ascent (ignore the left fork and a few minutes later, ignore the right fork that crosses over the water canal). From time to time you will discover small *red* marker posts at the edge of the path. The ascent over a carpet of needles in the semi-shade of the pines is mostly very pleasant. About 25 minutes from the tarmac road, cross an open dry water canal. The camino now keeps to the left, continues up through the pine wood and then zigzags uphill. After a good half an hour (you have left the forest behind just before), the trail hooks to the right (stones in a row, *white arrow*; straight ahead, in just a few minutes, reach the former **Refugio de Las Arenas** ❸).

In the alpine valley: Montaña de las Arenas and the impressive Pico de Cho Marcial.

The trail now ascends through a exceptionally beautiful lava sand landscape, dotted with gnarled chestnut trees, whilst opening up beautiful views of the coast and the neighbouring island of Gran Canaria, and then also of the black volcanic cone of the Montaña de las Arenas. Shortly before a barrier, our trail joins a sandy track. A good 100m past the barrier, a distinct path flanked with rows of stones branches off straight ahead at a junction and then soon rejoins the track ❹. Before continuing uphill on the path opposite, it is worthwhile to take a short excursion along the

The final ascent through reddish volcanic cinder is somewhat arduous.

track to the left into the beautiful alpine valley behind the **Montaña de las Arenas** (Volcán de Arafo), 1589m. The valley is blocked to the south by the massive rock faces of Pico de Cho Marcial, 2023m, and also to the northeast, by equally impressive mountains; to the west, the valley extends right up to the ridgeline of the Cumbre Dorsal with Montaña de la Crucita.

Our trail leads just off to the side of the black lava terrain through the pine forest. Later, climb briefly through a small treeless *barranco* whilst ascending, and then zigzag to the left uphill through another pine wood. A quarter of an hour after leaving the track, cross over it again and continue along the narrow trail. A good 5 minutes later, cross the track again and 10 minutes after that, cross it once more. On the left, above the next bend in the track, you see layers of rock shimmering in colours ranging from red to black. The camino climbs a mountain ridge and opens up a fantastic panorama of the entire mountain valley. The route now becomes a bit steeper, also stonier.

About 20 minutes later, the wood thins out – you are now ascending through reddish volcanic debris. This panoramic section over slippery, sandy ground is the most strenuous part of the walk. Soon, past a tiny shrine, cross the track again – the camino continues a few metres further on the left. It now takes only another 10 minutes (above on the track, turn right) to reach the **Mirador de La Crucita** ❺, 1988m, on the mountain road which follows the Cumbre Dorsal ridge. 30m further on the left and on the other side of the ridge, the Candelaria trail continues its way to Aguamansa – midway along this stretch you can turn right onto a steep path and climb in 10 minutes to the highest point of **Montaña de La Crucita** ❻ and from there, although somewhat hindered by pine trees, enjoy a spectacular view of the Orotava Valley, Teide and the Güímar Valley.

TOP 11 Ventanas de Güímar

↗ 200m | ↘ 810m | 13.0km
5.25 hrs

Not for the weak-kneed: a spectacular canal route through the rock face

This adventurous, spectacular tunnel route through the sheer rock faces of the Barranco de Badajoz is hard to beat – not only due to the quality of the experience, but also due to the challenge it presents: the canal path is often extremely narrow and precipitous and, from time to time, an excellent sense of equilibrium is demanded whilst maintaining balance along the canal rim. Also needed is a bright torch or headtorch, since not all of the tunnels (some with a length up to 500m) boast an aperture. Another tip: if you prefer to avoid the overgrown canal path and the descent to Güímar, turn around at Fuga de Los Cuatros Reales.

Starting point: Ladera de Güímar at the end of the tarmac on the Pista de Anocheza, next to the first radio masts, 887m (parking shortly before or just afterwards along the track). The road, steep, narrow and 2.5km long, forks away just before the *mirador* on the road for the *ladera* at Km 29.9 of the TF-28 Güímar – Fasnia (5.5km from Güímar; Marrera bus stop for lines 033, 035, 037; then, by foot, a good 1hr to the end of the tarmac).
Destination: the taxi rank at the Plaza de las Flores in Güímar, 275m. Return to the starting point by taxi (about € 10).
Grade: the canal path is sometimes vertiginous and precipitous; absolute sure-footedness and a perfect head for heights demanded. At times, you have to balance along the rim of the canal. Only during stable weather, never during storm or rainfall (danger of falling rocks)!
Refreshment: in Güímar.
Alternative: return via Galería La Paloma: at the fork before reaching the 10th tunnel, turn right through the short aperture tunnel into the narrow, canyon-like, deep-cut Barranco de Badajoz. Along a very strenuous and overgrown path (long trousers recommended) head up the valley to the Galería La Paloma (¾ hr). To the left, a farm road ascends steeply to the ridgeline of the *ladera* (a good ¾ hr). Here, meet up with a track, only to leave it again in a right-hand bend along an unpleasant, steep and slippery trail forking left. Now keep steady along the ridgeline to return to the starting point (1½ hrs).
Important notes: the canal path is officially closed so undertaking this walk is at your own risk! For the tunnels, up to 15 minutes in duration, a powerful torch or head torch is demanded.

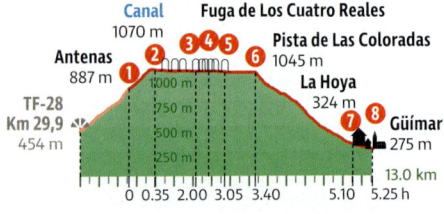

The radio masts often perch on the border of the cloud banks – view towards Gran Canaria.

At the end of the tarmac, at the **radio masts** ❶, continue ascending straight on along the steep main track to reach the next tall radio mast next to the **Pino Don Tomás** (not quite ½ hr). Again at the following fork, continue along the track heading straight on (flanked by cedars) and, 130m on, turn right along the distinct path (prohibition sign; see Important notes), which traverses through rockroses to reach the abandoned **water canal** ❷ on the edge of the slope. And now the adventure begins: already after walking a short stretch, the canal leads along the dauntingly sheer rock face of the Ladera de Güímar, setting the picturesque Güímar Valley, spectaculary

The spectacular centrepiece of the walk – the Ventanas ('windows') de Güímar.

framed by mountains, below our feet. The trail usually leads directly along the covered canal, however, many of the plates are broken so that you have maintain balance whilst walking along the canal rim, often a fairly vertiginous undertaking. A quarter of an hour later, reach a wrecked excavator, behind which the entrance to the **1st tunnel** is located. Pay close attention to the overhanging rocks on the ceiling but also on the side; you have to walk stooped-down for most of the way in the tunnel, about 210m in length. Afterwards, we find ourselves almost smack in the middle of a breathtaking natural amphitheater, fantastic! The section that follows – steadily along the path below the canal – is strenuous, undulating and overgrown, but nevertheless marvellous, not least due to the gorgeous flora, and especially the ever-present, trailing tendrils of bellflower. 10 mins later, the **2nd tunnel** awaits (140m in length; you have to reckon that some

water will be present in the canal so that you usually need to walk next to it). Just afterwards, the **3rd tunnel** follows (100m; here, too, water will be lying in the canal), already provided with three apertures. Afterward, cross over the deep-cut Barranco de Chamoco and then enter the **4th tunnel** (160m), which is easy going thanks to the numerous apertures for light. The canal trail now leads for a longer time in the open air and delights the walker with its marvellous plants and flowers as well as with the views it offers. Past a ledge, we get a glimpse of the heart of the walk, the Barranco de Badajoz with its dramatic alignment of rock faces, especially the Fuga de Los Cuatro Reales. A backwards view shows that the Puerto de Güímar has appeared. Then the **5th tunnel** ❸ (115 m), follows, also provided with apertures – and immediately afterwards, once the steep *barranco* has been crossed, the **6th tunnel** (150m, without apertures) follows. **Tunnel 7** (not quite 200m), past the kink 100m on, is provided with apertures. Almost seamlessly continue on into the **8th tunnel** with the renowned apertures of the **Ventanas de Güímar**. The traverse of the sheer rock-faced *barranco* **Fuga de Los Cuatro Reales** ❹ is unmatched on Tenerife.

Just before the last apertures, the trail forks – here, we leave the apertures behind and bear left to enter the **9th tunnel** (200m, no apertures). Shortly afterwards, the **10th tunnel** (the last one) follows: at the fork, do not turn right along the bulky plastic pipeline (see Alternative), but instead turn left to enter the tunnel, about 500m in length, following a pipeline that provides pleasant warmth for the tunnel and fills it with the sound of gurgling water. Past the tunnel ❺ the canal trail crosses over the Barranco del Río, passing a couple of tumbledown buildings and then leads through a fragrant pine wood. During this stretch of trail, you must often tight-rope walk along the rim of the canal. As soon as the pine forest is taken over by scrub wood, the canal path also becomes overgrown– but fortunately, not for long, and then meets up with the **Pista de Las Coloradas** ❻.

Here, leave the canal behind and descend along the track in a straight line towards Güímar, taking in a marvellous view of the valley and to the coast. Not quite half an hour later, bear right at the fork in the track (or bear left and then descend along the camino later on) – the track crosses over a valley notch and then drops down in a direct course via a ridge, now tarmac-paved. During the long descent, pass numerous fincas and terraces for dryland farming. Just past the *plaza* at **La Hoya** ❼, in front of the 'bridge', climb down some steps to the right and then take the road (always straight on). In **Güímar** pass the church by bearing left and then meet up with the main street. Here, 150m to the left, reach a taxi rank and bus stop on the Plaza de las Flores ❽.

↗ 165m | ↘ 165m | 7.1km
2.00 hrs

12 Malpaís de Güímar

Pleasant coastal walk through an enchanting volcanic landscape

You sometimes get cool and even rainy days on Tenerife. This short, leisurely circular walk on the sunny side of the island is tailor-made for such days. It leads through the impressive lava landscape which nature has fabulously modelled in the Malpaís de Güímar Nature Reserve, stretching from the volcanic cone of Montaña Grande (just under 300m) to the coast.

Starting point: *plaza* of Puertito de Güímar, 5m (bus stop for the 120).
Grade: easy, leisurely coast walk, but with no shade!

Refreshment: bar/restaurants in Puertito de Güímar.
Tip: you want to be sure to bring along your swimming gear!

From the central *plaza* at the harbour of **Puertito de Güímar** ❶ follow the coastal promenade in an easterly direction and then Calle Marques de Santa Cruz which continues along the coast. After just under 10 mins, by the last little beach huts, the roadway ends and a beautiful path begins. It runs through an expansive lava field where there's lots to discover: lava tunnels, small rock arches, isolated sections of basaltic lava, tiny flat areas of sand and miniature salt-pans. Spurge, Candelabra plants (false cactus) and salt-loving plants provide bright, green patches of colour in the dark lava landscape. In good visibility, you can enjoy wonderful views of the Güímar Valley and the Anaga mountains.

After a good half an hour, the lava path ascends to the 30m high cliffs,

This consistently comfortable trail leads through a wonderful lava landscape.

the highest point of the walk along this stretch of the coast. Just under 10 mins later there's a fork in the trail ❷ (wooden post 'Montaña Grande'): carry straight on for a detour to the stony, not very inviting Playa de la Entrada (15 mins) and further on to El Socorro (just under 10 mins; bar/restaurants).

Otherwise leave the coastal trail along the path branching off left that leads directly towards the cinder cone of Montaña Grande. Not quite 10 mins later, the path becomes a roadway and the Candelabra cacti are now more plentiful in the lava landscape. Not quite 10 mins after that, meet a barrier. Here, ascend left along the path and a good 5 mins later, reach another fork at the foot of Montaña Grande (wooden post). You could go round the cinder cone on the right (about ¾ hour) although this route is severely spoiled by the noise of the nearby motorway. So keep left and then pass several volcanic vents and also a small viewpoint on **Morra del Corcho** ❸ (just under 10 mins). 5 mins later, there's a fork – go diagonally left here downhill. The path descends gently in the direction of Puertito de Güímar and runs more or less along the edge of the Malpaís de Güímar Nature Reserve. About 25 mins later, the path swings to the left – a fabulous stretch – and a few minutes after that, joins the coastal road. Go right along this road in 5 mins back to the harbour of **Puertito de Güímar** ❶.

↗ 730m | ↘ 730m | 9.6km

13 From Araya to Risco de la Vera

3.45 hrs

A walk, rich in diversity, along the foot of the mighty Cumbre Dorsal

The hinterland of Candelaria is one of the least known walking regions on Tenerife but nevertheless offers everything you need to satisfy your wanderlust: marvellous views, splendid cultivated landscapes, as well as wild and unspoilt barrancos and pine forests that lie at the foot of the towering Cumbre. We heartily recommend the walk described here which circles around the Barranco Achacay in a perfect combination of these elements.

Starting point: the church square in Araya, 363m (next bus stop for line 123 is on the TF-247, from there, it's 300m to the *plaza*); or, at the junction 'Cruz del Camino' (see below; 25 mins shorter).

Grade: this is mostly a pleasant walk, only somewhat steep from time to time, but nevertheless demanding sure-footedness and some stamina.
Refreshment: bar/restaurant on the TF-247.

From the church square in **Araya** ❶, follow the steeply ascending street towards 'Monte Los Brezos'. 600m on (a good ¼ hr) reach the junction **Cruz del Camino** ❷. Here, the circular walk SL TF 294 (*white/green*) sets off; turn right onto it, passing a little *plaza*. 200m on, leave the street behind (past the *barranco* bridge) by turning left onto the camino that forks away. After a couple of minutes of steep ascent, merge into a street and continue ascending along it. At the end of the street (Las Haciendas; a wine press to the right), the trail forks: straight ahead, the SL TF 296 breaks away towards Igueste, but we keep to the left along the SL TF 294 towards Los Brezos. The route leads along a roadway which ascends steeply at the next ridge and, past a finca, becomes a camino. Now continue climbing pleasantly but resolutely upwards along the ridgeline, soon passing through an open pine wood while taking in lovely views to the coast, of the deeply-incised

Ascent along the Barranco de Las Vigas – view of the coast and of Candelaria.

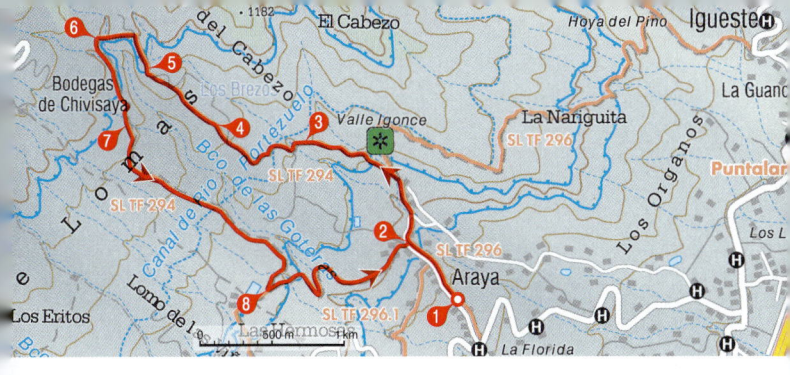

Barranco de Las Vigas and of the Cumbre. Not quite ½ hr past Las Haciendas, the camino merges into a track ❸ (50m to the right, a baking oven for bread). Turn left onto the track to cross over the Barranco de Las Vigas and, afterwards, turn right along a road. Some minutes later (100m past a sharp right-hand bend) the trail turns off to the right, following a camino as it ascends parallel to the road, then crosses over the road and, soon after, reaches the Ermita de San Isidro and the **Los Brezos** picnic area ❹.

Straight ahead, continue climbing steeply along the track but leave it behind again 300m on at the junction of tracks, heading straight on along the camino. Shortly after, this crosses over the track and then merges back with it again. Now pass the **Risco de la Vera** ❺ where you can get a downwards view of the mighty basin of the Barranco Achacay with a galería. 250m on, the trail again runs for a short stretch away from the track and, at the junction of tracks that follows (with a view of the Piedras de Carcho) bear left, passing a tumbledown cottage. At the next junction, turn diagonally right, passing through a chain barrier. A good 100m on, leave the roadway behind by turning right onto a path forking away that ascends for a stretch into the **Barranco Achacay** ❻ and then changes to the other side of the valley. There ascend for another short stretch and then continue in a traverse through a pine forest, crossing over a threshing circle. Afterwards, whilst enjoying a marvellous view of the coast, cross over a *barranco* and then descend

During the return, view of the basin of the Barranco Achacay with the Risco de la Vera.

along the ridge that follows, keeping always to the rim of the *barranco*. About 20 mins later, next to a rocky spur, a camino forks away towards the Galería Achacay ❼ – but our trail veers right, away from the *barranco* and then crosses over a secondary *barranco*. Some minutes later, at the junction, bear left. Now the camino descends in a direct line via the Lomo El Luchón, soon following the rim of the *barranco* yet again (a view of the basilica at Candelaria!). Just past a high tension pylon reach a trail junction at a water canal: the SL TF 294.1 forks off to the right ❽, but we turn left onto the SL TF 294, leading along the canal and then pass a bridge for the canal. Now descend for a short stretch along the ridge (enjoying a view of Araya), then the camino bears left to cross over the **Barranco Las Goteras**. On the other flank of the valley, ignore a trail forking away to the Fuente La Gotera and follow the trail to the left to reach a road. Cross over this road and then follow the roadway, subsequently always keeping straight ahead, to reach the **Cruz del Camino** ❷ and continue the descent to **Araya** ❶.

↗ 1060m | ↘ 1060m | 14.6km

6.40 hrs

From Realejo Alto to Chanajiga 14

Strenuous, panoramic circular walk through the Ladera de Tigaiga

The refurbished and newly marked circular trail from Los Realejos to the Chanajiga picnic grounds is one of the most attractive routes in the upper Orotava Valley. Highlights include a stretch through the Pavos laurel forest and the steep Tigaiga rock face which serves as a natural border for the western Orotova Valley – and, of course, provides marvellous views taking in the valley. However, it must be admitted that this route, because of its length, the many steep stretches of ascent and the numerous descents, is very strenuous and demanding as well.

Starting point: Plaza Viera y Clavijo in the village centre of Realejo Alto, 350m (bus stop for the lines 330, 347, 352–354, 390).
Grade: long, strenuous walk; some stretches via very steep caminos. Do not attempt during rainfall or strong winds!
Refreshment: only in Realejo Alto.
Alternative: via the PR TF 40.1, you can shorten the circular route by 1 hr: the lovely trail (for the turn-off, see below) crosses the Barranco La Calera, ascends through a captivating misty forest (at first along the *barranco*), veers to the right towards the steep flank of the Ladera de Tigaiga, and then ascends in zigzags. After a total time of a good ¾ hr, just before the Risco Miguel, merge into the track for the PR TF 40.
Linking tip: with Walk 15.
Important note: recently (2023) the PR TF 40.1 and the track/PR TF 40 between Chanajiga and Risco Miguel were officially closed due to rockfall.

Begin the walk at the Plaza Viera y Clavijo in the village centre of **Realejo Alto** ❶ above the parish church and next to the town hall (sign PR TF 40, *white/yellow*). The

65

route always ascends straight ahead along the Calle El Medio Arriba and passes a chapel 5 minutes later. 100m on, bear right at a fork to follow the narrow concrete road down into the Barranco La Calera (parking possible here) and then up the valley enjoying a view of the Ladera de Tiagaiga, which serves as the western border for the Orotava Valley. 10 minutes later, the track changes over to the right flank of the valley and 150m on, the PR TF 40 ❷ forks (sign). Take the left hand fork for the ascent via the Til de Los Pavos (to the right, your return route via El Asomadero) and, soon afterwards, at the end of the roadway at a Galería continue along the ascending trail. The lovely camino ascends quite heartily along the edge of a chestnut wood and heather trees, then meets up with a road way a good quarter of an hour later. Follow this sharp to the left, enjoying a view of the *ladera* and the viewpoint El Asomadero directly above you. Subsequently, reach the cluster of houses marking the village of **Palo Blanco** ❸ to continue climbing up along a street.

At the final houses, the street becomes a camino (beware: a short, extremely slippery stretch when wet!), and then merges into a road. Turn left here, enjoying a splendid view over the Orotava Valley all the way to the coast. The road remains on the level at first, then descends back to the *barranco* (below a poultry farm). Not quite 100m before reaching the floor of the *barranco*, a camino forks off to the right (sign) and ascends steeply through a deciduous forest. Some minutes later, ignore a path forking off to the right and then immediately afterwards, your trail crosses a secondary *barranco* and continues the ascent through an ancient laurel wood (Til de Los Pavos). At a fork, a few minutes later, bear right at a small bench. Shortly afterwards, pass the **Fuente del Til** ❹ – this is a marvellous stretch

During the descent, enjoy a lovely view of Los Realejos and Puerto de la Cruz.

of trail, not least due to the lively birdsong. 10 minutes later, leave the splendid wood behind and return to brushwood and the caterwaul of civilisation. Subsequently, the camino crosses two secondary *barrancos* and then forks immediately – turn right here (the Camino de Las Travesia turns left, heading toward Las Llanadas). 50m on, the trail forks once again ❺ – here, you can turn right along the PR TF 40.1 to shorten the circular route (see Alternative), but instead keep straight ahead towards Chanajiga. The camino ascends through the *barranco* and then continues steeply along a ridge. It takes about quarter of an hour for the route to level out somewhat (to the left: a forestry road). A good 10 minutes later, the trail leads left to become a broad forest trail which leads in a good quarter of an hour to the spacious picnic grounds of **Chanajiga** ❻ at a barrier and merges into a track road. The view from here taking in the Orotava Valley, is stupendous!

Now follow the track to the right towards Risco Miguel. 100m on, the PR TF 40 forks off to the left from the track to pass the playgrounds and then steepens for some minutes. Now, head right to cross the steep slope of the Ladera de Tigaiga, first through a pine wood and then through fayal-brezal forest. A good quarter of an hour later, the trail rejoins the track; turn left to reach **Risco Miguel** ❼ and the Choza Enrique Talg (¼ hr; 10 minutes later, the PR TF 40.1 merges). A good 50m on, the marked trail forks diagonally right onto a camino which leads in easy up-and-down walking through the densely wooded and steep slope – a splendid stretch of trail! A good half an hour later, the trail merges into a concrete road which leads to the right to the **Mirador El Asomadero** ❽, the most beautiful viewpoint of the walk.

30m on, your trail, the PR TF 40, forks off to the right (straight ahead, you could descend via La Corona to Icod El Alto). The trail descends very steeply, often over steps, in tight bends and, half an hour later, passes a *mirador* ❾ and, immediately after, two caves. Subsequently the camino leads past a mighty rock face. Now Los Realejos has come into view – as well as the Barranco La Calera. Here meet up with a road which descends to the right to the junction with the PR TF 40 ❷. Now, following the familiar approach trail, return to **Realejo Alto** ❶ (25 minutes).

15 From the Chanajiga picnic area to Fortaleza

↗ 1100m | ↘ 1100m | 18.5km
6.30 hrs

Extensive, panoramic ascent via the Ladera de Tigaiga

What a walk! Constantly hugging the rim of the sheer drop on the western wall of the Orotava Valley, this panoramic route climbs up to the uniquely beautiful 'lunar landscape' of the Cañadas. The ascent is admittedly very strenuous, but as compensation, you will be presented at the end with a breathtaking view of Teide along with the Montaña Blanca. – If you want to trump this walk (and you can lay claim to the necessary endurance) you could choose to tackle the route 0.4.0 'From Sea to Sky', that is, from sea level all the way to 4000m above – a major challenge for any ambitious and avid mountain walker (see Alternative).

Starting point: the picnic area, Chanajiga, 1182m. From the TF-326, between Palo Blanco and Benijos, turn off towards Las Llanadas to reach Chanajiga (5.5km; signed. Bus 330 to Las Llanadas).
Grade: strenuous hike, sometimes along steep trails and tracks.
Alternative: route 0.4.0 Playa del Socorro – Pico del Teide (PR TF 41, *white/yellow*, 12.20 hrs (officially 7–9 hrs!), 3800 metres of height): from the Playa del Socorro, ascend along the access road to TF-5. 50m past the underpass, the trail begins (sign) and ascends to Lomo el Boliche, then steeply descends to a track along which you ascend to a intersecting road in Tigaiga. Turn left onto it and continue for 350m then right to ascend the steep narrow road. Turn left at the next intersecting road and then right at the following junction. Past a bridge over a canal, the narrow road becomes a cobbled camino that climbs up to the TF-342. Turn

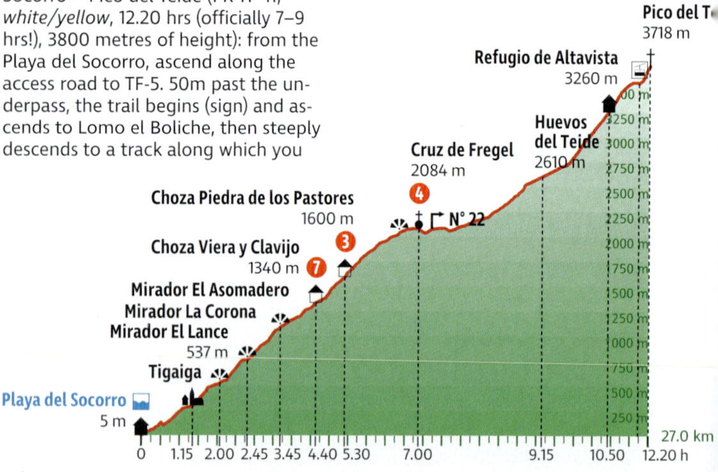

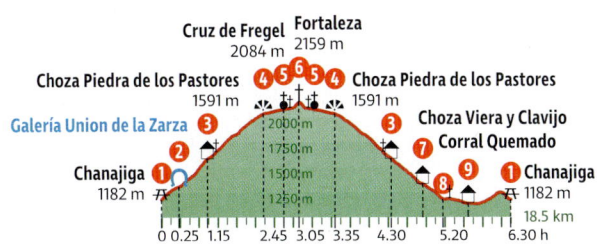

right to follow this path to the Mirador El Lance at the village limits from Icod el Alto (bus line 354). 150m on, in a left-hand bend, turn sharp left onto the Carretera Transversal 1 El Lance. 200m on, turn sharp right to ascend along the steep village street. A good ¼ hr later, a roadway branches off to the left, tarmac-paved at the outset, and ascends to the Mirador La Corona (paraglider launching point; a splendid downwards view). Ascend parallel to the sheer drop at the rim of the Orotava Valley (steadily straight on), passing the Fuente Pedro (excursion path, 20 mins later). Reaching the next junction (a good 5 mins on) turn left to ascend to the Mirador El Asomadero. The steep roadway twice crosses a track, then follows it (some mins later, keep left). A good ¼ hr later, reach a major junction of tracks at a stone pillar (Corral Quemado). Here straight on (bear right/left), ascending along the track, passing by the Choza Viera y Clavijo (25 mins; 50m to the left) to reach the Choza Piedra de los Pastores (½ hr). Now follow the description below to the Cruz de Fregel. On the other side of the saddle, descend to the Cañada de los Guancheros. Here turn left via trail No 1 to the National Park Visitor Centre El Portillo, 2050m (1 hr from Cruz de Fregel, bus lines 342/348 are to the left at the road junction, 5 mins) or, some mins later, turn right via trail No 22 (Walk 85) to ascend to the Teide road and then further with Walk 86 onto Teide.
Linking tip: with Walk 14.
Important note: recently (2023), the track between Risco Miguel and Chanajiga was officially closed due to rockfall (attempt at your own risk).

At the large trail board at the **Chanajiga** picnic area ❶, behind the track roundabout, turn left to ascend the wide steps and again left up the broad trail, passing picnic tables and a waterworks (now the trail narrows). Soon afterwards, meet up with a stony roadway and turn right onto it to continue the ascent. At a road junction 10 minutes later turn right and reach, a few minutes more, the **Galería Unión de la Zarza** ❷ (a splendid view of the Orotava Valley and the picnic area). The roadway now becomes a camino ascending in zigzags through a pine forest. Three-quarters of an hour later (en route crossing over a forestry road) reach the rim of the Ladera de Tigaiga where the camino merges into a track following the PR TF 41 (*white/yellow*). Turn left onto the track and, 100m on, meet up with the **Choza Piedra de los Pastores** ❸.
To the left, a forestry track continues towards Cañadas, but we follow the forestry road which continues ascending straight ahead over the ridgeline. Then leave this behind by taking the trail that runs parallel to the forestry

road. 20 minutes later, the trail merges once again with the forestry road — here, at the fork, bear left to continue ascending. Suddenly the pine forest recedes and we can now enjoy an unhampered view of Teide in all of its splendid glory, as well as the mountain ridge of the Fortaleza. Now bushy broom lines the trail and we can spot a forestry house off to the right. Not quite an hour past the Choza Piedra de los Pastores, the trail merges into a forestry track that is ascending from the right. But already past the next bend, leave this behind again by turning left onto the roadway forking away (No 29). 10 minutes later, meet up again with the track and, this time, turn left to follow it — but, in the next bend, turn left for a short stretch to enjoy a marvellous view of the Orotava Valley ❹ (see photo above): the boundless view reaches from the coast over the vast belt of forest all the way to the Cumbre Dorsal. The track now keeps almost on the level as it crosses over to the Degollada del Cedro, 2084m. Here, at the little chapel **Cruz de Fregel** ❺, find yourself a cosy spot for a break to savour the lovely view of Teide. By keeping straight ahead, you could continue on to Teide or to El Portillo (see Alternative). We,

however, turn right along the pleasantly ascending roadway. When this ends, turn left onto a lovely trail flanked by rows of stones and climb up to the highest point on top of the **Fortaleza** ❻ – the view reaches from Teide all the way to the Orotava Valley. The return to the **Choza Piedra de los Pastores** ❸ follows the same route as the approach. If you would prefer to get back to Chanajiga as quickly as possible, 100m past the shelter, turn right onto the path from the approach route (1 hr shorter). We, however, continue on along the track at the rim of the Ladera and use this to descend, always heading straight on. Not quite half an hour later, pass the **Choza Viera y Clavijo** ❼ (the shelter is located 50m along the forestry road turning right; just past the shelter is a splendid viewpoint taking in the Orotava Valley). About 20 minutes later, reach a major junction of tracks ❽ (Corral Quemado). Here turn off to the right and not quite an hour later (about 25 mins en route, pass the Choza Enrique Talg am Risco Miguel ❾; beautiful viewpoint!) reach the picnic area **Chanajiga** ❶.

Just before reaching the Cruz de Fregel: Fortaleza (right) and Teide.

16 From Barranco de Ruíz to San Juan de La Rambla

↗ 450m | ↘ 450m | 8.5km
2.40 hrs

Varied circular walk along the north coast

San Juan de La Rambla has one of the most beautiful sections of coastline in the north of the island – beyond the narrow coastal plain with its picturesque villages there are some huge towering rock faces. Terraces characterise the hillsides at the foot of Teide another level further up. This splendid, not very demanding circular walk takes in all these landscapes.

Starting point: Zona recreativa (picnic area) Barranco de Ruíz, 120m, at Km 44.5 on the TF-5 road Puerto de la Cruz – Icod de los Vinos (bus stop for the 108, 325, 363).
Grade: all in all, an easy walk on sometimes rather steep caminos (avoid the walk when wet or stormy) and a hardly used road.
Refreshment: Finca San Juan, bar/restaurants in San Juan and in Las Aguas, kiosks at the Barranco de Ruiz picnic area.
Tip: maybe take your swimwear.
Alternative: The old trail from La Vera to Icod el Alto (a good hour), closed due to a rockslide, is extremely overgrown and obviously no longer being

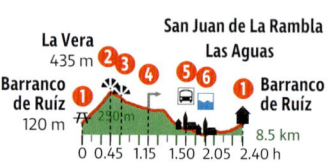

maintained: follow the road on the left uphill; leave it after 5 mins (20m after it joins a broad road) and take the path turning off diagonally left. After a good 15 mins it reaches the bottom of the Barranco de Ruíz and ascends through laurisilva forest (go left at the fork a few minutes later). After 20 mins, the camino passes a waterfall and, a good 10 mins after that, on the plateau at the edge of the gorge, joins a narrow road which, in 15 minutes, climbs up to the right to the TF-342 near Icod el Alto (bus stop for the 345; you can also turn left onto the narrow road to reach Icod el Alto)
Linking tip: with Walk 3.

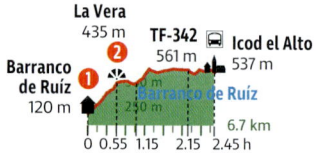

Start the walk at the western end of the **picnic area** ❶ and climb up some steps to a camino which ascends through the striking Barranco de Ruíz. 10 minutes later cross over a water canal and in just under a quarter of an hour pass the foot of a rock face, overhanging in some places. Then the stone-paved path ascends in zigzags up to the plateau above the *barranco* which you reach at a small *plaza* in **La Vera** ❷.
The view from here is fantastic – on one side, the magnificent Teide, on the other, the enormous *barranco* and the coast. Beyond the *plaza*, you come to a street. Leave the trail here which continues up the *barranco* (see Alternative) and walk to the right over the road down between terraces.

After just under 10 minutes, pass the **Mirador El Mazapé** (❸; youth hostel, wonderful view along the coast). After a bend further on, the little-used road heads left towards the slope (a fabulous view at the bend). A good 20 minutes later, a road turns off sharp right ❹ to the country hotel Finca San Juan (with bar/restaurant).

Here, one should already descend to San Juan de La Rambla (recommended for walkers who would prefer the shortest and most leisurely path: 5 minutes after the hotel on the left, you come past the tennis court to a gully where a path descends and soon afterwards, at the edge of a plateau, becomes a stone-paved camino and leads directly down to the road bridge in San Juan de la Rambla).

Alternatively, you could also stay on the road straight ahead and, just under 10 minutes later, cross over a

The ascent in the Barranco de Ruíz.

Descent to San Juan de la Rambla.

larger *barranco*. 2 minutes after the *barranco* bridge, a roadway turns off right to a transformer tower 10m away from the road, from which a camino (unfortunately, progressively overgrown) sets off down the *barranco* and immediately goes past an electricity pylon and a large cross. The trail leads over a ridge down between two steep-sided *barrancos*.

After a good quarter of an hour, the trail changes over onto the left side of the *barranco* (at the fork following just after, keep to the rim of the *barranco*). Shortly afterwards, you meet a road at the first houses of San Juan. Follow this road downhill to the right to the bridge over the coastal road, TF-5 (just before this, the camino from the country hotel merges with the road). At the fork in the road after the bridge, keep right and a few minutes later a paved road descends left to reach the *plaza* of **San Juan de La Rambla** ❺ with the church.

Now follow the road to the right and after a few minutes, at the fork before the merge with the TF-5 (bus shelter) turn off left in the direction of Las Aguas. 10 minutes later, reach the seaside promenade of **Las Aguas** (❻, bar/restaurants, small pebble beach with boat mooring). A wonderful camino sets off along the steep coast. This leads in 20 minutes to **La Rambla** ❼. Here, at the Plaza de La Rambla next to the Ermita del Rosario, go right up the steps to the village road, turn left and in 10 minutes return to the **Barranco de Ruíz picnic area** ❶ on the TF-5.

The wonderful coastal trail from Las Aguas (photo) to La Rambla.

↗ 500m | ↘ 500m | 5.8km

17 From Garachico to San Juan del Reparo

2.30 hrs

Leisurely old camino above the former harbour town

Before the devastating eruption of Montaña Negra (see Walk 18) in 1706, Garachico was one of Tenerife's most important merchant and harbour towns. Two lava flows destroyed the harbour as well as extensive parts of the little town, which was rebuilt afterwards. Today, Garachico is one of the most delightful and unspoilt places on the island and a must for every tourist. A visit to the town can be combined ideally with a walk to San Juan del Reparo – the old, stone-paved trail leads through superb pine forests while following a lava flow and presenting views of Garachico, lying right at your feet.

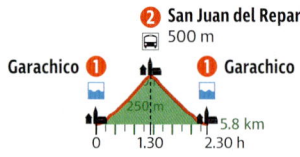

Starting point: Garachico, 17m, Castillo San Miguel on the coastal road next to the seawater pools (bus stop for the 363).
Grade: leisurely walk along an ancient cobblestone path.
Refreshment: bar/restaurants in Garachico, bar in San Juan del Reparo.

Start the walk in **Garachico** ❶ near the Castillo San Miguel on the coastal road and head towards the town and the parish church of Santa Ana (before it, on the right, a pretty little park with the Puerta de Tierra; here, ignore the PR TF 43, which turns off to the right). Immediately past the church (eastwards) reach the spacious Plaza de la Libertad where the Iglesia de Nuestra Señora de los Ángeles is located; on the right, next to it, the Convento de San Francisco and the town hall

From the trail you are afforded marvellous views of the delightful little town of Garachico.

(*ayuntamiento*). Now ascend to the right of the town hall, up Calle 18 de Julio. The street soon becomes a paved trail and, after a few minutes, meets a road – turn right along this road for 20m to then continue your ascent up left (PR TF 43, *white/yellow*). After 10 minutes the trail joins a road again which passes a barrier on your right after 2 minutes. 2 minutes after that, a lovely camino turns sharp right, bordered by low stone walls, and ascends in zigzags up the gentle slope covered in pine trees. The camino regales you again and again with marvellous views of the town.

After just under 1 hr, at the first houses of **San Juan del Reparo** ❷, the broad camino merges with a road that brings you in 10 minutes up to the church on the main road (bus stop for the 325, 392, 460; bar). From here, you could continue up along the PR TF 43 to La Montañeta (1¼ hrs; to the right of the church, ascend steeply along the village main street), otherwise turn back along the same trail to descend to **Garachico** ❶.

↗ 380m | ↘ 380m | 12.7km
3.50 hrs

18 From Arenas Negras to Chinyero

Short excursion into the island's more recent volcanic history

The rest area Las Arenas Negras is the perfect starting point for excursions into the extensive volcanic and woodland belt lying to the north-west of the Teide massif. Slopes of pitch-black lava flow, cinder cones and bright green, shimmering pine forests are set in contrast – a picture postcard landscape!

Location: La Montañeta, 950m (bus stop for the 360).
Starting point: Zona recreativa Las Arenas Negras (picnic area), 1225m, approach via a bumpy track road, 2.2km in length, that forks off from the TF-373 at Km 9 (800m from La Montañeta/Ermita San Francisco). If you are taking the bus for the approach, get off at the Ermita San Francisco at the upper village limits of La Montañeta and climb up the *white/yellow* marked PR TF 43 to reach the picnic area (¾ hr from La Montañeta).
Grade: easy walk.
Refreshment: bar in La Montañeta.

At the end of the track with the car park for the recreation area **Las Arenas Negras** ❶ a roadway, enclosed with boulders, branches off to the right and leads in a few mins to a sandy plain at the foot of the Volcán Garachico (the ascent of the volcano is prohibited for reasons of nature conservation). The roadway now turns into a trail, bordered by rows of stones, which runs along the edge of the plain and then at the foot of the Volcán Garachico. About 10 mins later, the trail bears left and then becomes a path which ascends for a short stretch towards a mountain ridge (to the left and above a trig point post). The path leads in easy up-and-down walking between the mighty lava flows which the volcano spewed forth towards Garachico in 1706. Afterwards, the path drops down into a sandy terrain, broken up by young pine

78

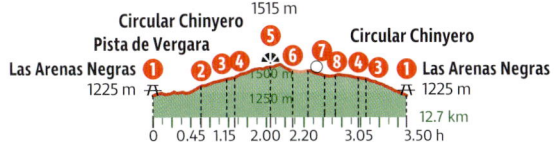

trees; bear slightly to the right to traverse this area. After a total of half an hour, enter a pine forest and soon afterwards meet up with an intersecting trail, flanked by rows of stones (PR TF 43.1, *white/yellow*) – turn left onto this trail and ascend. Some minutes later, at the western ridge of the Volcán Garachico, reach a roadway which follows the Vergara watercourse ❷.

If you prefer a short circular walk, turn left to follow the roadway for a good 10 mins and then turn left along the intersecting trail PR TF 4, to return to the starting point (¾ hr). We, however, turn right 50m further on, following the trail PR TF 43.1 to cross over the watercourse (sign: 'Chinyero'). The trail ascends gently through open pine forest and then merges 20 minutes later with the PR TF 43 ❸ (the return route later on turns left here). Just under 10 minutes later, the trail crosses over a track – this is the beginning of the **Chinyero circular route** ❹ (Circular Chinyero) which we follow in a clockwise direction. The track leads in a broad bend around the twin peaks of Chinyero and then forks a good 15 mins later – turn right here. A good 15 minutes more, the trail crosses over a farm road and ascends for a short stretch to reach a lovely rest area/viewpoint beneath a spreading pine tree ❺. 10 minutes after that, bear right at a fork to ascend and some minutes more, cross over a track ❻ (left leads in 5 mins to the **TF-38** at Km 14,9). A good 5 mins later, the trail semi-circles around a group meeting area. 10 mins after that, merge into a track ❼ – turn right here, following the PR TF 43 (the PR TF 43.3 forks to the left to Santiago del Teide). 10 mins more, the trail forks yet again ❽ – turn right here with the PR TF 43 to cross through the marvellous Chinyero lava field (straight ahead, the PR TF 43.2 forks away to Los Partidos). 20 minutes later, the trail merges into a track. 50m past this point, reach the outset of the circuit route ❹. Turn left here to return to the next junction ❸ and then turn right (PR TF 43) towards Arenas Negras. 15 minutes later, the trail crosses the Vergara watercourse and the track. Another quarter of an hour brings us back to the picnic area **Las Arenas Negras** ❶.

The very colourful Chinyero is Tenerife's youngest volcano (1909).

↗ 270m | ↘ 270m | 5.0km

19 Montaña de la Botija, 2122m; Montaña Samara, 1936m

2.00 hrs

Volcano walk at the foot of Pico Viejo

Montaña de la Botija and Montaña Samara tower up from the expansive lava landscape at the foot of Pico Viejo. This circular walk passes several craters and lava flows.

Starting point: *mirador*/car park at Km 7.7 on the Cañadas road Chío – Boca Tauce (TF-38), at the southern foot of Montaña Samara.
Grade: mostly leisurely walk on trails and paths. The rim of the crater of Montaña Samara is narrow in the upper section and precipitous – in stormy weather you should therefore not continue on to the summit. In poor visibility there could be route-finding problems.
Alternative: extended circular walk via Cuevas Negras (an additional 1¼ hrs): after 10 mins, turn diagonally right onto trail No 32. Soon cross over a lava flow and, 40 mins later, reach a little pine wood. Here, trail 9 forks off to the left. A good 10 mins later, on a plateau with stone walls, trail No 38 turns left towards Cuevas Negras. 15 mins more, at the hook in the trail, pass the first tubo (lava tube) and, subsequently, even more of these. Afterwards, the trail crosses a field of lava and merges with trail No 13 at the Reventada turn-off (see below).
Tip: at Km 10 on the TF-38 (at the km signpost) a path turns off to the east leading, 100m further on, to a lava tunnel, about 3m high and 30m long.

From the **mirador** ❶ follow the distinct trail that forks 30m on at a signpost – turn right onto trail No 32 which leads eastwards towards Teide. The sandy trail runs fairly parallel to the road and after 5 mins leads left past a rain gauge. 100m on, ignore a path forking off to the left. A few minutes later, at the fork ❷ bear diagonally left along trail No 13, following the left

At the start of the walk – Montaña de la Botija with Pico Viejo and Pico del Teide.

hand edge of a lava field (trail No 32 turns off diagonally right in the direction of Pico Viejo, see Alternative). The trail ascends through a gully on the right of the black volcanic cone of Montaña de la Botija. Behind you, in the distance, you can see the island of La Gomera, behind this to the left, El Hierro, and further right, with the double hump, La Palma.

15 mins after the last fork the trail levels out – the massive Pico Viejo now appears and Teide is just emerging behind it. The path continues towards these peaks and soon leads along the left hand edge of another vast lava field in a flat valley. Gradually, after a total of a good three quarters of an hour, reach the top of a volcanic sand ridge – to the left and somewhat below, you can see a young, solitary pine tree. Here the trail turns sharply off to the left in the direction of Montaña de la Botija ❸ (the trail straight on to the nearby Montaña Reventada has been closed off due to conservation).

The path descends along the edge of a rugged lava flow coming down from Montaña Reventada. After a good 5 mins, keep left on the main path with trail No 13 which now diverges further away from the lava flow on a slight incline and a few minutes later reaches a small col ❹. The summit detour onto **Montaña de la Botija** has also been closed off, but you can instead climb up the neighbouring summit and from there enjoy a far-reaching view of western Tenerife.

The path now dips slightly, keeping to the left, down across the gritty volcanic flank of Montaña de la Botija. After a quarter of an hour, reach a junction (straight on, after a few metres, meet up with the approach trail) – turn sharp right here with trail No 13 to a small group of rocks. Then the trail, edged with lines of stones, leads for the most part leisurely descending towards Montaña Samara and soon follows a wide right hand bend. After a quarter of an hour, the trail forks just before the volcanic crater. On the left, the return trail turns off to the starting point nearby but before that, you can continue straight on to the crater and ascend directly left across the wind-exposed ridge up to the highest point of **Montaña Samara** ❺, 1936m (just under 10 minutes).

The Teno mountains and the South
Untamed barrancos and sensational coastline cliffs

The Teno mountains in the extreme north-west of the island offer a wonderful, virtually untouched walking terrain. Like the Anaga massif, the Teno massif is one of the oldest mountain ranges on Tenerife and boasts numerous dramatic gorges – especially in the west on the steep coastline which plunges almost vertically to depths of up to 600m ('Acantilado de Los Gigantes') – the most famous of these is the Barranco de Masca, one of the island's classic walks. Also in the north, the Teno massif, cut by deep *barrancos*, drops extremely steeply down to the fertile coastal plain near

Buenavista and Los Silos. The Teno mountains reach an altitude of about 1000m and are virtually treeless with the exception of the slopes on the north-east side where a few dense laurisilva forests are still located – an archaic, often wind-scoured and cloud-covered landscape which seems, on the barren Teno plateau at least, almost odious. The Palmar Valley and, even more so, the Masca Valley with its picturesque palm groves are exceptions to the rule. Towards the south, this region is bordered by the south-west coast, superbly developed for tourism but in some places somewhat spoiled as a result. Los Gigantes and Puerto de Santiago, the sunniest seaside resorts on the island not only boast a wonderful sandy beach at Playa de la Arena but are also ideal bases for holidaymakers wishing to limit their walks primarily to the western part of the island; on the other hand, Las Américas, Los Cristianos and the other seaside resorts on the southern coast have the advantage of motorway access to Santa Cruz. The caldera rim mountains slope gently down to the coast on this side, sometimes furrowed by seemingly bottomless *barrancos* such as the Barranco del Infierno. In the regions around Adeje, Arona and the Valle de San Lorenzo, there are also a few imposing rocky mountains, which are attractive places for walking.

BARRANCO DEL INFIERNO

In spring 2015, Tenerife's second most popular gorge (next to the Masca Gorge) has been limited to a certain number of walkers and an entrance fee of € 11 is demanded. Because of this, the route is no longer presented in this walking guide. The walk begins near the bar/restaurant Otelo at the upper edge of the settlement of Adeje and ends at the island's highest waterfall, dropping down 80m in three tiers and running the entire year through. Walking time: 2¾ hrs; height difference: 300m; grade: easy; information: www.barrancodelinfierno.es

20 From Los Silos to Erjos

↗ 960m | ↘ 960m | 16.4km
5.15 hrs

On old caminos through the laurel woods of Monte del Agua

The primeval laurisilva forests of Monte del Agua above Los Silos are among the most unspoiled on the island. Marvellous old caminos and shady forestry tracks open up this densely forested area of the Teno mountains to mountain walkers. If the route from Los Silos to Erjos and back down to Los Silos is too strenuous, you could choose instead to begin the hike in Erjos – this shortens the time needed to only about two hours but still includes most of the outstanding features of the walk.

Starting point: *plaza*/church in the centre of Los Silos, 109m (bus stop for the 363).
Grade: all things considered, this is a strenuous walk, but most of the individual stretches are leisurely, following beautiful ancient caminos and forest roads.
Refreshment: bars in Los Silos and in Erjos.
Alternative: from Las Moradas to Las Portelas: at the turn-off (see below) along the roadway to the right. At a barrier it joins a broad track with the PR TF 52 (*white/yellow*) which leads left to Erjos and right (keeping along the track) to Las Portelas (1 hr from the turn-off, bus stop for the 355, 366).

A narrow road leads on the right past the church of **Los Silos** ❶ and heads for the mountains – Calle Susana. 100m on, the road crosses the new main road (bus stop) and 100m after that, a concrete path branches off to the right in the direction of Las Moradas (PR TF 54, *white/yellow*). It becomes a lovely camino after 100m, which leads along beside

View back to Los Silos from the ascent path – on the left the Barranco de Bucarón, on the right the Barranco de los Cochinos.

the stream bed of the Barranco de Bucarón. After a quarter of an hour, change over onto the left hand side of the valley across a bridge. 5 minutes later, the camino switches back to the right hand side of the valley which then gradually widens. A few derelict stone houses – **Las Moradas** ❷ – appear up on the ridge on the left of the valley to which the camino leads. From there you can enjoy a lovely view down into the deep, untamed and rugged Barranco de los Cochinos – you can get an even better view if you climb up to the small summit (498m) on the left which takes 5 minutes. The camino continues up past the houses and then crosses over to the left onto the slope above the Barranco de los Cochinos. After a good quarter of an hour, pass a derelict building on the left, covered in blackberry bushes – **Moradas de Arriba** ❸. Subsequently, cut through a secondary valley. The trail now enters a sparse scrub wood. This is mostly a pleasant stretch, somewhat narrow at times, ascending steadily across the slope. At the end, climb up via a little valley notch until the trail joins a forest

road ❹. By turning right, you can reach Las Portelas (see Alternative), but turn left instead with the PR TF 54 in the direction of Monte del Agua. After 5 mins, pass the ruins of a building. A few minutes later, the forest road leads through a small valley. Here, the waymarked trail branches off to the right. It meets an intersecting trail some minutes later; turn left to ascend across the slope to the broad **Pista del Monte del Agua** ❺ (½ hr from the forest road; a rocky resting place at the junction). Now follow the PR TF 52/54 (*white/yellow*) along the forest track to the left. Gradually it enters a beautiful laurel forest. After a quarter of an hour, ignore a roadway turning off left on a left hand bend (post). Not quite half an hour later, pass a *mirador* ❻ (starting here, the forest road has been made accessible for mobility-impaired persons). 5 minutes after that, the wood thins out – you can already see ahead the village of Erjos (do not descend to the left here). On the next right hand bend the waymarked trail turns off diagonally left and takes a shortcut across the wide bend of the track. After just under 10 minutes, it joins a roadway which, to the left, ascends into the village. After the first houses, meet up with a road (left, your descent trail later on, in the direction of Cuevas Negras). Head straight on to the church square of **Erjos** ❼ – behind the church, on the main road, you will find a bus shelter (bus stop for the 325, 392, 460) and two bars (on the right along the main road).

From the church gate go back straight on again past the church square and keep right following the PR TF 53 (*white/yellow*) down the road. At the last house in the row, a camino zigzags to the left down into the Barranco de Cuevas Negras – between times it turns into a roadway. A water conduit runs along beside it which has replaced the derelict water canal. 20 minutes after Erjos, leave the overgrown garden terraces of the village behind and enter an open brushwood. The broad camino, lined with moss-covered stones and crossing through the forest, is one of the most beautiful in the Teno mountains. 25 minutes later, pass a farmstead and more abandoned gardens. On the other side of the slope more houses appear. Below them the camino switches to the right hand side of the valley once again and leads through the hamlet of **Las Cuevas Negras** ❽ – most of the houses are in a state of disrepair.

Just before Erjos with Teide in the background.

In the village centre, a trail turns off to the right in the direction of Tierra del Trigo (PR TF 53.1), but follow the PR TF 53 straight on downhill in the direction of Los Silos. The gorge becomes more and more dramatic: the camino descends very steeply below an overhanging, extremely furrowed rock face. Huge Euphorbia line the edge of the path and Los Silos appears ahead.

After just under half an hour, reach the bottom of the *barranco* with the first houses ❾ – the massive Barranco de los Cochinos turns off left. You are greeted by what is truly a little paradise: between lush orchards with orange, almond, fig, medlar and palm trees, later also banana plantations, a roadway leads down the valley soon crossing a bridge and switching to the right valley flank. 50m afterwards follow the PR TF 53 to the left across a bridge and reach on the other side a roadway (Calle Susana) which brings us back to the main square in **Los Silos** ❶.

Kiosk on the plaza of Los Silos.

21 Cruz de Gala, 1347m

↗ 540m | ↘ 540m | 10.9km
3.45 hrs
🚌 👣

Enchanting route through laurel woods and over panoramic summits

This interesting circular walk over the Gala peaks is characterised by magnificent, ever-changing panoramic views.

Location: Erjos, 1000m.
Starting point: Restaurante Fleytas on the main road 1.5km above Erjos, immediately before the turn-off of the road to San José de los Llanos (car park, bus stop for the 325, 460).
Grade: apart from the rather vertiginous stretches along rock faces on Little Gala, a predominently easy walk.
Refreshment: bar/restaurant Fleytas (closed Wednesdays), bar/restaurants in Erjos.
Linking tip: with Walk 29.

From the bus stop at the **restaurant** ❶ descend 50m along the main road towards Erjos and then turn left onto a track road. This leads in wide bends down onto a plain then, after 10 mins, merges with an intersecting road. Follow this to the right. 50m further on, the road forks – straight on leads to Erjos, but turn left instead onto the PR TF 51 (sign), passing between two ponds that are often without water. Stay on the main track at the following forks (i.e. a good 100m further on, turn right at the first fork and 20m after that, take the middle trail ❷ on the right next to the earth wall; the PR TF 51 cuts away here to the left). Now ascend on the other side of the valley straight up to the ridge (on the way, you pass a chain barrier).
At the top of the ridge (it's a total of a half an hour to this point), keep left. After 35m, you have to make a decision ❸: if visibility is good, we recommend that you ascend directly over the panoramic ridge (the trail always leads along the ridgeline and merges again later, at the iron gate, with the main trail). However, we fork off to the right along a distinct path which leads through the laurisilva forest, while keeping about at the same height.
A quarter of an hour later, bear diagonally left ascending along the main trail, and in not quite

another 10 minutes, reach a forestry road. Turn left along this road and, not quite 10 minutes later, pass an iron gate ❹ and then meet up with a tarmac road ascending to the **Cruz de Gala** ❺. The ascent to the summit with transmitter towers (the fire lookout tower has been torn down) takes 15 minutes and presents a fabulous view: practically the whole of the Teno mountains lie at your feet (directly south-west you can see the prominent rocky summit of Pico Verde) and the volcanic terrain at the foot of Pico Viejo lies spread out before you.

View from the Degollada de la Mesa towards Cruz de Gala.

You can descend from the highest point directly to the Degollada de la Mesa (a good 10 minutes, some easy scrambling in places), otherwise go back along the road to the iron gate ❹ (a good 10 minutes) to continue left on the level forest road. After a good 10 minutes, the forest road veers off to the right. But stay on the trail straight ahead (after 30m left) which, a minute later, joins the Sendero de la Cumbre ❻ (PR TF 51/56, *white/yellow*). Follow this panoramic trail to the left and, after about a quarter of an hour, reach the **Degollada de la Mesa**, 1247m, the col between the Big and the Little Gala. At the point where the main trail leads on the left downhill, a path turns off to the right, ascending and keeping to the ridge and, in not quite a quarter of an hour, onto **Little Gala** ❼ (Pico Verde, 1318m; at the summit, some light scrambling is required). The view of Masca, the mighty Masca Gorge and La Gomera is exquisite!

Back at the Degollada de la Mesa, continue descending the main trail. After 10 minutes, this becomes a wide forest track (the PR TF 56 turns away here to the right) that, 25 minutes later, joins the road that leads up from the Erjos to the Cruz de Gala ❽. The PR TF 51 leads opposite on the left along a lovely path down into a small valley notch. After a good quarter of an hour, it joins a roadway that, 5 minutes later, on the alluvial plain, joins your outward route: right, then left between the mostly dry ponds, afterwards right at the fork and after 50m, left up to the main road at the **Restaurante Fleytas** ❶.

22 From Buenavista to Masca via El Palmar

↗ 830m | ↘ 340m | 10.1km
3.30 hrs

Varied valley walk and ridge crossing

A walk could hardly be more diverse: the ascent through the Palmar Valley leads you through a rural, still mostly unspoilt Tenerife. Afterwards the panoramic crest of Cumbre del Carrizal awaits. A delightful descent then leads down to the palm groves of the beautifully situated village of Masca.

Starting point: bus station in Buenavista del Norte, 129m, or the turn-off of the road in the direction of El Palmar (bus stop for the 355, 363, 365, 366, 369).
Destination: Masca, 620m (bus stop for the 355, 365).
Grade: a leisurely walk throughout, partly along roads, mostly however on beautiful caminos and paths.
Refreshment: several bars and restaurants along the way (in Buenavista, El Palmar, Las Lagunetas, Las Portelas, Cruz de Hilda and Masca).
Alternative: detour from Cruz de Hilda, 780m, to Morro de la Galera/Roque La Fortaleza (a good 3½ hrs; a fantastic walk, but only for the surefooted walker with a perfect head for heights, only in good weather!): from the top of the pass, a roadway ascends westwards then ends after 5 mins. Keeping left, a distinct, pleasant trail continues with a magnificent view of Masca and the Roque de Masca. The trail soon switches to the right hand side of the ridge. Somewhat exposed, this leads briefly over a narrow rocky ridge. Some mins later, the ridge broadens again. The reinforced trail now leads down and slightly to the right, passes a small rocky plateau and then reaches a level, rocky ridgeline. The sometimes precipitous, and sometimes also exposed, alpine path continues gently downhill then runs constantly up-and-down across the rock face before steeply ascending in tight zigzags. A short traverse follows 10 mins later, then you continue up a steep incline to reach the crest of the ridge. Follow the ridge, keeping to the left-hand edge (at the outset, enjoy a view of Teide and the Playa de Masca!), descending arduously and almost completely pathless (at the cistern, ascend to the right and keep to the rocky ridge) until reaching the Morro de la Galera (Roque de Abajo), the final hillock before the steep coast. From here, you also have a view of the Punta de Teno, but the Playa de Masca, on the other hand, is out of sight.
Tip: the walk can be shortened as desired (e.g. to/from Las Portelas). Each village along the route can be accessed with the No 355/365 bus Buenavista – Masca.

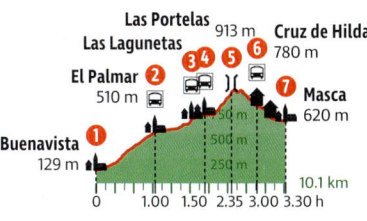

Walk from the bus station ❶ up to the main road and follow this for a good 100m to the right to reach a left turning of the main road to El Palmar and Masca; ascend this road for 5 mins. On the first left hand bend turn right onto the narrow road heading straight uphill. After 10 minutes, meet the main road once again. On the other side, a cobblestone trail continues which subsequently crosses or touches the main road several times (after 10 mins, you have to follow the main road for 40m). About 20 mins later, complete a left-hand bend and then fork away by continuing straight ahead along an access road which, after passing a dam, leads steeply uphill through the village of El Palmar.

In a good 20 mins, where the mountain valley of El Palmar begins, once again cross the main road and continue straight on along the narrow road. 100m on, in the village centre

View from the Cumbre del Carrizal of El Palmar Valley.

of **El Palmar** ❷ meet up again with the main road (bus stop, bar) but carry straight on. After 50m pass the church at the right hand side and follow the village street Calle La Cruz (later Calle Los Llanitos) with the PR TF 52.2 (*white/yellow*) straight on uphill (after 10 minutes the PR TF 57 turns off right to Teno Alto across the main road, see Walk 23). Now pass a massive volcanic hill, rutted by deep furrows – the lava sand surface has been sliced like pieces of cake. After a good 15 minutes, the *white/yellow* marked trail turns left onto a road which you follow straight on uphill. After a good 15 minutes, pass a right hand loop in the main road and go straight on following the *white/yellow* waymarkers along the village road (Camino El Ojito) of **Las Lagunetas**.

At the church square ❸ (we recommend the *Bodegón*) turn right with the PR TF 56 (*white/yellow*) onto the narrow road (Calle de La Cruz) that soon comes to an end. To the left a meadow path passes through terraces and merges with the main road at the community library of **Las Portelas** ❹ (bus stop).

Cross the main road and continue uphill along the road to the right (Calle de Fuera) with the PR TF 59 (*white/yellow*). After 100m, on a left hand bend, a meadow path branches off to the right which leads down into a small *barranco* (the last section is concreted) – walk along this to the right for 25m and on the other side along a lovely camino steeply up to a road. Follow this uphill and after 4 minutes (25m after a left hand bend) turn right onto a distinct path that in a few minutes reaches the main road. Across the road, diagonally to the left, the *white/yellow* waymarked camino continues, leads gently uphill in wide bends and after 15 minutes reaches the top of the ridge of the **Cumbre del Carrizal** ❺. The meteorological divide runs along the ridgeline, separating the rainy north from the sunny southwest – accordingly, the vegetation changes abruptly at the ridgeline: behind you, the tree heather-covered slopes of the upper Palmar Valley and, in front of you, the succulent-blanketed slopes of the Carrizales Valley.

Cross the ridgeline path (PR TF 51; it ascends to the left over Cumbre de Bolico up to the Cruz de Gala and to the right to the Tabaiba Pass) and keep following the PR TF 59, which leads on the other side of the ridge towards Cruz de Hilda/Masca. This soon passes a rock outcrop with a panoramic view of Los Carrizales and the *barranco* of the same name, as well as beyond to the Hilda Pass. The route continues as a beautiful high mountain walk, passing a spring, to reach **Cruz de Hilda** ❻ (beautiful viewing terrace with café, closed on Fridays). To the right of the road, a roadway branches off and after some minutes becomes a spectacularly panoramic cliff face path (see Alternative) but you can also enjoy a marvellous view over the Masca Valley from the top of the pass.

Now, in front of the *mirador*, follow the narrow road that branches off to the left in the direction of Masca. Two minutes later, directly above a palm tree, a rocky trail branches off to the right, descending away from the palm trees. Soon walk below a few houses, then descend in zigzags. After a quarter of an hour, the trail merges with the main road at the Masca bar/restaurant in the district of **La Vica** (bus stop).

It takes only 10 minutes to reach **Masca** ❼ along the main road to the left where several attractive bars and restaurants offer refreshment. Countless palm, orange, lemon and almond trees thrive in this sun-drenched valley, protected on all sides by steep rocky mountains. Is there a more beautiful place on earth?

The descent path from the Cumbre del Carrizal to Masca.

TOP 23 — From El Palmar to Teno Alto

↗ 650m | ↘ 650m | 10.1km
3.40 hrs

Circular walk over the Teno plateau and Cumbre de Baracán

Expanses of meadowland, cultivated terraces and the occasional hamlet characterise the barren plateau of Teno Alto, the first destination of this walk. The undisputed highlight is the ensuing walking trail over the Cumbre de Baracán, one of the most beautiful trails on the island.

Location: El Palmar, 500m (bus stop for the 355, 365 and 366).
Starting point: turn-off to Teno Alto, 530m (bus stop, car parking along the road).
Grade: mostly easy, but now and then rather steep.
Refreshment: bar/restaurants in El Palmar and in Teno Alto.
Linking tip: with Walks 22 (from the Tabaiba Pass), 24 and 25 (from Teno Alto).

Begin the walk in **El Palmar** ❶ at the turn-off to Teno Alto. Next to it on the left the trail (PR TF 57, signpost to 'Teno Alto', *white/yellow*) starts uphill between stone walls. After almost a quarter of an hour, cross a road (the picnic area Los Pedregales is located on the right hand side at the road) and now begin a steeper ascent. A few minutes later, cross over the road leading towards Teno Alto. The trail now ascends steeply through light scrub and pine wood to a col on the ridgeline of the **Cumbre de Baracán** ❷ (20 minutes).

Here you meet the road again but do not cross over to it. The camino which you now take runs parallel to the road. Then cross a valley notch and ascend for a short time to a rocky mountain ridge (keep right here) and walk downhill on the other side of the ridge. After 10 minutes, reach the bottom of the valley. The trail now leads across the slope again, bearing left and over a rock outcrop, slightly ascending to a terrace where the camino widens into a track. Some minutes later, on a sharp left hand bend in the track, the cobblestone camino continues straight on and shortly afterwards crosses the Teno road and immediately after that, finally merges with it. Keeping left you soon reach the church square of **Teno Alto** ❸ (Los Bailaderos) where two bar/restaurants are located.

Next to the church square, turn left following the PR TF 51 (*white/yellow*) onto the ascending street. After a good 10 minutes, pass a barrier and a few minutes later, the trail forks off to the left. It soon bends left away from the crest of the mountain ridge and leads across a slope through a wood of tree heathers. Some minutes later, the trail again returns to the other,

Backwards view from the ridge trail to Teno Alto.

The ridge trail leads past the verdant dome of the Baracán to the Tabaiba Pass.

treeless flank of the ridge, now with a beautiful view of Los Carrizales and the west coast as well as of La Gomera. The trail switches sides twice more and, one hour from Teno Alto, reaches a stone bench – there's a detour to the left here to the summit of **Baracán** ❹ (1003m, not quite 10 minutes; trig point). A good 5 minutes after that, the camino sweeps back to the left hand side of the ridge, now with a pretty view of the Palmar Valley. Almost a quarter of an hour later, the trail once again touches the crest of the ridge (there are nice spots for a break on the other side of the ridge) and soon after, you reach the **Tabaiba Pass** ❺ and the Masca road.

20m before the road, a distinct camino branches off to the left into the Palmar Valley – this descends only a short distance then leads on the level across the slope below the road and over to a house. From there, descend 30m on the track and, on the right next to it, along a meadow path which soon passes another house on the left. Cross a track (5m to the right) and soon afterwards reach a wide road; descend along this to the main road and the upper district of the village of **El Palmar** ❻ (bus stop). To the left, this road brings you back to the starting point ❶ in 10 minutes. If you wish to avoid the main road, you can follow the trail opposite: at an intersecting road, turn right to the village road of El Palmar and descend left here with the PR TF 52.2 until, after 5 minutes, a road turns off left to meet the main road 10m away (directly at the turn-off to Teno Alto).

↗ 740m | ↘ 740m | 8.1km

4.00 hrs

Risco alpine path – from Buenavista to Teno Alto

TOP 24

Spectacular cliff path to the Teno Alto plateau

'Risco alpine path' – what a fitting name! – the cliff face path leads right across the steep, rock walls of the Teno mountains, with plunging, sometimes sheer drops, down to the plain of Buenavista – a thrill like no other, rewarded by breathtakingly beautiful downward views.

Location: Buenavista del Norte (bus stop for the 355, 363, 365, 366, 369).
Starting point: barrier on the road from Buenavista to Punta de Teno (TF-445) at Km 2.5 (bus top for line 369). Parking possible on the side of the road.
Tip: from the barrier, the road to Punta de Teno is only open for bus and taxi.
Grade: some very steep stretches along a somewhat exposed cliff face path to the Teno plateau; when wet or during strong winds, this walk is not advisable.
Refreshment: bar/restaurants in Buenavista and in Teno Alto.
Alternative: ideal to combine with Walk 25 (return transport from Teno Bajo via hourly bus 369 service until 17.25). – From Teno Alto you can continue to El Palmar, Buenavista, Las Portelas or Masca (bus connection see Walks 22, 23).

2.5km from Buenavista, the road crosses the vast Barranco del Monte. At the **barrier** ❶ the PR TF 58 (signpost, *white/yellow*) branches off to the left and, after 100m, leads past a larger water storage tank on the left. The camino now runs for about 15m at the edge of the *barranco* and then turns right towards the smaller stream bed of the **Barranco de la Torre** to leave it after 10 minutes to the right and climb steeply over the nearby mountain ridge.

After a total of about 25 mins, a path branches off to the right at a small terrace, however, ascend straight on (left) up some steps (shortly after, bear right at the fork). Soon,

a couple of metres of exposed ascent lead up steps cut into the rock. Somewhat later, traverse the slope to skirt left around a rock outcrop, pass a cave then reach a steeply plunging *barranco* – this is a somewhat precipitous stretch which can be very tricky when wet. The camino now continues to ascend along the steep, gully-like *barranco* for about 20 minutes and then leaves it again to the left, while climbing up along the rim of the Barranco de la Torre. After about 15 minutes, the trail leads to the left below a small rock wall and, soon after, continues to the right over a broad reddish ledge of rock. Some minutes later, reach the Teno plateau at the **Puerta del Risco** and then immediately after, reach the site of a circular gathering place of the ancient Guanche people ❷ which is enclosed by low stone walls. To the right of the site a distinct path continues traversing the slope. After 5 minutes, in front of a little summit block, the path descends to the right into a beige/red-coloured, eroded landscape (now without a distinct path). About 10 minutes from the summit block reach **Roque El Toscón** ❸ (also known as Roque Marrubio), a small, detached pulpit rock, 600m, that plunges vertically down towards the coast (fabulous viewpoint; easy scramble at the end).

Back at the Guanche cult site ❷, follow the camino (*white/yellow*) – coming from below – ascending past the cult site on the left. The sometimes

The rocky alpine path to the Teno plateau is very demanding, especially when wet.

Just before the Teno plateau, the trail pulls out all the stops.

paved trail bears to the right past a colourful area of tuff rock formed from consolidated volcanic ash, and then, keeping right, leads to a flat saddle. Past the saddle the trail leads to the left, slightly ascending, traversing the slope and over to a flat mountain ridge. Cross over the ridge then descend to a road junction (10 minutes). Now following the 'Teno' signpost ascend beyond the junction straight on up the eroded gully (it's better to follow the road ascending on the right if wet). A good 5 minutes later meet up with the road again; turn left to reach **Teno Alto** ❹ (Los Bailaderos) in 5 minutes.

25 From Teno Alto to Punta de Teno

↗ 720m | ↘ 720m | 9.5km
4.15 hrs

Descent to the north-western tip of Tenerife

The descent from Teno Alto to Punta de Teno, the north-western tip of Tenerife, is one of the most popular walks in the Teno Mountains. The route leads through the barren fields of the Teno plateau, furrowed by rugged and eroded gullies as well as pleasant valleys – a remote, archaic strip of country providing magnificent views of La Gomera when visibility is good.

Starting point: church square of Teno Alto, 780m, on the plateau of the Teno mountains (no bus connection, access on foot with either Walk 23 or 24). If you wish to approach by bus, begin the walk in Teno Bajo (bus line 369 from Buenavista).
Grade: predominently gentle walk, but with a rather laborious ascent.
Refreshment: bar/restaurants in Teno Alto.

Alternative: from the Ermita de El Draguillo at Km 6.9 on the Teno Bajo – Buenavista road (a few minutes from Teno Bajo) resolute, sure-footed walkers can follow a camino, ill-maintained at the outset (a good 1 hr later, from the cataract, the trail is not distinct) along the Barranco de la Sobaquera back to Teno Alto (about 2¾ hrs in ascent).
Linking tip: ideal to combine with Walk 24 (refer there; return via bus).

From the *plaza* in **Teno Alto** ❶ a street leads straight on (PR TF 51, *white/yellow*) passing the bar/restaurant La Piñata and forks after 10 minutes on a flat mountain ridge with a few houses. Descend straight on here down the roadway and at the fork 10 minutes later keep right downhill. A few minutes later the roadway joins a road. The waymarked trail crosses this and descends along the old, sometimes paved camino on the left-hand side of the road. It runs along beside a water conduit at the right hand edge of the Barranco de las Cuevas. A few minutes later it rejoins the road, only to leave it once again past a farmstead while bearing left along the *barranco*, parallel to water conduits ❷. Agaves, prickly pear cacti, Euphor-

The Teno plateau with the hamlet of Los Dornajos. – Below: Roque Chiñaco.

bia and geraniums line the trail which then leads between tumbledown houses. The trail heads directly towards a cluster of houses and 10m before the first one, turns left, descending to the bottom of the *barranco*. Here, meet up with the roadway again and turn left to cross over to the other side of the *barranco*. The roadway now leads steadily downhill between terraces (on the way, close the gate behind you!) until it ends a quarter of an hour later at a spur of land at **Roque Chiñaco** ❸. You can see the Punta de Teno with a lighthouse ahead.

At the end of the roadway, a camino continues down to the left. Soon pass a rock tower and, about 25 minutes later, a water distributor ❹ (by following a large water conduit to the left, you could take a shortcut to Punta de Teno – a good 15 minutes on, the path joins the TF-445 next to a plantation; ¼ hr along the road to the lighthouse). The path forks after 5 minutes – continue left here on the main trail which, 5 mins later, next to the Luz de Teno agricultural cooperative in **Teno Bajo** ❺ (Caserío Las Casas; bus stop, an hourly bus service until 17.25 for line 369 to Buenavista) merges with the Buenavista – Punta de Teno road (TF-445).

If you wish to make a detour to the lighthouse on Punta de Teno, follow the road (or the trail above the road) to the left (2km; ½ hr).

101

↗ 270m | ↘ 270m | 5.6km

26 Abache alpine path

2.20 hrs

🚌 🚶

Pleasant and panoramic – the high trail above the Carrizales valley

The Abache alpine path is one of the most beautiful – and easiest– walking trails in the Teno mountains. This leads along a marvellous high mountain trail above the dramatic Carrizales gorge. Two little peaks also provide delightful scenic viewpoints.

Starting point: Los Carrizales, the turn-off for the walking trail is in the first hairpin bend of the access road, 645m (bus stop for lines 355/365 on the TF-436 Buenavista – Masca, Km 13, at the turn-off for the access road; from here, 200m to the starting point for the walk).
Grade: mostly a pleasant (but sometimes a steep) camino, which demands sure-footedness and a relatively good head for heights; from the tumbledown house, some sections more overgrown.

Start off in the first **hairpin bend** ❶ of the access road from Los Carrizales; take the lower trail that forks off from here. The narrow road is concrete for the first metres as it leads pleasantly through the slope whilst opening a view of the wild and idyllic Carrizales valley, dotted with almond trees. Before the road reaches the crest of the ridge, a camino forks off to the right. This lovely high trail passes below the Roque de los Catorce Reales. Afterwards, as a cleverly laid camino traversing the rock face, it passes the Roque la Barbita. This is a fantastic stretch of trail that also presents a view of La Gomera and La Palma. The trail leads, more or less, directly over the crest of the ridge as it now opens a view to the nearby Roque Fortaleza as well as to the Cumbres Carrizales and Baracán. At the onset of a gently sloping plateau, pass a little peak, **El Paso** ❷, which provides for a panoramic rest break. Afterwards,

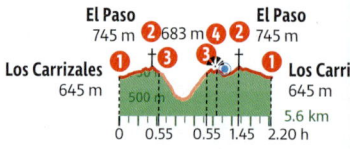

The destination for this walk is a tumbledown house with a threshing circle – opening up a view of La Gomera.

continue by descending along the plateau whilst bearing left and then soon keep to the left of the plateau along the crest. At a tumbledown **house** ❸ meet up with the next pretty spot for a break. Crossing over the threshing circle a trail continues on to the Roque Bermejo, perched on the steep coastal cliffs, but this is often hard to follow and can therefore only be recommended to the adventurous walker. On the other hand, an absolute must is the excursion to the nearby Abache ridge: behind the house, climb down along the terraced plateau and cross over to the adjacent ridge (here, straight away, on the other side of the ridge, a camino forks off diagonally to the right, very overgrown for the first metres, and leads to a spring). Follow the crest of the ridge to reach a 'peak' with a pole marker ❹ – a marvellous viewpoint with a view taking in the Gigantes rock face all the way to the southwest coast, of the Carrizale valley, to Punta de Teno and of La Gomera and La Palma.

For the return, you could either take the approach trail (passing the house) – or continue on along this ridge (mostly a path marked by cairns) and, at the upper end of the plateau, meet up again with the main trail.

↗ 550m | ↘ 550m | 6.9km

27 Guergue alpine path

4.00 hrs

Classic walk high above the Masca Gorge

The path leads along the mountain ridge which divides two of the most monumental gorges in the Teno mountains, the Barranco de Masca and the Barranco del Natero. Combined with the dizzying downwards views, framed by the two sheer faces of the gorges, you can also expect a fabulous view of the steep coastline at the abandoned Finca de Guergue near Los Gigantes. On top of that, La Gomera seems only a stone's throw away.

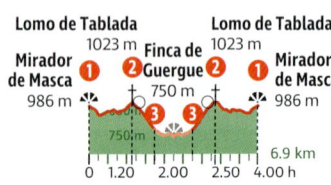

Talorte: Masca, 620m (bus stop for the line 355, 365), and Santiago del Teide, 930m (bus stop for the lines 325, 355, 460–462).
Starting point: Casas de Araza, 970m, on the Santiago – Masca road (bus stop for the 355); parking possible at the Mirador de Masca (400m below the Cherfé Pass).
Grade: a sometimes steep camino which requires surefootedness and a lack of vertigo. Overgrown path on the Guergue plain.
Refreshment: bar/restaurants in Masca and in Santiago del Teide.
Important note: the trail has been closed beginning 2019: at the start of the walk, at the Casas de Araza, a property owner has erected barriers and acts aggressively as well. It is not certain when or if this historically significant trail will be reopened. Information available at the visitor centre Los Pedregales, tenoparque@tenerife.es. As an alternative until then we can recommend the route from Cruz de Hilda to Morro de la Galera (Alternative Walk 22) or Walk 26.

Threshing circle on the Lomo de Tablada with a view of Teide.

Walk down the road from the **Mirador de Masca** ❶ for about 200m to the next right hairpin bend where a roadway branches off on the left to the **Casas de Araza**. On the right, next to it, a path turns off right which leads down over the mountain ridge to a weakly defined col (just under 10 mins, do not turn left to the Barranco del Natero). The camino, marked by cairns and sporadic *orange* waymarkers, now runs gently undulating, then keeps

The Guergue high plain as seen from the sheer drop at the rim of the Masca Gorge.

uphill on the left hand side of the ridge (partly over rock where you need to keep an eye open for cairns) – now and then you are afforded spectacular views down into the Masca Valley.

After a total of almost half an hour, reach the ridgeline and a few minutes later pass a small cave. Shortly afterwards the trail descends steeply to a small notch. The camino ascends again through a gate and then, at times on the level, at times steeply up and down, continues on the left hand side of the ridge. Not until just before a striking rocky peak, the highest point of the walk, the usually reinforced mountain path changes for a few minutes onto the right hand side of the ridge (a bit precipitous) to switch back again just before the summit onto the left hand side. Reach an extensive meadowland plateau sloping down to the south-west, the **Lomo de Tablada** ❷, with a few houses at the upper end. Before walking down to the houses, you should climb up the few metres to the Cabezada, 1023m. The rocky peak affords fabulous views of the Barranco de Masca and vast areas of the Teno mountains as well as of Teide and Pico Viejo. After a total of 1½ hrs reach the houses at the right hand edge of the plateau. A threshing circle shows that grain has been cultivated here in the past.

If you would like to continue downhill to the Finca de Guergue, follow the sometimes somewhat overgrown path that leads past the threshing circle on the left. After 30m, directly below a cistern, it bends to the right and then keeps down along a mountain ridge, for the most part between abandoned terraces. You can see two solitary, dilapidated farmsteads below – the first one is reached after not quite a quarter of an hour, the second, the **Finca de Guergue** ❸ (Los Pajeros Grandes, 750m), a quarter of an hour later. From there, enjoy a splendid view of the coast between Los Gigantes and Las Américas.

If this is not enough, you can also take a detour to the rocky peak, lying off to the side to the south-west (½ hr one way) or to the precipice at the Masca Gorge (20 minutes one way).

Downwards view of the Playa de Masca.

TOP 28 — Masca Gorge

↗ 690m | ↘ 690m | 10.0km
5.45 hrs

Daring descent through the rocky labyrinth of the Barranco de Masca

The chasm-like Masca Gorge, surrounded by rock faces several hundred metres high, presents one of the island's most popular walks: passing through Masca's orchards and following a small brook, enter into an incredible labyrinth of crags and barrancos, until finally the sound of the sea becomes ever louder – fantastic!
Sadly, in 2020/21, the walking path was thoroughly renovated and long stretches have been secured so that its adventurous flair has been lost in the process. On top of that, you have to reserve a time slot – because of this, please enquire as to the access regulations well in advance.

Starting point: Masca's centre, 620m (bus stop for the 355, 365), above the chapel. If you choose to use boat service get on the 462 bus from Los Gigantes to Santiago del Teide (Mon–Fri only) and from there take bus 355 (or a taxi) to Masca. You can only park for a maximum time of 2 hrs in Masca, from 9 to 14.00, (for this reason, be sure to use bus transport or taxi for the approach!)
Grade: strenuous walk along an exceptionally well-constructed trail that demands sure-footedness. In times of inclement weather, the gorge may be closed (if this is the case, you will be contacted).
Refreshment: bar/restaurants in Masca.
Return by boat: when the sea is not too rough, there's the possibility of returning from the Playa de Masca by boat to Los Gigantes. The website camino-barrancodemasca.com offers relevant services; alternatively you can also join an organised walking group.
Please note: presently, no ferry service is being permitted but 2023/24 reopening of the boat docks is planned.
Tip: don't forget your swimming gear!
Important note: since March 2021, the trail through the Masca gorge is strictly regulated with restricted visitor access and prepaid reservation; more information and bookings at caminobarrancodemasca.com. At the moment (2023) access is limited to Saturdays, Sundays and holidays. Required equipment: helmet (lent-out for free), hiking footwear, sufficient water and a fully-charged mobile phone.

Start of the gorge adventure.

From the main road go down to the chapel of **Masca** ❶. Head left past the chapel and descend to the village district situated on the mountain ridge between the Barranco de Masca (left) and the Barranco Madre del Agua (right). The trail into the Barranco de Masca branches off at a check point on the mountain ridge. It leads between agaves and palm trees resolutely down to the stream bed. After a good quarter of an hour, cross over a small bridge (25m after that on the left, above a scree-blanketed slope, the entrance to a tunnel leading over into the Barranco Seco). 10 mins later, cross over again onto the right hand bank of the stream. The idyllic trail passes some terraces and crosses through rushes and reeds to return to the left bank. After a total of 40 mins – leaving the cultivated terraces of Masca behind – the trail returns again to the right bank. The rock faces are now getting closer together. Descend to a small weir where a water canal begins on the left. Then the trail continues next to the stream bed and skirts to the right around a rock barrier. You are now in a veritable labyrinth of rocks, one of the most striking stretches of the walk – small *barrancos* merge from all sides, one mountain ridge after the other en-

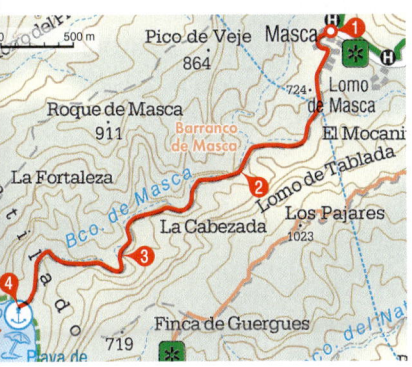

Destination of this spectacular gorge walk – the Playa de Masca.

croaches with steep, sometimes overhanging, rock walls. After 10 minutes, pass an iron gate and shortly afterwards, the route is blocked by a large boulder. The path descends bearing right through the rock arch ❷ (chain handhold), then the trail crosses back and forth over the stream bed. Three quarters of an hour later another giant boulder blocks the path ❸ (cascade) – turn right here to descend. 10m above the *barranco* floor you now see a rock arch. The path then switches sides several times. Gradually, the sound of the sea grows nearer. Finally, the trail leads left through the rock face, passing a gigantic overhanging rock. The steep walls now recede and the sea appears ahead. To the left, where the gorge merges into the sea, a little finca can be seen – to the right, a narrow footbridge leads to a rock in the sea (where boats are moored).

The **Playa de Masca** ❹ is covered in gravel and smoothly polished rocks but 100m to the left (depending on the surf and season) a strip of sand can be found which, when the sea is calm, is a perfect spot for a swim (at your own risk, danger of falling rocks!). In addition, you can enjoy bathing near the boat landing.

Left: just before the Playa, pass an enormous rock overhang.
Right: a backwards view into the barranco.

↗ 330m | ↘ 640m | 8.5km

29 From Santiago del Teide to Masca

3.00 hrs

Popular ridge walk with numerous possibilities for alternatives

This ridge walk over the Cumbre de Bolico, the meteorological divide between the damp North and the dry South, is one of the most beautiful and popular walks in the Teno mountains. The leisurely walk offers spectacular views and, in the winter, presents a sumptuous display of countless Canary Bellflowers. In the end, at Cruz de Hilda and in Masca, some cosy little places to enjoy a meal are waiting for you. The only pity is that you have to take the bus back from Masca to Santiago del Teide.

Starting point: junction near the church in the centre of Santiago del Teide, 930m (bus stop for the 325, 355, 460–462).
Destination: Masca, 620m (bus stop for the 355, 365).
Grade: easy walk on predominantly good, pleasant trails.
Refreshment: bar/restaurants in Santiago del Teide, at the Cruz de Hilda and in Masca.

Linking tip: the walk can be combined with Walks 21, 22, 30 and 31.
Important note: because of the construction work for the motorway tunnel that passes through the Teno mountains, the trailhead is closed until further notice. You could (very strenuous) follow the construction fence without a distinct path. Past a stream bed you reach the walking trail. But it is better to begin the walk at the Erjos Pass (Puerto de Erjos, bus stop for the 325, 460) and follow the forestry track. 20 minutes later (fork) bear left. 25 minutes on at the end of the track reach the walking path as in the description below.

View from the Cruz de Hilda towards Masca and Pico Verde (above left).

Start the walk in the centre of **Santiago del Teide** ❶ near the church and, on the other side of the main street, follow the walking path PR TF 56 (*white/yellow*) which, on the far side of the picnic area, runs parallel to the main street. This narrows to become a path and then runs directly along the main street; 5 minutes later, both the path and the street hook to the left. 5 minutes later, you come to a right hand bend — here the trail used to bear left before the construction of the motorway began (see Important note). The beautiful but virtually shadeless camino ascends along the edge of a pine wood and, after half an hour, meets a forest road which ends at this point — turn left here to follow the PR TF 51/56 uphill to the **Degollada de la Mesa** ❷ (a good 10 minutes), the col between the Big and Little Gala. For surefooted walkers we recommend a detour left onto Little Gala (Pico Verde, 1318m; just under ¼ hr, rather precipitous in places, some easy scrambling at the summit) — the view of Masca, the Masca Gorge and towards La Gomera is one of the best on the island!

Carry straight on along the waymarked main trail (do

View of Gala from the Santiago Valley.

not descend left) that runs leisurely across the slope and opens up your first views into the Masca Valley. After a good 10 minutes, the trail forks – continue left here over the **Cumbre de Bolico** (on the right a possible ascent to the Cruz de Gala, see Walk 21). Not quite 5 minutes later the trail goes between a threshing circle (lovely spot for a rest) and a derelict building (a forestry road forks off to the right, heading towards Las Portelas as the PR TF 56). 5 minutes later, a path turns off diagonally left from the PR TF 51 ridge trail to a fabulous rocky viewpoint ❸ where you not only catch a tiny glimpse of Masca, but also, to the right, the Palmar Valley and the continuation of the cumbre over the Tabaiba Pass towards Teno Alto.

After the detour, continue along the main trail which consequently leads along the right hand side of the ridge through scrub wood. After a quarter of an hour, the path ascends for a short while to a panoramic rise in the ridge ❹. You should spend a bit of time here and enjoy the magnificent view of Masca. The next large rise in the ridge is circumnavigated on the right – a marvelous stretch through laurisilva forest with trailing Canary Bellflowers. Eventually, reach a large junction on the **Cumbre del Carrizal** ❺ (25 minutes) – leave the ridge trail at this point by taking the PR TF 59, turning sharp left to Masca (you could also continue straight ahead on the PR TF 51 to Teno Alto whilst, to the right, there is a possible descent via the PR TF 59 to Las Portelas).

After a few minutes, the trail comes past a rock outcrop from where there's a wonderful view of Los Carrizales with the *barranco* of the same name and of the Hilda Pass. This beautiful high mountain walk continues past a spring to the **Cruz de Hilda** ❻ (lovely viewing terrace with café, closed on Fridays). Now follow the narrow road that forks off left before the *mirador* (trail board). After 2 minutes, directly above a palm tree, a trail turns off to the right and, a quarter of an hour later, near the Masca bar/restaurant in the district of **La Vica**, merges with the main road (bus stop). It takes only another 10 minutes or less to walk left along the main road to **Masca** ❼ where you will find some attractive bars and restaurant.

↗ 500m | ↘ 500m | 11.2km

3.45 hrs

🚌 ✕ 👥

From Tamaimo to Santiago del Teide 30

Through the Santiago Valley on ancient paths between villages

This pleasant circuit through the Santiago Valley follows ancient connecting paths – walkers will be enchanted by outstanding views of the dramatic landscape and, when almond trees are in bloom in the spring (from about mid-January to the end of February/beginning of March), slopes are completely covered in white and pink blossoming trees.

Starting point: the major intersection in the village centre of Tamaimo, 570m (bus stop for the 325, 460–462).
Grade: easy walk along old trails connecting the villages.
Refreshment: bar/restaurants in Tamaimo, Arguayo and Santiago del Teide.
Note: along the stretch Arguayo – Santiago del Teide, the walker is very exposed to the clamour of the motorway traffic.
Linking tip: with Walks 29, 31–34.
Important note: due to motorway construction the stretch between Santiago del Teide – El Molledo is closed until further notice (alternatively, use the main road to El Molledo). For this reason, we recommend, just past waypoint ❺, to turn left and take the trail to El Molledo. At the bus stop shelter cross the main road and continue along the village street, passing the church. Follow the *white/yellow* markings to the trail junction on the other side of the village (see below).

From the major intersection in **Tamaimo** ❶ follow the main road in the direction of Guía de Isora and after 200m, just before the bus stop, turn left onto the steeply ascending village road Calle La Rosa (PR TF 65, *white/yellow*). After passing the last house, the road becomes a wide camino and crosses over a water canal after 50m. About 20 minutes

115

View to Tamaimo with the Guama – the Risco Blanco appears in the middle of the photo.

later, next to Montaña del Ángel, reach the Arguayo plateau and meet a tarmac road ❷. Follow this road for 50m to the left and then continue straight on along the camino. This leads gently uphill, turns left to cross under the new motorway via an underpass and, after a good quarter of an hour, reaches the main road in **Arguayo** ❸. A trail continues opposite. After 40m, it meets the Carretera General (the *plaza* with the church is straight on) which brings you up and left in 3 minutes to the 'Museo Centro Alfarero' (pottery and Guanche artefacts, Tue–Sat 10 am–1 pm/4 pm–7 pm, Sun 10 am–2 pm).

Directly after the museum pass a little bus stop shelter (bus stop for the 461, 462) where – by crossing over the main road – the trail to Valle de Arriba turns off left (PR TF 65.5 towards El Molledo). 30m along this steep, ascending concrete trail reach a junction next to a water storage tank – continue diagonally left. The camino leads across the western slope of the Montaña de la Hoya, offering a magnificent view of the Santiago Valley and the south-west coast.

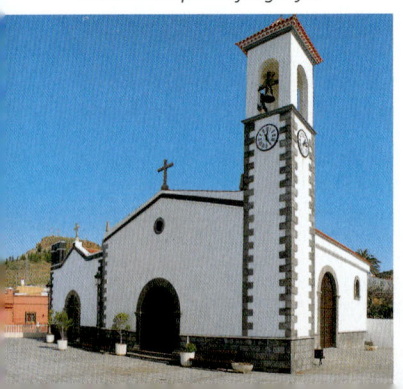

The church square of Arguayo.

20 minutes later, pass over a small rocky ridge ❹ – where a view opens up ahead of the village Las Manchas with Montaña Bilma in the background. Now the trail descends into the broad Santiago Valley and then leads along the motorway, crossing

over a track (on the left, a bridge). A good 5 mins later, the camino crosses the motorway via an underpass ❺, then runs to the right of and parallel to the motorway. A few minutes later bear right at the fork (the trail bearing left heads to El Molledo). Soon after, the camino crosses over two water canals, then converges to the right with the main road between Santiago del Teide and Arguayo. On the other side of the road a distinct path continues on through the lava and leads on the right of a high stone wall. Not quite 10 minutes later reach a road; follow this to the left, passing the cemetery, and after the playground go right to reach the church on the main road of **Santiago del Teide** ❻ (not quite 10 mins; bus stop for the 325, 355, 460–462).

Turn left onto the main road and descend to the petrol station (5 mins). 30m after passing the petrol station fork to the right onto the broad trail leading to Los Gigantes (PR TF 65, *white/yellow*). 10 mins later, this passes above **El Molledo** ❼ and then forks – bear left here (to the right, the PR TF 65.1 leads to Risco Blanco and the PR TF 65.3 to Degollada del Roque) and at the next fork 50m further on bear right. The camino now descends along the right rim of the Barranco de Santiago. Not quite half an hour later (just before, the PR TF 65.3 merges), ignore a camino forking left into the *barranco*. Not quite 15 mins later, a wide cobbled trail forks off to the left – but keep straight ahead here for 50m along the PR TF 65 then turn left at the junction of the PR TF 65.2 (see Walk 32) to continue through the *barranco*. At the following fork turn diagonally left via the PR TF 65.2 to cross over to a village road and the first houses of **Tamaimo**. Continue straight on along the road (bearing right at the first fork) to the church square and pass this to the left. Walk along Calle Santa Ana to the main road which leads back to the intersection ❶ 30m to the right.

↗ 380m | ↘ 360m | 9.4km

31 Ruta del Almendro: Arguayo – Santiago del Teide

3.10 hrs

A 'must' when the almond trees are in flower

During the flowering season of the almond tree (Jan./Feb.), the trail 'Ruta del Almendro en Flor' counts as one of the island's most beautiful. We wouldn't recommend this walk in other times of the year even though the walking trail is diverse in variety and presents panoramic views as it leads between the almond trees and lava fields.

Starting point: Museum Centro Alfarero in Arguayo, 915m (bus stop for the lines 461 and 462).
Destination: Santiago del Teide, 930m (bus stop for the lines 325, 355, 460–462). If you have to return to Arguayo, it is best to take a taxi (ask in a bar or tel. +34 922 860840).
Grade: an easy walk the entire way along caminos and paths; at the end also via a roadway.

Refreshment: bar/restaurants in Arguayo and Santiago del Teide.
Linking tip: with Walk 30.

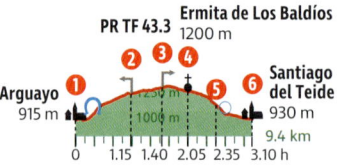

Across from the Centro Alfarero (pottery museum) in **Arguayo** ❶ and the bus stop shelter, the signed PR TF 65.4 (*white/yellow*) to Santiago del Teide begins. The trail follows the Calle El Carmen through the prim village. At the old wine press, turn off diagonally right. At a roundabout with a tree in the middle, meet up with a broad road. 30m further on, the waymarked and signed trail forks off to the left, following a roadway, and is immediately embraced by the almond tree covered slopes. 100m after that ignore the SL TF 201 to Chio that forks to the right. Another 50m on, keep to the right along the main trail (diagonally left 'por Las Tierras' is a little shorter). Now the roadway becomes a camino, scree-slippery underfoot, and after passing a galería (follow the waymarkers to the right) ascends more steeply for some minutes via zigzags, flanked by solitary pine trees and spurge whilst opening a lovely view of Arguayo and all the way to La Gomera (later on, even to La Palma). Now the trail levels out and traverses the slope while bearing left, soon crossing a sprawling field of lava and then terraces covered in almond trees – sheer visual poetry! A couple of minutes later, the trail hooks off to the right and subsequently crosses a massive field of lava (a splendid view of Teide and Pico Viejo). Passing a wall of lava, three metres in height, spot Santiago del Teide for the first time to your left. Now the trail keeps steady on through open pine forest, heading directly

View over the terraces of almond trees towards Arguayo and the island of La Gomera.

for the volcanic dome of the Montaña Bilma and, a few minutes later, merges with a trail ❷ approaching from the left, coming from Las Manchas. Pass by more lava fields and groves of almond trees, then continue at the edge of a pine forest to cross over to the next oasis of almonds – here, you really should find a pretty spot to take a break. Now the trail crosses over a couple of lava flows and just before the foot of the **Montaña Bilma** merges with the PR TF 43.3 ❸ – here turn diagonally left to continue. Teide appears once again. The trail leads along the backside of the Bilma, directly along its

View of Santiago del Teide (photo above) and of Teide (photo below).

foot, at first next to and then crossing over a field of lava. Immediately past the lava field meet up with a track and turn left along it to continue (at the fork 250m on turn left again). Passing between fig trees and solitary almond trees off to the one side and the lava flow on the other continue in a gentle descent to the **Ermita de Los Baldíos** ❹, which was erected here in gratitude at the terminus of the Chinyero lava flow in November 1909.

The trail continues to the left along the roadway that passes more almond trees as it descends downwards. Soon the trail becomes a lovely trail of volcanic sand. A half hour past the chapel the PR TF 65 to Valle de Arriba ❺ intersects, but we keep to our trail, turning right/left and dropping down to the valley floor. In front of the triangular water reservoir, turn left onto the narrow trail that shortly before reaching **Santiago del Teide** crosses over what is most certainly the loveliest almond grove of the entire route. At the first houses, the trail merges into a street; turn right onto the street and, past the playground, right again, to reach the church on the main street ❻.

↗ 480m | ↘ 480m | 5.4km

2.30 hrs
From Tamaimo onto Guama — 32

Panoramic walk above the Santiago Valley

This mostly leisurely circular walk onto the ridge above Tamaimo opens up wonderful views of the valleys and gorges on the south-west coast.

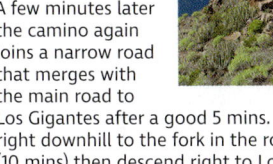

Starting point: major crossroad in the centre of Tamaimo, 570m (bus stop for the 325, 460–462).
Grade: predominently easy walk on caminos and paths, one short section is steep and rocky.
Refreshment: bar/restaurants in Tamaimo.
Alternative: continue downhill to Los Gigantes (1¼ hrs from the PR TF 65, see below): on the return trail turn right onto the valley trail (PR TF 65, *white/yellow*). After 25 mins it joins a track. Keep following this track straight on downhill along beside plantations. At the end of the track after 10 mins continue left along the trail beside the plantation. A few minutes later the camino again joins a narrow road that merges with the main road to Los Gigantes after a good 5 mins. Go right downhill to the fork in the road (10 mins) then descend right to Los Gigantes (¼ hr to the harbour; 50m beforehand, a trail turns right to the Playa de Los Guios; bus stop for the 325/473 in the village centre).
Linking tip: with Walk 30.

From the major junction in **Tamaimo ❶** walk 30m along the main road uphill in the direction of Santiago del Teide and turn left onto the Calle Santa Ana. After the street hooks to the right reach the church. Calle El Agua continues straight ahead (sign 'Cruz de los Misioneros', PR TF 65.2, *white/yellow*) which you leave 3 minutes later along the first narrow street turning off to the left. This immediately becomes a camino which brings you to the Barranco de Santiago and, via the same route as

View from the ridge at Cruz de los Misioneros of the jaunty Risco Blanco.

the PR TF 65 crosses the stream bed below a threshing circle. High above on the ridge, you can already see a large white cross to which, from the junction on the other flank of the valley, the PR TF 65.2 turns off to the left.

With Tamaimo far below pass by a few basalt rock faces. After ascending a good quarter of an hour pass a hidden cave ❷ (10m on the left of the trail, a spring gushes from the rock wall).

The trail now runs on the level for a short way to the right and then leads all the way up to the top of the ridge from where there is a fantastic panoramic view, especially of the Barranco Seco and the impressive Risco Blanco directly opposite. Now bear left and soon pass below the **Cruz de los Misioneros** ❸ to which a trail turns off to the right shortly after (sign). Now, Teide and Pico Viejo also appear.

After the detour continue following the main trail that ascends the slope on the left (20m on, via steep rock steps; cable-secured) to the ridgeline. Along the ridge reach

the highest point of the **Montaña de Guama** ❹ (small rock outcrop) some minutes later.

Continue along the ridgeline keeping at the left edge of the gently sloping and terraced summit plateau. The trail regales you with wonderful views of the Santiago Valley and the south-west coast (the harbour of Los Gigantes also appears) – and towards La Gomera. After a good 10 minutes, a path forks off to the right to the rock arch, 'El Bujero' (not quite 10 minutes later, descend to the left over a ridge to a crag, ¼ hr; from here, the route is very demanding). A good 10 minutes later, the trail forks about 200m before reaching a rock spike. You really should carry on here for about another 5 minutes down along the ridge to a rock barrier just before the **rock spike** ❺ of basalt, 575m – from here, enjoy a wonderful view to Los Gigantes and the huge rock arch (El Bujero) on the neighbouring ridge.

Back at the fork, continue descending the main trail to the **Degollada de Tejera** ❻ (a good 10 minutes). Here the trail turns away from the ridge and turns left down into the Santiago Valley where, after a good 10 minutes, it meets the valley trail ❼ (PR TF 65, white/yellow). You could descend on the right to Los Gigantes (see Alternative, 1¼ hrs), otherwise turn to the left to return to **Tamaimo** ❶ along the trail. 20 minutes later, shortly before the first houses, the camino runs through the *barranco* floor for a short way and leaves this after 25m by turning right onto a road which ascends in a few minutes back to the church square.

El Bujero (left) and a downwards view of Los Gigantes (below).

↗ 920m | ↘ 920m | 11.5km

33 Barranco Seco – from El Molledo to Playa Seco

6.20 hrs

Classic tour for fit and experienced mountain walkers!

The walk through the Barranco Seco ('dry gorge') to the beach of the same name is a real alternative to the very busy Barranco de Masca. The gorge is admittedly not as spectacular and impressive as its famous neighbour and, due to the lack of boat mooring, there is no boat connection, but to make up for that, the trail is wonderfully unspoilt, not to mention, truly adventurous in spots. And, backed by huge towering rock faces, the beach can certainly compete with the Playa de Masca!

Starting point: church square in El Molledo, 880m, a little village on the TF 82 between Tamaimo and Santiago del Teide (bus stop for the 325, 460–462).

Grade: long, challenging walk that demands surefootedness, a lack of vertigo, good physical fitness and a certain amount of route-finding skill. Only to be undertaken in absolutely safe, stable weather, and never in the heat!

Refreshment: nothing en route, bar/restaurants in Tamaimo/Santiago del Teide.

Alternative: excursion climbing the Risco Blanco (¾ hr, one-way): at the junction (see below) bear diagonally right, following the PR TF 65.1 in up-and-down walking to a finca with a threshing circle. Now turn left, descending to a saddle at the foot of the Risco Blanco. If you wish to climb to the summit (only for skilled, experienced scramblers!), turn left to climb down along the camino for 50m and then turn right to ascend cross-country through a steep, scree-slippery, rocky terrain (cairns).

Linking tip: with Walks 30 and 34.

Important note: from February to August (nesting season for the osprey) the walking path to Playa Seco is prohibited starting at waypoint ❹.

From the church in **El Molledo** ❶ follow *white/yellow* waymarkers on the level along Calle La Calzada crossing over to the Barranco de Santiago and meet the valley trail on the other side of the valley (PR TF 65; 3 mins). Carry straight on along this trail up to the next fork (50m; straight on) and 15m afterwards the trail forks again. Here turn diagonally left onto the PR TF 65.3 (diagonally right, the PR TF 65.1 leads to Risco Blanco, see Alternative). The trail runs slightly downhill across the slope and after a good 10 mins passes an abandoned goat farm. A good 10 mins after that cross over the ridge ❷

The path through the dramatic Barranco Seco. On the left: Risco Blanco with the Barranco Seco.

and descend along the other side – with a lovely view towards La Gomera and of Risco Blanco which, from here, only appears as a broad lump of rock. A few minutes afterwards, just before a striking rocky knoll, the camino turns back again to the ridgeline (Degollada del Roque; here, the PR TF 65.3 turns left), then finally turns towards the slope on the right of the ridge. It soon descends noticeably in zigzags and forks after a few

After 2 hours you reach a water canal – Walks 33 and 34 part company here.

minutes (there's a shortcut straight ahead; on the right the camino passes a rock spur which offers a nice resting place and viewpoint). A quarter of an hour later, the trail forks again (shortcut diagonally right) and a few minutes after that, it crosses a conspicuously chalky white **water canal** 550m (50m to the left is a tunnel to Tamaimo). Some minutes later keep right at a fork, then the trail turns left towards the slope and crosses a chalky white *barranco* gully to wind downhill soon afterwards at the foot of a dark rock wall into the bottom of the Barranco Seco with the **Galería de la Junquera** ❸.

Soon after that, the trail changes over onto the right hand side of the valley and after a good 5 minutes turns back again onto the left hand side. A good 10 minutes later the camino meets a covered **water canal**, 215m. Follow this canal for 50m to the left until a distinct camino branches off right downhill ❹ (Walk 34 continues straight on along the canal to Los Gigantes, a nice alternative for the return). Sometimes the camino is somewhat loose under foot and has even slipped away as it descends in 3 minutes into the *barranco* floor. 2 minutes later, pass a huge lump of rock and, via a camino to the right, skirt around the next outcrops in the stream bed. After a few minutes this descends again, keeping left, onto the rocky and eroded stream bed (easy scrambling) that you cross directly above a rock step. A distinct camino continues on the other side and soon leads back into the scree-filled stream bed. Continue the descent via the stream bed (keep

an eye open for cairns; now and then, a path makes a shortcut along a ridge). The gorge becomes more and more striking – but be sure to leave the sheer, sometimes overhanging gorge walls quickly behind you (danger of rockfall)! After a quarter of an hour you reach the crux of the walk below an overhanging rock face (bird droppings): a rather exposed, cable-secured traverse with little foot and hand holds must now be negotiated. 5 minutes later, the path reaches the stream bed again at a large conduit and switches over onto the left hand side of the valley and, 5 minutes more, returns to the right hand side. Now, you cannot fail to hear the surge of the surf at the **Playa de Barranco Seco** ❺ close at hand. The 500m long, stony beach soon appears ahead.

This is a wonderful place for a swim, but only in absolutely calm seas! One problem is the constant stream of excursion and 'pirate' boats that sometimes anchor in the bay, which is encompassed by huge rock faces. There is no boat's mooring on this beach so, unfortunately, no chance of getting a lift, even though Los Gigantes is only a stone's throw away. If you need convincing, walk to the other end of the beach at the mouth of the Barranco del Natero (not quite 10 minutes; be careful at the foot of the rock faces where there is a risk of rockfall!).

The narrow, extensive Playa Seco is enclosed by massive rock faces.

TOP 34 From Tamaimo to Los Gigantes

↗ 600m | ↘ 600m | 14.9km
5.00 hrs
🚌 ✕

Hair-raising tour through the dramatic Gigantes rock face

A walk could not be more spectacular and adventurous. This circular walk takes you through two long pitch-black tunnels with water canals (take a torch!) and a secluded gorge. Without a doubt, however, the highpoint is the roughly 45 minute exposed stretch traversing the steep rock face of Acantilado de Los Gigantes – a breath-taking 100m above the coast, giving a constant view of Los Gigantes with its harbour and the marvellous Playa de Los Guios.

Starting point: major junction in the centre of Tamaimo, 570m (bus stop for the 325, 460–462).
Grade: a very challenging walk which demands absolute surefootedness and a lack of vertigo (long precipitous passages along the steep coastline). Should only be undertaken in totally safe and settled weather!
Refreshment: bar/restaurants in Tamaimo and Los Gigantes.
Important notes: the trail between the Barranco Seco and Los Gigantes is officially closed – tackle this walk at your own risk! The entrance to the tunnel Tamaimo – Barranco Seco ❷ was open just recently. If closed, then circumvent it by taking the first tunnel coming from Tamaimo: just at the outset of the walking trail, 100m into the Barranco de Santiago, the trail crosses a water channel, which you can easily ascend to shortly afterwards. This leads through the 1-km long Túnel 1 Boca Norte (be careful, you have to frequently stoop a little!) to enter into the Barranco Seco. Continue right along the canal to the walking trail 50m away, which decends through the Barranco Seco.
The canal tunnel to Los Gigantes (between ❺ and ❻) has been fitted with iron gates. If the tunnel is closed, you can only go from Tamaimo to ❺ or in the opposite direction from Los Gigantes only to ❻ and then you must turn back again.
For both of the tunnels (a good 20 and 15 minutes) you need a bright (head) torch.
Be sure to bring along your bathing gear!
Linking tip: with Walks 30 and 33.

From the major crossroad in **Tamaimo** ❶ walk 20m up the main road in the direction of Santiago del Teide and turn left onto Calle Santa Ana that brings you straight ahead to the church of the same name. On the other side of the *plaza* turn left into Calle Real and keep right at both of the following road junc-

View across Los Gigantes to the steep rock face of Acantilado de Los Gigantes.

tions. Past the last houses reach the stream bed of the Barranco de Santiago; continue the descent along the PR TF 65 (*white/yellow*; past a canal on the right hand flank of the valley). 5 mins later pass a house (now via a roadway) and 5 mins after that, the roadway branches off right to two sheds. Directly after the first building look for the entrance to a 1388m-long **tunnel** ❷ that leads over into the next valley. It is easy to walk through and after a good ¼ hr descends for a short stretch (now, the roof of the tunnel is lower so watch out for jutting rocks at head level!). Another 5 mins and then you can see daylight again in the **Barranco Seco** ❸ – and the Risco Blanco high above.

Now descend an indistinct path along a *barranco* gully, first follow-

The breathtaking trail runs right across the middle of the huge steep face of Acantilado de Los Gigantes.

ing the left-hand rim, some minutes after directly in the *barranco*, passing rusty mine trolleys (beware: do not change over to the right side along a path) until reaching a cascade on a rock face. If you are an experienced scrambler, you could continue climbing down from here – but it is better when, 10m before the drop-off, you turn left, following the faded *red* waymarkers, climbing up diagonally for a few metres along the slope. Traverse the slope about at the same height, then descend slightly with the *red* waymarkers. The distinct alpine path merges somewhat above the **Galería de la Junquera** ❹ with the valley trail coming from El Molledo; follow this down the valley (see Walk 33). The trail soon changes over onto the right hand side of the valley and a good 5 mins later switches back onto the left hand side. A good 10 minutes after that arrive at a covered **water canal**, 215m. Follow this canal to the left (after 50m, on the right, Walk 33 turns off to Playa de Barranco Seco) and, about 5 mins later, reach the entrance to the second, just under 1km long **tunnel** ❺ – this time accompanied by a water canal with a conduit. The end of the tunnel is visible from the start. Walking through the tunnel takes a quarter of an hour and then you find yourself back at the steep rock face of **Acantilado de Los Gigantes** ❻ a good 200m above

the Atlantic. Descend directly from the exit of the tunnel following the *green/orange* waymarkers (left) and later bear right to cross the slope. At a distinct fork turn left to descend to the boulder-strewn *barranco* gully and change to the other side of the valley. The path, always narrow and exposed, runs across the steep slope (sometimes disconcertingly precipitous) and regales you with wonderful views along the coast to Los Gigantes and La Gomera. After crossing over a projecting rock (10 mins) a view also opens up of the huge rock faces in the direction of Punta de Teno. Pay close attention: soon after follow the *green* waymarkers to bear left at a fork, then ascend over rock (the right-hand path, leading through impassable, dangerous terrain, is blocked by a row of stones). Half an hour later the precipitous traverse ends at a roadway which 100m on, at the first houses of **Los Gigantes** meets Calle Tabaiba ❼ (right). Follow the road keeping straight ahead through the village. (After 5 mins you can descend a street on the right, then carry straight on down some steps to the harbour ❽, 10 minutes; 50m before the harbour you can take a worthwhile detour to the right to the Playa de Los Guios; bus stop for the 325, 461, 462, 473, 477, 493, 494 in the centre of the village.)

After a good 10 minutes Calle Tabaiba/Avenida Jose Gonzalez Fortes merges into the TF-454 main road which you follow straight on uphill and 5 minutes later, pass the **Mirador de Archipenque** ❾. 5 minutes after that, 25m before the junction with the main road to Tamaimo (bus stop), turn off left up a steep, narrow road (the PR TF 65; *white/yellow*). This becomes a trail 10 minutes later which you keep following straight ahead uphill (another 10 minutes later, a track between plantations then, in a right-hand bend, turn left onto a camino). After three quarters of an hour pass the two sheds again with the tunnel entrance ❷, and, 25 minutes later, return to the starting point in **Tamaimo** ❶.

The marvellous Playa de Los Guios awaits you next to the harbour of Los Gigantes.

35 From Guía de Isora to Chirche

↗ 320m | ↘ 320m | 6.0km
2.10 hrs

Ancient connecting trail to one of the south-west island's most beautiful villages

Chirche is set in a particularly panoramic location – from here, the view not only takes in a splendid vista of the southern island but also captures the Pico Viejo. Physically fit walkers can continue an ascent along the waymarked trail towards the Cañadas, but we take the pleasant climb, an hour in duration. For the ambitious, sure-footed 'sleuth' we recommend tackling the return route via the Finca Ramallo instead.

Starting point: the church square of Guía de Isora, 591m, above the main road (bus stop for lines 417, 460, 490, 492–494 on the main village street next to the tourist office; signs point out a car park 150m above the church square, past the police station).
Grade: easy walk along a good camino.
Refreshment: bar/restaurants in Guía de Isora and in Chirche.
Alternative: return via Finca Ramallo (a good 2 hrs; challenging, some stretches very overgrown): from Chirche walk back along the trail but, at the turn-off for the PR TF 70 to the right, keep straight on along the roadway traversing the slope. At the next fork, turn right and pass a finca 100m on. The roadway becomes a camino and forks at the next ridge – continue along the camino traversing the slope, then (ascending at the end) cross over a *barranco*. At the following ridge, the camino passes the abandoned Finca Ramallo. With the finca to your left, keep bearing somewhat left while climbing down the ridge and, past a solitary pine tree, the trail turns left towards the next *barranco* and begins to descend steeply shortly after. On the other side ascend steeply for a short time then keep bearing right to climb up to the basalt rock faces.

Continue along the rock faces until an alpine path ascends to the left over rock to climb up to the ridgeline (3 crosses). Descend for a short stretch directly over the ridgeline (at first a short stretch over the ridgeline to the left, then bear right via a terrace to cross to the right-hand ridgeline, now follow the *white/green* marked SL TF 206). Some minutes later, the trail veers slightly to the left onto the terraces and, at the same height as a villa, crosses over a canal. Later, next to a finca with goats, cross over another canal and soon afterwards reach the main road TF-82. Before the merge the camino turns right through the *barranco* and, on the other side, continues in an ascent. The camino forks on a ridge – turn left to descend to a roadway and then ascend along this to the merge of the PR TF 70 (threshing circle); turn left to return to Guía de Isora.

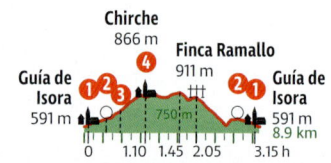

Because of its marvellous location Chirche is well-worth visiting.

From the church square in **Guía de Isora** ❶ climb up the Calle Los Chorros (30m further on, a sign: PR TF 70, *white/yellow*). At the following junction at the police station turn right and, at the large car park, keep right along the street. Bear left at the following fork. This street becomes a lovely little camino (sign: 'Aripe') at the final house and ascends through a wild and idyllic landscape with solitary almond and pine trees while opening a view of the Pico Viejo. A good 10 mins later pass by an old threshing circle and, 80m after that, meet up with a roadway ❷ (left) that becomes a camino again after passing a finca. A quarter of an hour later the trail forks in front of a finca ❸. Straight ahead you could continue on to Aripe with the PR TF 70.1 – we, however, bear right onto the PR TF 70. The camino soon climbs up over a ridge next to the pretty mountain village of Aripe, following along conduits and passing old brick kilns. A half hour later, next to **Chirche** ❹, the camino merges into a roadway (to the right Alternative, return route). Turn left onto the roadway, passing orange plantations, and head into the settlement. By turning right and keeping straight ahead, then taking a street to the left you can make an excursion to the Mirador de Chirche (bar/restaurant; 10 mins).

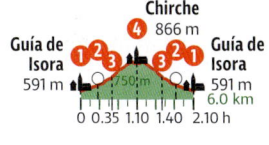

On the village street, 250m past the church and to the left, we can recommend the bar/restaurant Romero (open daily, from 11 am; closed on Mondays). From here you can continue descending along the street to Aripe and then turn left via the PR TF 70.1 to reach the approach route and return along it to **Guía** ❶.

↗ 185m | ↘ 185m | 10.4km

36 From La Caleta to Playa Paraíso

2.45 hrs

Pleasant seaside promenade to the Bird of Paradise beaches

Not long ago, only a stone's throw away from the monstrous resort hotels of the southern island, you could find Tenerife's hippy enclaves. In simple huts, caves and tents, numerous societal drop-outs were living and sojourning on two of the island's most beautiful beaches, before they were driven away. In El Puertito, a lovely beach is also awaiting us before we finally reach the holiday complex of Playa Paraíso

Starting point: the seaside promenade at La Caleta, a former fishing village north of the Playa de Las Américas (bus stop for lines 448 and 467).

Grade: an easy walk.
Refreshment: bar/restaurants in La Caleta (seafood!), El Puertito, Playa Paraíso.
Note: take along your bathing gear!

Begin the walk on the southern end of the bay at **La Caleta** ❶ next to the restaurant Celso and ramble along the promenade to cross over to the other side of the bay. Past the bar/restaurant El Varadero a coastal trail sets off. This ascends along the cliffs to the plateau above and then continues pleasantly along the coastline – opening up a lovely view of the mountains at Adeje, of the Cumbre and even to La Gomera; also the destination for the walk, Playa Paraíso, with its unmistakable high-rise buildings can be easily spotted. Soon the trail leads to a splendid cliff-enclosed cove with a pebble beach ❷ (Playa de Los Morteros) which is an absolutely wonderful spot for a swim. Past the cove, the trail ascends once again to the cliff tops and then, soon after, at the

Once a favourite for societal dropouts – Playa de Los Morteros (above) and Playa Diego Hernández (below).

splendid two-section split sandy beach **Playa Diego Hernández** ❸, returns again to the sea. Afterwards the coastal trail leads along a plantation wall then leads over a headland to reach the grand sandy bay of **El Puertito** ❹, connected via a road (Bodegón Pepe y Lola at the end of the road). You could skirt around the steep slope which follows by using the road. Then, keep to the paths heading towards the multi-storey settlement of **Playa Paraíso**. Skirt around the holiday complex by keeping left along the coastline, then cross over a *barranco* with a pebble beach (Playa Las Salinas). Immediately afterwards, meet up with a road where, to the left, a bus stop for the lines 471/473 and two restaurants are located ❺ – in the cove that follows, you might be tempted by the beach and a man-made bathing area.

↗ 200m | ↘ 200m | 4.8km

37 From La Quinta to Boca del Paso

1.45 hrs

Cheerful stroll in the quiet hinterland

This circular walk high above the south-west coast enjoys a widespread popularity, not only because of its short length but also due to the pleasant trails and the views taking in the coastline as well as the Cumbre with Teide.

Starting point: car park at the church of La Quinta, 929m, a village situated in a panoramic position high above the southern coast. **Approach:** along the TF-82 Adeje – Guía de Isora to Los Menores, then via the TF-583 to Taucho (7km) and continuing to La Quinta (1.5km). No bus service.
Grade: easy circular walk, only a short stretch of the trail demands a little sure-footedness.
Refreshment: bar/restaurant in Taucho.
Linking tip: with Walk 38.

From the church in **La Quinta** ❶ (trail board) take the Calle La Serrería to follow PR TF 71.1 (*white/yellow*) in the direction of Boca del Paso. At the fork, 50m on, bear right – the street now becomes a farm road that, in the next bend to the left, is left behind by heading straight on along a camino. This is flanked by agave plants and utility poles as it traverses to the next ridge along which the trail (a farm road at this point) crosses two water canals next to a finca. How lovely is the upwards view from here, taking in the Cumbre and Teide! Now, the waymarked trail leads away from

View from the Boca del Paso to the Cumbre and Teide as well as back to La Quinta.

the farm road (which continues to the left) and soon enters an open pine wood (beforehand, a lovely view of the coast opens up) then crosses a small *barranco*. At the next major ridge, reach a trail that turns right to traverse the **Boca del Paso** ❷ (marvellous view taking in the southern coast!) and continues to Adeje.

We, however, turn left onto this trail to ascend pleasantly (PR TF 71, *white/yellow*). 20 minutes later, the trail crosses a narrow canal that has been hewn into the rocky terrain – here, bear diagonally left along the waymarked trail that follows the canal. Some minutes later, reach a trail junction ❸ (sign), to bear left with PR TF 71.2 (*white/yellow*) towards La Quinta. This descends for a short stretch and then bends to the right towards the slope; above, we can spot the tumbledown houses of El Aserradero. Subsequently, follow a conduit as the trail now becomes unpleasantly slippery and rocky underfoot for a short stretch. Then the trail is pleasant again as it crosses a valley notch and two water canals. Gradually, the houses of La Quinta and Taucho begin to appear before us. To the right, we can once again enjoy a lovely view of the Cumbre. At the first house, the walking path crosses a narrow road and leads in a bend over the Barranco de la Quinta (Taucho is perched on the next ridge) to return to the car park in **La Quinta** ❶.

↗ 640m | ↘ 970m | 16.1km
5.45 hrs
🚌 ✕

38 From Arona via Ifonche to Adeje

Fabulous mountain walk above the south-western coast

The heights above Arona and Adeje present walkers with a beautiful walking Paradise, full of variety, and frequently opening up magnificent views down to the coast near Las Américas as well as into seemingly bottomless barrancos. If the walk from Arona to Adeje seems too long for your taste, you can also start off in Ifonche (no bus connections!)

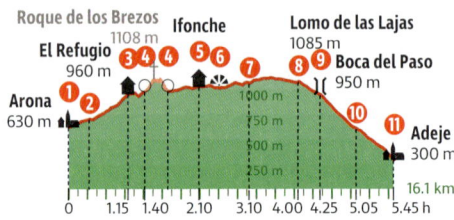

Starting point: Arona's centre, 630m (bus stop for the 342, 474, 480, 482; or the bus stop at the upper end of the village on the main road in the direction of Vilaflor); or the turn-off of the track at the restaurant 'Olivers' (very little parking, better to park before the last road bridge or after the next bend in the road).
Destination: Adeje, 300m (bus stop for the 417, 447, 448, 460, 471, 473).
Grade: a long, but all things considered, an easy walk.
Refreshment: Possibly El Refugio (tel. +34 637830738, el-refugio.com), bar/restaurants in Arona, Ifonche and Adeje.
Alternative: walkers who wish to save themselves a couple of metres of altitude could begin the walk at the bus stop on the turn-off for Ifonche in Escalona (a good ½ hr along a *beige*-marked camino to reach El Refugio).
Linking tip: with Walks 40 and 42.

View back from the trail to Arona and the south coast.

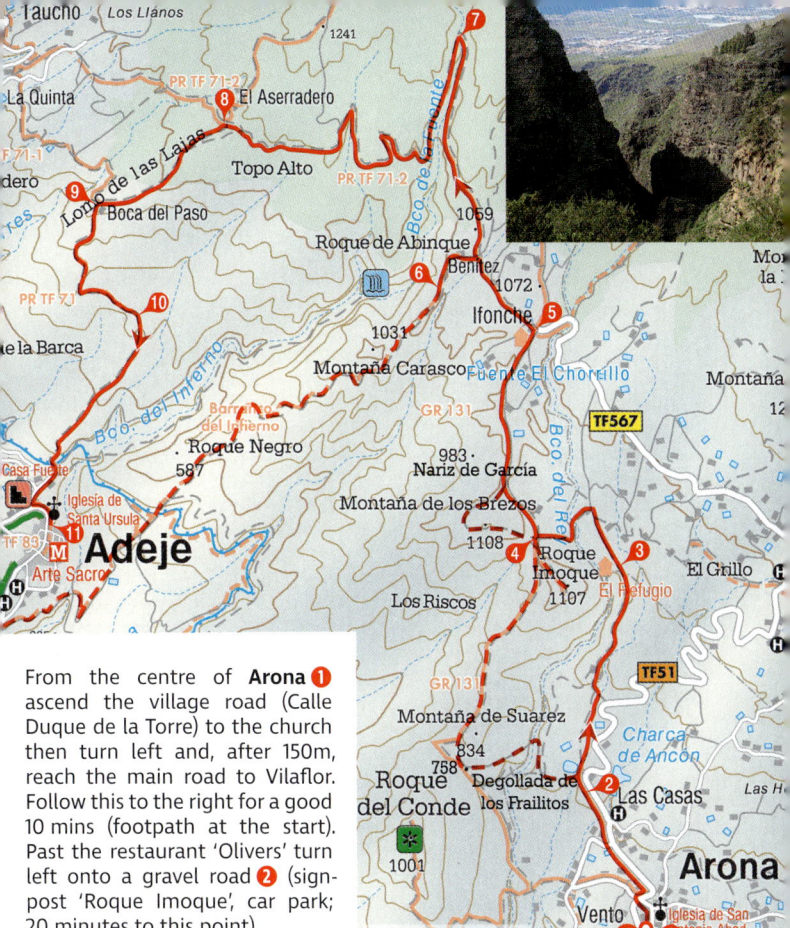

From the centre of **Arona** ❶ ascend the village road (Calle Duque de la Torre) to the church then turn left and, after 150m, reach the main road to Vilaflor. Follow this to the right for a good 10 mins (footpath at the start). Past the restaurant 'Olivers' turn left onto a gravel road ❷ (signpost 'Roque Imoque', car park; 20 minutes to this point).

The gravel road (sign 'Ifonche') soon crosses the Barranco del Ancón – directly afterwards, the Camino del Topo turns off right before a water storage tank (signpost, *white* waymarkers). Ascend gently along the ridge at the edge of the Barranco del Ancón and, just under half an hour from the main road, pass a run-down finca. Behind the building keep right following the *white* waymarkers, cross the water canals and follow these uphill. The beautifully formed Roque Imoque towers up on the left. The path continues temporarily between the water canals (do not cross over

Refreshment is available in the Restaurante El Refugio (left) and in Ifonche (right).

left to the track), then ascends the slope keeping right. After 10 minutes meet up once again with the water canals — at this point you should cross left over the canals and have a look at the sheer drop down into the Barranco del Rey.

Now continue ascending up beside the water canals and almost 10 minutes later, pass the welcoming bar/restaurant '**El Refugio**' ❸ (only open from time to time). Stay on the track for another 5 minutes and then turn left at a house. Descend along the trail straight on beside a conduit into the Barranco del Rey (possibly 'privado' signs which you can ignore). Keep left here (heading down the *barranco*, an excursion is worthwhile to the Fuente de las Pilas in a good 5 minutes) and then ascend on the other side of the valley, to the left of a steep rock wall, up to the nearby mountain ridge. Continue ascending along the ridge past a derelict house to a large threshing circle ❹ on the col between **Roque Imoque**, 1107m (on the left) and the **Roque de los Brezos**, 1108m (on the right, 20 minutes, see Walk 40). From the col offering a wonderful view of Las Américas, it is also possible to descend the Camino de Suárez to Arona (see Walk 40).

Here, meet up with the GR 131 (*white/red*). This leads to a farmstead and a tarmac road — turn left onto the road and ascend. The road keeps heading straight on, for a short while with a lovely view of Adeje, the coast at Playa Paraiso and towards La Gomera, to reach the 'El Dornajo' bar/restaurant (open daily from 1 pm onwards, closed Thursdays) in **Ifonche** ❺. Here, leave the GR 131 behind as it continues to Vilaflor, and, at the junction, turn left

with the PR TF 71.2 (*white/yellow*) onto the road. 100m on turn right onto a roadway, leaving this again 100m later (signpost) by turning left onto a pretty trail leading above a water canal. The distinct broad camino enters a sparse pine wood. After 5 minutes, a solitary farmstead appears ahead on a mountain ridge; the path heads towards this, passing to the right of terraced meadows. 200m before the farmstead the camino crosses a roadway and, just after that, crosses another one – here it is worth making a detour to the Infierno viewpoint (the walking trail subsequently continues straight on): turn left along the roadway to the farmstead then descend along the ridgeline to an old threshing circle ❻. From the knoll at the end of the mountain ridge you can enjoy a beautiful view of the dramatic Barranco del Infierno (even if you can barely spot the waterfall) and the coast as well. By the way, to the right and below, a camino descends from the mountain ridge towards Adeje – a nice alternative (2 hrs; the camino is not maintained in places – it is somewhat stony and overgrown; sure-footedness and a perfect head for heights are required!).

After the detour, continue along the marked trail which leads uphill through an open pine wood and, after a few minutes, along a wonderful high mountain trail crossing the slope above the deeply furrowed Barranco de la Fuente (now with *green/white* waymarkers). After not quite 20 minutes, reach a fork in the path – here ascend to the right (the trail to the left leads down to a spring and the floor of the *barranco*). Some minutes later, the trail descends to the bottom of the *barranco* ❼ and then bears left to leave it again. After about 10 minutes, reach the crest

Backwards view of the Roques from the plaza in Adeje. – Below: Barranco del Infierno.

of a mountain ridge; here, continue sharp right, traversing the slope. In easy up-and-down walking cross numerous, mostly small valley notches. 45 minutes from the *barranco* there's a fork in the path – carry straight on here, ascending the waymarked trail (you can also continue left across the slope) to a trail junction on the treeless mountain ridge which follows, the **Lomo de las Lajas** ❽.

The waymarked trail to La Quinta (PR TF 71.2) continues straight on but you turn left here with PR TF 71, descending the flat, rocky ridge beside a narrow water canal cut into the rock. 20 minutes later, reach a mountain spur with a fantastic view down below of the south-west coast between Los Cristianos and Los Gigantes (**Boca del Paso** ❾, see photo bottom of page 140) – the PR TF 71.1 branches off to the right here towards La Quinta but keep left and descend the wide camino which leads in zigzags directly towards Adeje.

After a good 45 minutes, keeping left, reach a broad ridge with almond trees ❿, and half an hour after that, a road directly below a radio mast. Follow this road to the left downhill to **Adeje** (on the very first right-hand bend, a trail branches off to the left into the Barranco del Infierno see photo left). Descend the steep village road, bearing left at the first junction, and reach the village centre 5 minutes later ⓫ (bus stop 50m further down from the church).

↗ 145m | ↘ 145m | 4.4km

1.20 hrs
Ifonche short circular walk — 39

Popular short walk with an exciting choice of summits

If you are looking for a circular walk that is brief but rich in variety, we can warmly recommend this one from the mountain village of Ifonche to the Fuente de El Chorrillo. Be pampered by the breathtaking views of the southern coast and of the Cumbre; on top of that, the walk offers a couple of bonuses.

Starting point: the bar/restaurant El Dornajo in Ifonche, 1033m, at the end of the TF-567 (from Arona, along the TF-51 towards Vilaflor, 6km on, at the entrance to the village of La Escalona, turn left onto the TF-567 and continue for a good 3km). No bus service (the nearest bus stop for lines 342, 419, 474, 482 is in La Escalona/Las Casas at the turn-off of the TF-567 from the TF-51 Arona – Vilaflor.
Grade: an easy circular walk, only some short stretches and the optional summit excursions are more demanding.
Refreshment: bar/restaurant El Dornajo in Ifonche (daily from 1 p.m.; closed Thurs).
Linking tip: with Walks 38 and 40.

At the road intersection (Restaurant El Dornajo) in **Ifonche** ❶ continue straight on along the street following the PR TF 71.2 (*white/yellow*) and, 100m on, turn right onto the roadway for another 100m (sign). Then turn left onto a lovely trail above a water canal to leave the roadway behind. The distinct broad camino then enters an open pine forest. 5 mins later, you can spot a solitary farmstead in front of you, perched on a mountain ridge (to the left, on the neighbouring ridge, some caves); the trail crosses over to the farmstead, passing to the right of terraced meadows. 200m before the farmstead cross over a roadway and then another one just afterwards – here, turn left onto the roadway leading to the farmstead and continue along the ridge, descending to an ancient threshing circle. The trail continues further along to reach a knoll at the end of the ridge ❷ from which we can capture a lovely view into the untamed Barranco del Infierno (even though the waterfall is hardly visible) as well as of the coast. Afterwards, retrace your tracks back towards the threshing circle and, at the halfway point, turn left onto the Camino Carrascogen (*white arrows*).

143

The marvellous alpine trail leads below the rock faces and through the slope.

This descends diagonally at first through the slope and afterwards along the foot of the mighty rock faces to cross to a *beige*-coloured eroded saddle ❸. Ambitious sure-footed walkers could take an excursion from here onto the Montaña Carrasco (on the opposite side of the saddle, turn right and, 30m on, turn right again to a circular col and then continue over the ridgeline to reach the summit). We, however, bear left on the eroded saddle and continue steadily straight on along the slope at the foot of the rock faces. During this stretch, pass solitary caves and cave dwellings – this is an especially beautiful section of trail! Not quite a quarter of an hour later, reach the **Fuente de El Chorrillo** ❹. A couple of bends further on, then the trail ascends steeply to a plateau. If you wish to include a visit to the Nariz de García, just before reaching the plateau, turn right onto a nondescript path – this crosses over to the dramatic rocky ridgeline and ascends over it to reach the apex (the summit lies directly adjacent to a paraglider launch site and is therefore a superb observation point). On the plateau, meet up then with a road and turn left onto it to return to **Ifonche** ❶ in a quarter of an hour.

The Nariz de García is a superb viewpoint.

↗ 600m | ↘ 600m | 9.6km

3.45 hrs

Roque de los Brezos, 1108m   40

Thoroughly enjoyable walk around the Roque Imoque

This route, on the whole a gentle one, possesses everything a walker's heart could desire – a beautifully scenic ascent trail, an abandoned finca with elaborately laid terraces, a fabulous panoramic summit – and, to top it all off, welcoming refreshment which awaits you when you arrive in the restaurant El Refugio.

Starting point: the centre of Arona, 630m, (bus stop for the 342, 474, 480, 482; or the bus stop at the upper end of the village on the main road in the direction of Vilaflor); or the turn-off of the track at the restaurant 'Olivers' (very limited parking, better to park before the last road bridge or past the next bend in the road).
Grade: predominently easy circular walk.
Refreshment: possibly 'El Refugio' (tel. +34 637830738, el-refugio.com), bar/restaurants in Arona and Ifonche (short detour).
Alternative: you can also begin the walk in Vento (see Walk 41) and reach the Degollada de las Frailito via the GR 131.
Linking tip: with Walks 38 and 41.

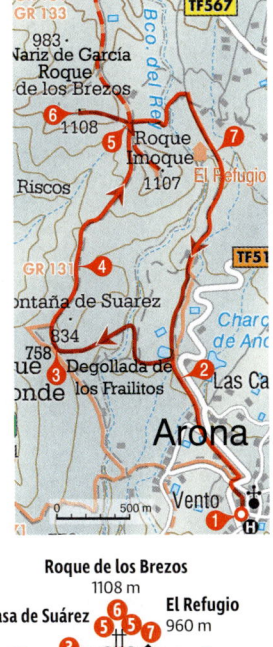

From the centre of **Arona** ❶ follow Walk 38 past the restaurant 'Olivers' ❷ as far as the Barranco del Ancón. Ignore the Camino del Topo turning off right here (your return route) and carry straight on (right) along the Camino Suárez (*white/green*). At the next fork (the main trail hooks off to the right) keep straight on to continue along the camino and pass the Casa El Ancón (old stone oven) to then enter the dramatic Barranco del Rey. At the floor of the *barranco* keep right and after 30m, ascend up to the next mountain ridge. The trail now heads left, traversing the slope above the deeply furrowed *barranco*, and then merges with the GR 131 (*white/red*) three minutes later. Follow it to the right through a small valley notch up to the **Degollada de los Frailitos** ❸ (¼ hrs) – from the col next to the Conde, enjoy a marvellous view of the south-west coast.

The Roque de los Brezos is a fabulous panoramic mountain – summit view of the coast.

The GR 131 ascends to the right along the ridge and, after a few minutes, through a peculiar karst-like rocky terrain. A good 20 minutes later, reach a col with a threshing circle and **Casa de Suárez** ❹, surrounded by terraces – a wonderful spot for a rest. Not quite half an hour later, you come to another **col** ❺, 983m, with a large threshing circle. Walkers with a head for heights can climb up to the right to the Roque Imoque, 1107m (a good ¼ hr, some scrambling on the summit block). Otherwise go left to the **Roque de los Brezos** ❻, 1108m – the ascent takes 20 minutes and the distinct path is waymarked with *green dots* and cairns. From the summit, enjoy a fabulous 360 degree panorama.

Also worthwhile is a walk onto the nearby summit dome, although noticeably more demanding, where the entire south-west coast lies at your feet (¼ hr there and back; diagonally right over the main ridge, an alpine path continues to reach the sheer drop in front of the two Varitos rock spires with a rock arch; 20 minutes).

After a well-deserved rest, return to the col ❺ and from there, take the distinct trail (sign: 'Fuente de las Pilas') through an eroded gully over to an abandoned finca. The *green*-marked trail now keeps left downhill into the Barranco del Rey (here, an excursion to the right is worthwhile to the Fuente de las Pilas, a spring surrounded by ferns at the foot of a basalt rock face; a good 5 mins) and leads up the other side to the next mountain ridge (possibly 'privado' signs which you can ignore) where you meet a track. Follow this track to the right and, a few minutes later, pass the bar/restaurant **'El Refugio'** ❼ (only open from time to time) – after that, the track becomes an eroded trail (Camino del Topo) that leads downhill, parallel to conduits and water canals while keeping always to the ridge. After a good 20 minutes, pass a derelict finca (20m below, turn left onto a path) and a good 20 minutes after that, past a dam wall, meet the track from the start of the walk. Follow this to the left, back to **Arona** ❶.

↗ 510m | ↘ 510m | 5.2km

3.15 hrs
🚌 👣

Conde, 1001m — 41

On Tenerife's southern landmark

Conde, the most distinctive mountain in the south of the island, is doubtlessly one of the most beautiful panoramic summits on Tenerife. From the mountain plateau you can enjoy not only a magnificent view of the south-west coast between the Reina Sofía Airport, Los Cristianos and Los Gigantes, but also of the south-western caldera rim and Teide.

Location: Arona, 630m (bus stop for the 342, 474, 480, 482).
Starting point: Vento, 650m. From Arona's centre ascend the village street (Calle Duque de la Torre) up to the church then turn left to the main road Los Cristianos – Vilaflor. Diagonally opposite, Calle Mazape forks off left to Vento (bus stop; ¼ hr on foot to Calle Vento, No 78). The access by car is signposted starting at the upper end of Arona.
Grade: easy to moderate walk on caminos, some stretches along steep paths.
Alternative: return route via the Degollada de los Frailitos (1½ hrs, only for the absolutely sure-footed and vertigo-free mountain walker!): from the trig point at the summit, follow the left hand (southwards) path for a good 50m. Immediately after the little rock ledge on the level plateau fork left to reach the edge of the plateau. Follow the rim for 25m to the right (do not turn left into the boulders!) until just before an old threshing circle, a distinct, waymarked trail branches off to the left along the steep slope. This leads well below the rock faces through the slope, descends along a little outcrop of rock (easy scrambling) and then merges onto a path that is no longer serviceable. Now another outcrop follows. After that you continue on the diagonal climbing down via boulders to reach a larger rock ledge. Here begins a rocky vertiginous traverse, then pass an overhanging boulder block to reach the ridgeline that leads downwards to the Degollada de los Frailitos. Turn right along the GR 131 (Walk 42) to return to Vento (to the left Walk 40).
Refreshment: in Arona bars/restaurants.

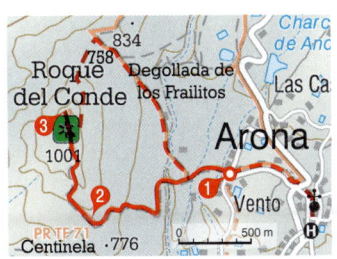

From the village street (Calle Vento) in **Vento** ❶ a trail branches off in a westerly direction beside house No 78 (sign; SL TF 218, *white/red/green* way-markers). The trail crosses the Barranco de las Casas, and afterwards, the little Barranco del Ancón. Then the trail forks — the *white/red* marked GR 131 bears right, but bear left instead along the *white/green* marked trail. After 100m, it descends to the right into a third, noticeably deeper gorge — the Barranco del Rey — a stunning *barranco* typical of the South (if you walk a few steps downhill in the bed of the *barranco*, you will find a striking cataract).

After walking for a total of 20 minutes, you will have left this gorge behind as well. The path forks on the other side — continue here to the left along the distinct path which climbs uphill briefly

Above: The camino through the Barranco del Rey. – Below: On the way to Conde.

Vertigo-free, sure-footed walkers can climb down through the steep, rocky eastern flank of the Conde and return to Vento (see Alternative).

and then leads left along the edge of the *barranco*. After a few minutes, the trail passes to the right of a solitary derelict house. Beyond the house, the camino continues its ascent, passing two old threshing circles, and leads up between overgrown terraces. At the upper end of the terraced slope, the camino becomes a path and not quite half an hour after passing the house reaches the crest of a mountain ridge leading down from Conde, the **Centinela** ❷. Starting now, enjoy a marvellous view below of the holiday resorts at Playa de las Américas and Los Cristianos.

Now traverse the slope ahead over to the next (western) mountain ridge. The path is still well-marked (cairns; *green* dots) and ascends the mountain ridge. After a good quarter of an hour, reach a rocky ledge below a low wall. Continue across the ledge to the left, and bearing left, ascend the camino, sometimes over rock. After a quarter of an hour, reach the broad, sloping summit plateau of **Conde** (keep this point in mind for the descent!). Surprisingly enough, you can see that terraces had been constructed here years ago where meadows have long since taken over again.

Only 5 minutes more bring you up to the summit ❸ (trig point) with some nice little spots for a rest stop. Also worthwhile is the circular walk along the sheer drop at the rim so that you can savour the unparalleled parade of peaks at all points of the compass.

↗ 420m | ↘ 1200m | 17.6km

42 From Vilaflor to Arona

5.20 hrs 🚌✕

A long and somewhat dreary descent route

The GR 131 leads along one of the most historically significant connecting trails for the island's northern and southern regions. The stretch between Vilaflor and Arona, although by no means spectacular, is nevertheless worthwhile – usually the route descends pleasantly and, until reaching Ifonche, mostly passes through a marvellous pine forest.

Starting point: the church square of Vilaflor, 1415m (bus stop for the lines 342, 474, 482). From the bus stop on the main street walk 10 mins along the Calle Sta. Catalina, then left at the end.
Destination: Arona, 630m (bus stop for the lines 342, 474, 480, 482).
Grade: this is basically an easy but a long walk that requires a good amount of physical fitness.
Refreshment: bar/restaurants in Vilaflor, Ifonche and Arona.

Begin the walk in the village centre of **Vilaflor** ❶. At first, ascend to the *plaza* up above and then, past the church, turn left onto the Calle Los Molinos (sign: GR 131, *white/red*). A few minutes later the street crosses the main road and, afterwards, passes the **Ermita de San Roque** ❷ with the village of Vilaflor lying at our feet. 5 minutes later, at the Hotel Vill'Alba, bear left and, where the tracks fork, continue on straight ahead into the pine forest. Passing terraced fields meet up with a fork on a col – here turn diagonally right to continue climbing up, soon passing a waterworks. 100m on, the trail forks diagonally left onto a camino and leads about on the level through the open pine wood. Cross over a ridge and, shortly afterwards, at the **Salto de las Corujas** ❸ cross over a

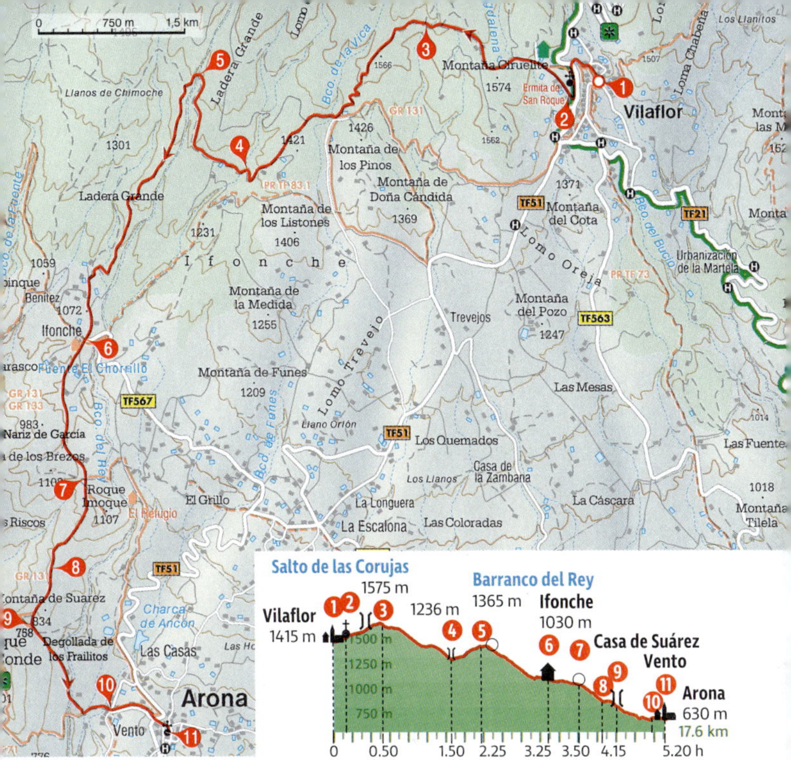

The loveliest stretch of the walk: descent via the ridge to Ifonche.

151

Spectacular sheer drop on the Salto de las Corujas.

barranco – the view reaching over the sheer drop at the rim, taking in the southern coast, is breathtaking! The trail continues, traversing the slope and then leads out onto a ridge; this is a lovely stretch, opening a view of Gomera and Hierro. Now the route continues pleasantly descending in broad bends to reach a fork – turn right here to pass a water distributor. Just afterwards, at some dryland fields, the camino merges into a forestry road. Continue straight on along this road through the pine forest and, at a major junction, continue the route by turning onto another camino. This leads out via a ridge and then descends along it, crossing over a roadway in between (30m right) and passing more dryland fields. Shortly after, yet another highlight awaits us: the rock-faced *barranco* of Las Goteras which is spanned by a bridge, the **Puente de Guayero** ❹. Cross over and then the camino begins another gentle ascent, crossing terraced fields and passing a reservoir. After that, climb up once again along a ridge until the camino crosses over the little rocky **Barranco del Rey** ❺. Via the following ridge, continue descending straight ahead and soon enjoy a view of Ifonche. A couple of bends follow then the ridge narrows and the trail leads through a small *barranco* to reach a roadway on the other side. This brings us to **Ifonche** ❻ (we can recommend the bar/restaurant 'El Dornajo'; open daily from 1 pm; closed on Thurs).

The final stretch is reigned over by the Roque Imoque. – Below: The Barranco del Rey.

Now take the GR 131 which continues along the road (soon a lovely view of the coastline at Adeje). Before a farmstead turn right onto a trail to a nearby **saddle** ❼ (threshing circle) situated between the brazen Roque Imoque (left) and the Roque de los Brezos (right, see Walk 40).

On the opposite side of the saddle the GR 131 continues traversing the slope of the Roque Imoque (splendid view of the southern coast). About 20 minutes later, pass the **Casa de Suárez** ❽, an abandoned finca, surrounded by terraced fields. 15 minutes later, in front of the saddle ❾ on the Conde, the trail veers away to the left towards the valley. Keep straight on, passing a tumbledown finca, and cross over the Barranco del Rey. Afterwards, pass another tumbledown farmstead, cross two more *barrancos* and reach the houses of **Vento** ❿. Turn left here, then take the first street to the right to reach the main road TF-51 in **Arona**. On the other side, reach the *plaza* with the church in a few minutes. Then continue on to the bus stop in the village centre near the main street ⓫.

153

↗ 140m | ↘ 140m | 13.0km

43 From Los Cristianos to Las Galletas

4.00 hrs

Marvellous coastal walk to the southernmost tip of Tenerife

Those who think that the South of Tenerife is just a bleak desert covered in scree will be proved wrong on this walk. Just a stone's throw away from all the hustle and bustle of Los Cristianos, the walker can look forward to some wonderful coastal landscapes, in some places totally remote and unspoilt, with spurge and cacti, lava crags and volcanic cones, tidal pools and coves that boast some sandy beach and are inviting places for a swim when the sea is calm.

If the surf is high, be patient until you reach Las Galletas – a comparatively quiet and relatively natural tourist resort with a beach by the harbour – where you can swim in the sea without any risk.

Walkers who feel that the stretch to Las Galletas is too long, can interrupt the walk in Palm-Mar or content themselves with an ascent of Guaza, Los Cristianos' native mountain (see Alternative).

Starting point: Los Cristianos' harbour (puerto), 5m (bus stop for numerous buses); or the south-eastern village limits at the end of the beach (Avenida de la Penetración; a good place to park).
Destination: Las Galletas, 5m (bus stop for the 415, 467, 468, 470, 486).
Grade: easy coastal walk, however, the path to Palm-Mar is rather steep and slippery.
Refreshment: bar/restaurants in Los Cristianos, Palm-Mar and Las Galletas.
Alternative: detour onto Montaña de Guaza, 428m: at the fork at waypoint ❷ ascend left along the main trail. After ¼ hr carry straight on along the ridge, walk at the edge of the terraced plateau, then ascend the track to the summit (radio masts, pylons; 1¼ hrs from the fork; if you prefer to walk along a path, leave the track, 30m on, by turning left and ascend the ridge directly to the summit). From here, it's a good 10 mins to a neighbouring peak (radio masts), from which you can enjoy a view of Los Cristianos.
Tip: don't forget your swimming gear!

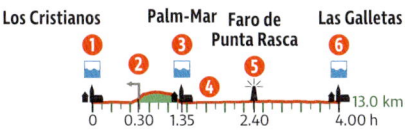

From the harbour in **Los Cristianos** ❶ follow the seaside promenade in an easterly direction. After a good quarter of an hour, pass a multi-storey building (Costa Mar). A broad gravel trail continues and forks after 5 mins at the end of the beach in front of the cliffs. Turn diagonally left onto the broad camino which gently ascends in a wide bend. 50m past the first right hand bend in the main trail, a path forks away, heading straight on ❷ (sign 'No pasar'): the main trail leads left up to Montaña de Guaza (see Alternative), but stay on the straight coastal trail that now ascends more steeply (keep an eye out for waymarkers). Some minutes later reach a high plateau. More or less on the level, just inland from the coast, pass through a barren, but nonetheless picturesque countryside dominated by spurge and later by cacti. 15 mins later, pass two little stone quarries (afterwards, keep right on the main trail). 5 mins after that, the trail forks in front of a

View back from the trail to Los Cristianos.

quarry at the edge of the slope above Palm-Mar. If you are not sure-footed, take the left-hand trail (then turn right soon after) that keeps following the plateau and then finally descends to the right to enter a small valley notch. Descend the notch, then later downhill to the right across the steep slope to the seaside promenade at the stony beach Playa de La Arenita.

At the end of the promenade of **Palm-Mar** ❸ meet a road and turn immediately right towards the coastal trail that leads pretty much on the level directly along the coast. 20 minutes later, before reaching a stony beach – **El Calladito** ❹ – the trail becomes a lovely path and, later on, enters the nature park 'Malpaís de la Rasca' – a delightful, virtually unspoiled, coastal plain at the foot of a volcanic cone. Later on, ignore a roadway turning off left and stay on the coastal path. Past a small strip of sand, you finally come to the **Faro de Punta Rasca** ❺ which roughly marks Tenerife's southernmost point.

A quarter of an hour past the lighthouse, leave the nature park behind and, near a huge banana plantation, meet a track lined with palm trees. After a quarter of an hour – you can already see Las Galletas ahead – the plantation track comes to an end. To the right of a wall, a pretty trail continues, usually flanked by rows of stones. This always leads directly along the coast while passing a couple of small, lovely strips of sand. Half an hour later, at a Red Cross building, meet the TF-66 main road which brings you to the right along the sand and pebble beach to reach the harbour at **Las Galletas** ❻. The bus stop can be found 30m on the left of the traffic island (No 467/470 bus stop on the left in the direction of Los Cristianos).

Just before Las Galletas the trail passes a few pretty strips of sand.

↗ 80m | ↘ 90m | 7.1km

2.00 hrs — From Costa del Silencio to Los Abrigos — 44

Gentle coastal walk with numerous places to swim

The starting route on Montaña Amarilla is the most spectacular part of this walk which otherwise has few highlights except for some beautiful stretches of coastline and (at times solitary) places for bathing. The second part of the coastal walk runs beside holiday complexes and golf courses, but as compensation, you can look forward to the Lunar Landscape of San Blas, a unique natural attraction (see Tips).

Starting point: eastern end of the Costa del Silencio holiday village, 10m (Las Galletas), at the foot of Montaña Amarilla (bus stop for the 467, 468). Access: from the motorway exit San Miguel drive in the direction of Las Galletas, then turn left in Guargacho to Costa del Silencio.
Destination: Los Abrigos, 5m (bus stop for the Buslinien 470, 483).
Grade: easy coastal walk on leisurely paths and promenades – only the section at the start at the foot of Montaña Amarilla is rather more demanding (but you can get round this by going over the ridge).
Refreshment: bar/restaurants in Costa del Silencio, Golf del Sur/Guincho and Los Abrigos (good fish restaurants!).
Tips: at San Miguel Marina you can take a trip in a submarine on an underwater safari, tel. +34 922 736 629, www.submarinesafaris.com.
The fabulous Lunar Landscape of San Blas can be found very close to the coastal trail. Unfortunately, there is a charge to enter; you can book by calling tel. +34 922 749 010 or email reservas.sanblas@sandos.com, € 15 per person; internet: www.sandos.com, Hotel San

Blas/activities. To the hotel reception: from Playa de San Blas turn right up the road to the roundabout at the back of the holiday complex – the hotel reception with the exhibition rooms is located here and the entrance to the Lunar Landscape is opposite).

At the eastern entrance to **Costa del Silencio** ❶ the Calle Chasna branches off from the main road (Calle Olimpia) at the end of which the Chasna C block of flats is situated. Start the walk here by going down the track to the foot of Montaña Amarilla near the seaside (parking possible). From here, there are two possibilities: you can either walk up to **Montaña Amarilla** ❷

The coastal trail along Montaña Amarilla is the climax of the walk.

and follow the trail at the top to the right, then go right to cross over to the coastal trail. However, depending on the surf and the tides (be sure to be careful!), it is a prettier choice to pass the kiosk and then descend to the seaside to continue walking along the foot of the marvellously formed tuff cliffs, shimmering in various, predominantly beige, colours. After 100m, you must negotiate a huge, smoothly polished rock sporting numerous etchings. Unfortunately, about 5 minutes later, the most beautiful stretch of the walk ends and, when Montaña Amarilla meets the sea (naturist beach) climb up over the rocks to the coastal plain. Now walk across the plain on a delightful and pleasant trail which keeps along the coast. At the outset, salt-loving flora dominate the landscape, but later, the terrain becomes more lush with spurge and cacti. For a rest stop among the coastal

rocks, you will find many small, inviting bathing spots, as well as nooks protected from the wind. After a good half an hour, reach the 300m long pebble beach of **Playa Colmenares** ❸. Meet a track here that forks after the first stretch of beach. If you prefer a short circular walk and do not wish to continue to Los Abrigos turn left here onto the roadway (see below).

Shortly afterwards, turn left onto the track to ascend (*white arrows*) whilst skirting around a 'fjord' via a broad bend. 100m on, turn right onto a path that leads to a holiday resort – here turn right along the road to descend to the coastal trail that now runs at the edge of the golf course **Amarilla Golf** ❹ (watch out!). A good 20 minutes later, pass the **San Miguel Marina** ❺ (see Tips). Now meet up with the coastal promenade of the **Golf del Sur** holiday complex where there are some small pebble beaches – inviting places to stop for a swim in the sea. 20 minutes later, reach the **Playa de San Blas** (the hotel on the right behind the beach has a fantastic Lunar Landscape, see Tips). 10 minutes later, pass the last pretty pebble beach of Playa Grande, then **Los Abrigos** ⑥ is reached – to walk to the harbour with its renowned fish restaurants, keep right along the roads. The bus stop is located on the left at the main junction before the harbour.

From der Playa Colmenares ③ **back to Costa del Silencio:** at the eastern end of the beach turn onto the roadway that leads inland (see above). After 5 minutes, it bends to the right and soon afterwards another roadway turns off left and leads past **Montaña de Malpasito** 20 minutes later (100m from the roadway, at the foot of the mountain, there's a brilliantly coloured quarry with a volcanic vent; it's also nice to make a detour onto the summit, 118m, ¼ hr). 2 minutes later a roadway turns off diagonally left and heads directly towards **Montaña Amarilla**. Keep following the main trail straight on until, at the eastern foot of Montaña Amarilla behind a wall, you meet a trail (¼ hr). This leads on the right to **Costa del Silencio** ①, but you can also ascend left after 2 minutes to the crater rim and descend along the other side to the village.

↗ 200m | ↘ 200m | 6.7km

45 From El Médano onto Montaña Roja

2.15 hrs

Dune beaches, fabulous rocky coastlines and a magnificent view from the top of the mountain

El Médano is not only a paradise for surfers, but also for those who love long sandy beaches, somewhat of a rarity on Tenerife. But this sun-drenched spot holds some scenic highpoints for walkers too – fantastic rock formations and, of course, Montaña Roja, a landmark for Tenerife holidaymakers arriving by plane. The volcanic summit drops almost vertically down to the sea and offers a fabulous view of the southern island and, lying directly below, the Playa de la Tejita which is definitely worth a visit.

Starting point: bus stop at the *plaza*/harbour in the centre of El Médano (Avenida José Miguel Galván Bello; bus stop for the 408–411, 470, 483).
Grade: easy walk – avoid the summit in stormy weather.
Refreshment: bar/restaurants in El Médano.
Alternative: Montaña Pelada (a total of 2 hrs; fabulous rock formations): from the bus stop in El Médano, follow the road eastwards and then the promenade running along the Playa de la Jaquita. Past the beach, a road turns off to the right and leads immediately on the left along the coast (now a track). Near a residential complex, it joins a seaside promenade which, past the holiday resort, becomes a track. A few minutes later, a path that leads down to the Ensenada de la Pelada. At the other end of the beach, the path ascends inland to a rocky ridge and runs over this to the Montaña Pelada (here you could add a circular walk round the Caldera de Pelada to your route).

Montaña Roja – an excursion to the Playa de la Tejita is worthwhile.

From the bus stop at the *plaza* in **El Médano** ❶ head towards the pedestrian zone which leads westwards in a few minutes to the actual *plaza* at the outset of the sandy beach. Follow the beautiful beach, at first beside sandstone rock formations then, after passing the village, beside dunes. The beach stretches all the way to Montaña Roja. After a good 10 minutes, cross a rocky ridge and 5 minutes later, pass a lagoon (Mareta Wildpret). The sandy beach ends after that. Now, past a low building, walk up to the right along the broad trail, lined with wooden posts (signpost to 'Montaña Roja'). After 3 minutes, reach a junction ❷: to the right, you can make a detour to the Playa de la Tejita (20 minutes one way) while straight on continues up to the trig point on the highest point of **Montaña Roja** ❸ (20 mins). After a rest stop on the summit, return along the ascent trail for a good 10 mins until meeting a distinct path, turning off to the right. This rather unpleasant, scree-slippery path meets a broad intersecting path 5 minutes later which is edged with stones. It's worth making a 5-minute detour to the right from here, passing marvellous sandstone rock formations sculpted by the wind, to reach the promontory at Montaña Roja (nice rest spots) before continuing along the path to the left. Just under 5 minutes later, a path branches off right onto the knoll of **Bocinegro** ❹ (trig point at the highest point) over which you descend to the coast. Walk along the coast back to **El Médano** ❶.

↗ 490m | ↘ 490m | 12.2km

46 From San Miguel to Aldea Blanca

3.45 hrs

Journey into the history of the South

The pretty little town of San Miguel, set panoramically above the southern coastline, is well worth an excursion on its own – a highlight is a ramble through the marvellously preserved Calle de la Iglesia, boasting 18th and 19th century houses. In addition, the continued route charms us with glimpses into the history of the pastoral southern island and also with splendid views of volcanoes and the coastline. Past the Centinela junction, the walk is not quite so rewarding – but, nevertheless, a splendid cobblestone trail returns unwaveringly back to San Miguel.

Starting point: church square of San Miguel de Abona, 612m, a pretty little town above the southern coast (bus stop for the lines 409, 416, 419 484). Approach from the southbound motorway at exit 62 'San Miguel/Las Galletas' (9km via the TF-65).
Grade: an easy walk along pleasant caminos. Hardly any shade en route!
Refreshment: bar/restaurants can be found in San Miguel as well as in Aldea Blanca.

The starting point for the walk is the panoramic Plaza de la Iglesia with the parish church in **San Miguel** ❶ (between the TF-65 and TF-28). Take the SL TF 231 (*white/green*), descending along the historic Calle de la Iglesia and, next to the Oficina de Turismo, cross over the TF-65. At another *plaza*, the trail forks – to the left, the Camino de Las Lajas (SL TF 231.1, our return route). Continue, however, straight ahead, following the SL TF 231. 50m further on, pass the museum of local history, Museo Casa de El Capitán (on the right). Some minutes later, reach a junction; here, follow the waymarkers left–right. 100m after that, bear diagonally right and pick up an ancient *Camino Real*, sometimes still cobbled, to descend pleasantly while enjoying a view of dryland fields and the striking Roque de Jama. The trail crosses over the Barranco del Lomo, a few minutes later, and then a view opens up of the coastline – a splendid stretch of

trail! We leave a road (left) behind, 50m on, by turning right and following the camino. This forks another 100m further on – here do not turn right to descend into the Barranco del Drago (an old bridge, spanning a canal), but instead keep straight ahead descending along the *Camino Real del Sur*. 200m past this point is another fork – follow the waymarkers to turn sharp right into the untamed and idyllic Barranco del Drago, enclosed by rock faces. In the *barranco* pass the **Fuente de Tamaide** ❷. Between the

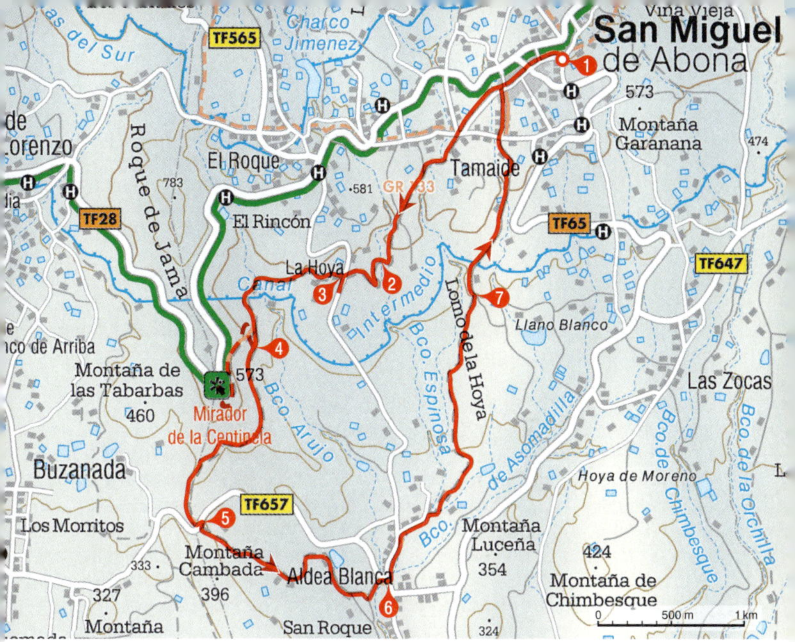

The Barranco del Drago with the Fuente de Tamaide; in the background, the Roque de Jama.

From the Mirador de La Centinela enjoy a fantastic panoramic view.

boulder blocks continue on to the other flank of the valley. There meet up with yet another camino. 200m further on, at the fork on the next ridge, keep sharp right, then come to a road. Turn left onto the road and, 50m on (100m further along the road is an old brick kiln), turn right to the **Caserío de La Hoya** ③, a cluster of old, beautifully-restored houses including a holiday resort complex. Passing a *charca*, continue descending into a valley basin at the foot of the Roque de Jama. On the other side of the valley pass a house (Casa del Gato). The camino now ascends a little, soon opening up a view to the **Mirador de La Centinela**, you can make an excursion to it by turning right along the abandoned roadway ④ (a good ¼ hr; one of the most magnificent viewpoints of the island with a view taking the southern island!). At the fork our camino continues straight ahead, cutting a wide bend as it skirts around the Centinela and opening up splendid views of the southern volcanoes. Then the camino leads out onto a ridge while taking in a view of a stone quarry (marvellous backwards view of Centinela and to the Roque de Jama) and then descends to the TF-657 ⑤ (Las Crucitas). Cross over the road by bearing right and then descend along the signed camino into the valley floor of El Ahijadero where the trail leads

Backwards view to the Casa del Gato at the foot of the Roque de Jama.

along a fence and then becomes a roadway. At a major junction by a large storage pond, bear right. 200m further on, at a power pylon, turn left onto a camino to climb down to **Aldea Blanca** ❻, reaching the village at a large *plaza* with a trail board. The walking trail SL TF 231 ends here.
Turn left to ascend Calle Valeria and reach the main street (cafeteria Ágora; to the right, on the TF-65, bus stop for the lines 484/486 to San Miguel or Las Galletas). Turn right on the main street to follow it for 30m and then turn left onto the Calle la Tosca. A few minutes later, pass a pretty *plaza* with a chapel, where the walking trail SL TF 231.1 passes by it. This continues on, ascending the street and, at the first crossing, turns right. Soon afterwards, the street hooks off to the left but we continue straight ahead along the Camino de Las Lajas. At first, the camino leads along a valley notch, but later, continues an ascent along the ridge where it reveals itself as a broad, ancient cobbled trail. A good half hour later, the camino crosses over an intersecting roadway ❼ (shortly after that, it merges with this roadway but then becomes a camino once again). Just afterwards, at the first houses, the camino merges into a street but we leave this behind again past a little valley notch by turning left onto another camino. Finally keep ascending along the street to reach the Calle de la Iglesia. Turn right onto it to return to the *plaza* of **San Miguel** ❶.

The splendid Camino de Las Lajas leads back to San Miguel.

47 From Cruz de Tea to the Paisaje Lunar

↗ 1030m | ↘ 1030m | 18.5km
7.00 hrs

Circular walks on the Cumbre of Granadilla

Thanks to its higher altitude at the foot of the pine forests on the Cumbre, the village of Cruz de Tea is an ideal starting point for walks. If you prefer taking it easy, you could restrict yourself to the circular walk to El Pinar. Ambitious walkers could choose the magnificent 'lunar landscape' as their destination. After the walk, heed the beckon for refreshment in the restaurant Cumbres de Abona, a very popular place for the locals as well.

Starting point: bar/restaurant Cumbres de Abona in Cruz de Tea, 900m (bus stop for the line 474). Approach from Granadilla: 3km along the TF-21 towards Vilaflor, then turn right along a narrow road for not quite 1km to reach the restaurant Cumbres de Abona in Cruz de Tea.
Height difference: 1030m – to El Pinar, not quite 400m.
Grade: a long, strenuous, circular walk, mostly following well-marked trails.
Refreshment: in Cruz de Tea bar/restaurant Cumbres de Abona (good and popular!) and Tasca El Horno (both closed on Mondays).
Alternative: you could also create two short circular walks from this route: Cruz de Tea – El Pinar (2½ hrs; easy) and El Pinar – Paisaje Lunar (4½ hrs).

75m along the street, before reaching the **bar/restaurant Cumbres de Abona** ❶, the PR TF 83 (*white/yellow*) forks away at the bus stop. The trail meets up with a street, 130m on. Turn left along this and ascend through the spruce little village. Pass a brick kiln (just past it, the Tasca El

Horno, closed on Mondays) and the Virgen del Buen Viaje chapel. 400m past the chapel the narrow street forks – turn right here. 40m on turn left onto a camino. The trail leaves the last houses behind and ascends mostly next to a roadway along a ridge while opening a lovely view of the Cumbre, covered in pine forests, and of the southern coast. Past a finca the roadway becomes a splendid cobbled trail, up to 5m in width. Soon afterwards pass an abandoned finca, distinguished by two towering palm trees at the entrance. The **Casa Los Malejos** ❷ is a lovely spot to take a break while enjoying a far-reaching view towards the coast. Now the camino is accompanied by a narrow watercourse until it enters the hamlet of **El Pinar** ❸ and crosses over a narrow street (not quite ½ hr).

If you are quite content with a short circular walk, turn left here and take the street to return back again (see below). We, however, pass the cross and ascend along the street past the widely scattered houses. At the last terraced vineyards the street ends and a camino continues onwards. This

Horno (above left), Casa Los Malejos (above right) and the camino to El Pinar (below).

From the mirador, it is only a stone's throw away to the lunar landscape.

crosses over the Barranco Silvestre and then forks at the next ridge. Turn left here to continue along the PR TF 83 (the PR TF 83.2 forks away to the right), and left again at the next fork 100m further on ❹ (to the right is our return trail later from Madre del Agua). The camino now goes on, climbing steadily up the ridge, mostly through an open pine wood and then passes a *mirador* with a view of a blindingly white finca (Casa Los Frontones). About at the same height as the finca, the trail crosses over a track and, some minutes after that, yet another one, the **Pista Madre del Agua** ❺ (La Florida, a popular starting point for the lunar landscape; the PR TF 83.1 forks off to the right). 5 minutes later, the trail meets up with a major trail junction – here, our trail merges with the PR TF 72, which we follow by turning right (10m on, turn left). This usually leads pleasantly through the slope. A good half hour later, a view begins to open up and then we reach a *mirador*, where the lunar landscape is laid at our feet; the southern coast also puts in an appearance. Now leave the waymarked trail behind and continue straight on along a path (at a fork, keep to the upper path). At the slope of black volcanic detritus, descend to the left to reach the fantastic minaret-shaped crags of the **Paisaje Lunar** ❻.

Now turn right onto a distinct path, somewhat off to the side of the upper cluster of crags, and climb down into the valley. Directly next to the lower lunar landscape cross over this valley. Pick up the path below the lunar landscape and head down the valley (*green* waymarkers). The path leads steadily through the slope above the *barranco* (a few minutes later, do not descend to the right) and soon crosses a slope of volcanic sand along a conduit. On the other side, descend in a straight line until meeting up once again with a conduit – turn left here towards the slope and follow the path, at first keeping about on the level, then bear right to descend along the ridge. Afterwards, the path climbs down to the left to a roadway. 15m on, in a bend, leave it behind again to descend along the ridge. Soon pass the first log cabins and you have reached **Campamento Madre del Agua** ❼. At the picnic area bear left to reach a barrier. In front of it turn right, keeping almost on the level (*green* waymarkers; at first without a distinct path, but soon rows of stones), then descend slightly to a low but 10m wide wall where the trail forks. Turn left here onto the overgrown roadway and descend to the Pista Madre del Agua 150m further on. Follow this briefly to the right until a camino, flanked by conduits, branches off diagonally to the left. The camino traverses the slope on the diagonal, descending pleasantly and, a quarter of an hour later, crosses over a roadway, the PR TF 83.1 (now the trail is signed). A half hour later, pass a vineyard and shortly thereafter merge into the ascending trail ❹. Take this trail to return back to **El Pinar** ❸ (20 minutes). At the cross keep to the road that traverses the slope to the right and then forks 10 minutes later – turn left here and follow the Calle Las Paredes to return to **Cruz de Tea** ❶ (½ hr later, this merges back into the approach route).

The marvellous lunar landscape is the undisputed highlight of the walk.

↗ 360m | ↘ 360m | 8.0km

48 Camino de Las Vegas

2.40 hrs
🚌 👫

Pleasant circular walk at one of the southern island's prettiest villages

Looking for a typical walk, rich in diversity, through the pastoral southern island? This circular walk at the edge of the Corona Forestal, the woodland belt of the Cumbre, should prove near to your heart. The walk is captivating due to its pleasant trails, pristine and idyllic rocky barrancos and pine forests, far-reaching views of the Cumbre as well as of the coast and a venerable cultivated countryside with irrigation canals and dryfield farming, a mill and a baking oven. Other highlights: the picturesque village of Las Vegas and the climber's rock faces of the Risco del Muerto, a worthwhile excursion.

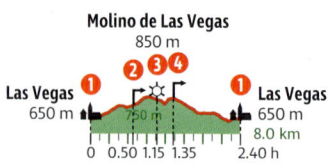

Starting point: church square of Las Vegas, 650m, picturesque village at the end of the TF-555 (next bus stop for lines 034 –36, 039, 430, 463 in Chimiche at the turn-off of the TF-555 from the TF-28, from there, a good 3km). Approach from the southern motorway at Exit 49 'Chimiche/ El Río' (8.5km via Chimiche to Las Vegas).
Grade: most of the way, this is an easy, pleasant circular route.
Refreshment: in Las Vegas bar/restaurant La Cantina (Wed–Sun 1pm–6pm), bar/restaurants in Chimiche.
Alternative: grand circular walk via Risco del Muerto and Pino del Guirre (1.30 hrs longer): At the fork ❷ keep straight ahead via the PR TF 83.1 ascending through the *barranco* (lovely rock faces on the left). 45 min later, you could loop diagonally right to reach the rock-climbing arena of the Risco del Muerto (sign, 5 mins). Ascending somewhat further, the trail merges again with the straight one and then forks on the plateau that follows. PR TF 83.1 leads to the left to continue on to the Paisaje Lunar – but keep to the right with PR TF 83.3 and follow the trail that mostly ascends, crossing a roadway 10 mins later. 15 mins after that, reach the highest point of the walk – here turn right to descend along the walking trail, passing a mighty pine tree (Pino del Guirre) until the trail joins the main trail at ❹ (45 mins).

The walk begins at the Las Vegas church with the 'belfry pine'.

From the church in **Las Vegas** ❶ (the pine tree next to the church serves as its 'belfry') climb up along the walking trail PR TF 83.1 (*white/yellow*) via the Calle Guajara. Soon leave the last houses of the tidy little village behind and the street becomes a roadway (enjoy a splendid view of the Cumbre and the Guajara). 10 mins later, turn right to continue the route along a camino flanked by rows of stones (straight ahead leads to the rock climbing area of Las Vegas). 5 mins later the camino crosses over a *barranco* and then forks at the next mountain ridge. Turn left here to climb up the panoramic ridge, covered in scrub vegetation and dotted with solitary pine trees. Subsequently, the trail crosses over a watercourse and soon after veers to the left towards the *barranco* while passing a cave dwelling. At the next ridge, meet up again with the roadway (right). 5 mins later the roadway forks in front of an almond grove ❷. We choose to undertake the shorter circular walk and continue by turning right with PR TF 83.4 (straight ahead is the long circular walk via PR TF 83.1; see Alternative). The trail starts off in an ascent and traverses the flank to the **Molino de Las Vegas** ❸ (roadway; 25 mins) – unfortunately, from the old water mill, hidden behind a large water reservoir, only a tower is still left standing. 100m further on, the trail veers again to the left to leave the roadway behind, then crosses the Barranco El Seco and finally meets a

The stalwart Pino del Guirre (Alternative).

The ascent leads over a panoramic ridge.

roadway ❹ next to a watercourse. The Caserío El Seco is situated to the left – but we turn right instead along the roadway and descend while enjoying a view of the Barranco del Río and Arico as well as the coastline. Quarter of an hour later, the trail forks off to the right onto a camino that crosses over the Barranco El Seco yet again and then passes some dryland fields. Afterwards the camino crosses over a roadway – now Las Vegas has already popped up in front of us. Shortly before reaching the settlement, the trail merges onto a road (shortly before that, a baking oven and an *aljibe* – a cistern – appear at the side of the trail). Take the road, or turn right along the waymarked camino and then left onto the road, to return to **Las Vegas** ❶.

The walk is particularly appealing during the almond blossom season.

↗ 1260m | ↘ 1260m | 22.7km

7.50 hrs

From Arico to El Contador 49

Spectacular circular walk through the heights at the foot of the Cumbre

This lovely circular walk, rich in diversity, through the heights above the villages and below the Cumbre is almost beyond belief. The only drawback is the fact that the walk is very long and very strenuous although it usually follows good and pleasant trails. For those preferring shorter walks, there are a number of options – the choices vary from a simple ramble between the villages of Villa de Arico and Arico Nuevo, a small circuit at the Lomo de Tamadaya (PR TF 86.3) and up the scale to the untamed, pristine rock climbers' barranco of Ortiz (PR TF 86.1). Of course, don't forget the linear walk to or from El Contador, which is possible to combine by road (by taxi or using two vehicles; approach from Villa de Arico). A thrill is guaranteed!

Starting point: bus stop shelter/car park on the TF-28 in Arico Nuevo, 387m (bus stop for lines 034–37, 039, 430). Approach via the southern motorway from the exit 'Arico/Porís de Abona' (6km to Arico Viejo, then 800m (left) along the TF-28 to Arico Nuevo).
Grade: very long, strenuous walk, mostly via good and pleasant walking trails.
Refreshment: bar/restaurants in Arico Viejo and in Villa de Arico. Water available at the picnic area El Contador.
Alternatives: a short circular walk: just past Casas de Tamadaya, take the PR TF 86.3 back to Arico Nuevo (a total of 2 hrs). – Village to village ramble from Villa de Arico to Arico Nuevo along the ancient *Camino Real* (a good 1 hr). – Excursion along the PR TF 86.1 into the rock climbers' *barranco* of Ortiz; return via the panoramic PR TF 86 (from Puente de Ortiz, not quite 1½ hrs). – To shorten the main walk, take the bus from Villa de Arico (a savings of 1¼ hrs) or begin or end the walk in El Contador.
Note: in 2021, this area fell victim to a ravaging forest fire.

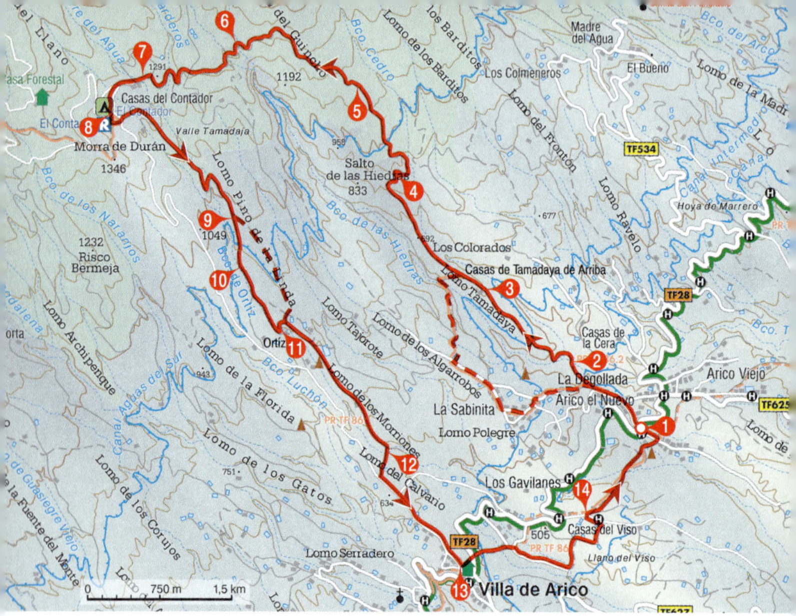

Begin the walk at the bus stop shelter (car park; trail board) in **Arico Nuevo** ❶ on the TF-28. Diagonally on the opposite side of the street, ascend along the PR TF 86.2 (sign 'El Contador', white/yellow) the Calle El Molino, at first cobbled, but tarmac later on. Past the district of La Degollada, the street hooks to the left — here, continue straight on. 10m further, turn right, following the PR TF 86.2 along a roadway (about on the level) as it heads up the *barranco* (the PR TF 86.3 forks off here as it heads straight on). Past a farmstead, the roadway becomes a camino that descends in zigzags into the Barranco de Tamadaya ❷ and leads along the gravel bed for 50m until it leaves it behind again, ascending between the two *barrancos* to Lomo de Tamadaya. Following the Lomo ascend pleasantly, soon passing the first pine trees while being accompanied by rock roses and a watercourse — and also a splendid view of the Cumbre. After a total of 1 hr, meet up with the solitary two-storey house **Casas de Tamadaya de Arriba** ❸ (also known as the Casa Quemada; warning: do not

174

explore the upper storey; there is a water-filled pit in the back!).
250m past the house the trail forks next to a large threshing circle — you could turn left here to follow the PR TF 86.3 via La Sabinita to return to Arico Nuevo. We however keep to the PR TF 86.2 along the ridge. A good 10 mins later descend for a couple of metres (to your left in the **barranco** a galería), then the camino begins to noticeably ascend — at first diagonally through the slope, then in zigzags through an open pine wood as it climbs up to the next ridge. Here a trail forks to the right towards Los Palomeros/Las Heritas ❹ (sign) — our trail leads for a short stretch out onto the ridge (a lovely sweeping view to the coast!) and then continues an ascent along the ridge while opening a view of a rocky cataract (do not fork off to the right towards this). 15 mins later cross a roadway and just afterwards a watercourse. The trail forks ½ hr later in front of the cottage **Casa Arenas de Tenesco** ❺. Turn left, following the waymarkers, and pass to the right of the cottage to continue. Some mins later the trail forks again — here do not continue ascending along the ridge but instead head straight on, traversing the slope. Now the valley walls of the *barranco* begin to gradually press closer. In the background the Casa Forestal appears. Now the ascent trail constantly steepens, leads for a short stretch along the foot of a rock face, then levels off. Another short burst of ascent climbs up to a breach in the rock, the highest point of the walk. Here, treat yourself to a rest stop and enjoy the far-reaching view.

Casas de Tamadaya de Arriba.

Ascent over the Lomo de Tamadaya; to the left, the barranco of the same name.

The rock face barranco at Ortiz is the best and most popular rock climbing area on Tenerife.

Now another short stretch of steep descent then the trail leads in easy up-and-down walking through the slope, crossing over a rock face *barranco* with the **Salto de las Yedras** ❻, then another one, just after. At the next ridge, bear right at the fork and cross over to a mighty conduit. Cross over it and, following the waymarkers, turn left through the slope. Some mins later, cross over a track. In front of us, we can already spot the terraces of El Contador. The camino leads over a ridge then descends to the right to reach a track. Leave this behind again 200m on by turning left onto a camino (30m after that, turn right towards Contador). Now negotiate another (harmless) *barranco*, then the trail merges into a track next to the **Casas del Contador** ❼. Turn left and pass the finca along its right-hand side to continue along the track. Shortly afterwards, the track merges into a tarmac road that leads left to the nearby **picnic area El Contador** ❽ – tables and benches as well as a source for drinking water are a tempting invitation to a rest break. Leave the road behind again at the large trail board by taking the PR TF 86.2, through the pine forest then pass by a threshing circle and finally meet up with PR TF 86. Turn left onto this and return back again to Arico. 100m further on, the PR crosses over the road, passes a building and then winds downwards parallel to a conduit via a ridge. Afterwards cross to the left over the Barranco la Puente and then, at the next ridge, continue descending until coming to a fork ❾ (sign; later on, the two trails merge together again at the Puente de Ortiz) – here you can either turn left, descending along the PR TF 86 via the Lomo Pino de la Linde (a beautiful view towards the coast!) or (much prettier!) turn right along the PR TF 86.1, climbing down into the Barranco la Puente ❿, where the trail continues a descent, flanked on both sides by the impressive rock faces of Ortiz, Tenerife's best rock-climbing area. Ramble through this rocky paradise for not quite 1km whilst meeting up again and again with rock-climbers, then ascend to a road bridge up above – **Puente de Ortiz** ⓫. Turn left for 100m until the waymarked trail PR TF 86 continues to the right. Be careful: a mere 10m on, at the trail board, fork off to the right onto the camino following a watercourse (not waymarked; 'privado' signs). The trail leads constantly along the rim of the *barranco* and, 20 mins later, passes directly on the left-hand side of an abandoned farmstead and a high tension pylon. Now the trail is once again waymarked *white/yellow* — and descends over a ridge which constantly becomes more narrow and then crosses to the right over the Barranco la Puente ⓬. Traverse the next ridge to reach a narrow street (Calle La Ermita) on the other side. The street descends in 15 mins to the church square of **Villa de Arico** ⓭.

If you would like to return by bus, continue descending straight ahead to the main road 100m further on (bus stop for lines 034–37, 039, 430) — but we turn left after passing the church, following the PR TF 86 (sign: 'Arico Viejo'). The trail crosses a street, then the main street and finally leads along the ancient, usually cobbled *Camino Real* which was once the connecting route for the villages of the south-east coast. The camino continues, opening a splendid view of the villages and to the Cumbre, as it climbs down into a valley notch and then becomes a roadway, ascending for a short stretch along a ridge. Here the trail forks off to the right onto a road which descends gently between solitary houses and dryland fields. A good 5 mins later turn left onto a camino (sign) that leads for a short stretch through a valley notch and, next to an aqueduct for the Canal del Sur, ascends to the next ridge. Now continue descending pleasantly along a roadway for a short stretch. Afterwards the camino merges into a narrow street. Turn left to reach a sports ground. Here turn left along the street and, past the school, turn sharp right onto the roadway ⓮ to follow this for 80m straight ahead until a waymarked trail forks off diagonally to the left. This heads directly towards Arico Nuevo and soon descends in zigzags into the Barranco del Lere. The trail crosses over to the other side and follows the rim of the *barranco* for a short stretch then turns off to the left, passing a stone quarry, to reach the church square in **Arico Nuevo**. To the right of the church, you could go on to Arico Viejo — but we turn left, ascending the pretty main street to return to the starting point on the TF-28 ❶ (5 mins).

Starting point and destination for the walk – the mountain village of Arico Nuevo.

50 Arco de Tajao

↗ 120m | ↘ 120m | 4.4km
1.30 hrs

Captivating barranco and coastline circular walk

The fishing village of Tajao is famous for its numerous seafood restaurants and fantastic pumice rock formations. One of them is even a minor walking attraction: the Arco de Tajao. But the walk to the gigantic rock arch has even more to offer – let yourself in for a surprising treat!

Starting point: car park at the harbour of San Miguel de Tajao (1km from exit 46 'Tajao' of the south motorway). Bus stop of the bus line 430 in Tajao, bus stop lines 111 and 711 at the motorway exit, from here it is only a stone's throw to the Arco de Tajao.
Grade: easy walk on good trails; during strong winds avoid the stretch along the cliff.
Refreshment: numerous excellent seafood restaurants in Tajao.

In **Tajao** ❶ walk past the harbour car park on the left and, after the last house next to the eye-catching rock, climb up to the left over the pumice cliff sculpted by the wind and the waves. Now continue over the ridge along the pylons (if you want, you can also choose to go diagonally along the cliff) until reaching the road again in the bend between the restaurants La Laja and Las Arenas (if the path over the cliff is too tricky, especially in strong winds, you can also join the walk here). At this point, an over-

The captivating Barranco de Bijagua.

grown roadway branches off to the right and leads down to the beach at the mouth of the **Barranco de Bijagua** ❷. Before turning left into the *barranco*, it is worthwhile to take an excursion along the coast, past the **Embarcadero de Bijagua** (a superb and exceptional site; the cave at the onetime jetty is restricted to private use) to the next beach, behind which there is a campsite (Caleta del Sordo, ❸).

Back at the **Barranco de Bijagua** ❷ follow the stone-flanked path that leads past the Pozo de Tajao (trough fountain) into the *barranco*. The *barranco* is soon flanked on both sides by rock faces – this is a marvellous stretch of trail. After 10 minutes, the *barranco* narrows to the left and leads to a rock outcrop – bypass this by returning to the path 80 metres beforehand, climbing diagonally right to the edge of the *barranco* and continuing there (already with a view of the Arco de Tajao on the other side of the *barranco*) until the path leads back down to the *barranco* floor. Here ascend a few metres up the *barranco*, then a path, bordered by rows of stones, leads up to the left to the nearby **Arco de Tajao** ❹. The rock arch is an excursionist destination that is easily accessed from the car park at the Tajao motorway exit and is, therefore, very popular.

The way back is along a distinct path that starts halfway up between the *barranco* floor and the natural arch. Always follow the *barranco* to return again to the beach ❷ – from there, take the approach route back to **Tajao** ❶.

↗ 175m | ↘ 175m | 5.8km

51 Barranco de la Linde and Arco del Jurado

2.00 hrs

Immersed in the tranquillity of one of the most beautiful of the southern barrancos

With its magnificent rock faces, caves and basalt columns, the Barranco de la Linde is an archetypical barranco of the island's south and, thanks to its first-rate accessibility and remoteness, is an ideal destination for a walk. In addition, a spectacular natural monument awaits us at the end of the walk: the largest basalt arch on the island, with a span of around 50 metres and a height of 25 metres.

Starting point: at the *plaza* or the beach of Las Eras (1km from exit 35 'Las Eras' of the south motorway). Bus stop lines 32/33 in Las Eras, bus stop lines 111 and 711 at the motorway exit (on the return stretch of the walk).

Grade: easy walk, but requires some scrambling over a rocky outcrop. Do not attempt this walk during/after rainfall!
Refreshment: we recommend the restaurant El Rincón (closed Tues/Weds); Cafeteria Tropin (closed Tues/Weds) in Las Eras.

At the beach of **Las Eras** ❶ the Barranco de la Linde empties into the sea – the *barranco* bed determines our ascent route. Hike up from the beach through the *barranco* which is bordered by rock faces on an easy-going, mostly sandy path to cross under the motorway after 10 minutes. The rock

The grandiose Barranco de la Linde – a rock outcrop requiring an easy scramble.

faces, where many pigeons are nesting, shield us from civilisation which only intrudes in the form of a few scattered wind turbines. A quarter of an hour past the motorway tunnel, pass a gigantic cave. A good 10 minutes later, a 5 metre high **cataract** ❷ awaits us – the rock outcrop requires some scrambling, but is not a serious challenge. Magnificent rock faces with countless caves now flank the *barranco* which widens out after half an hour (continue here along the right-hand side of the *barranco*). 5 minutes later, at a prominent scrawled sign 'Arco' at the floor of the *barranco* ❸, turn right onto a *white/green* marked path that climbs up to a small terraced plateau and, keeping to the right, continues to ascend to the upper rim of the *barranco* – along this to the left, touching on a roadway, to the nearby **Arco del Jurado** ❹ which is located below a wind turbine.

The best **return route** is to take the approach trail – but it is more pleasant to return to Las Eras along the road. This can be reached by turning right onto the path 5 metres before the rise of the rock arch. The path leads on the level at first, then slightly ascends to a roadway and finally reaches the road.

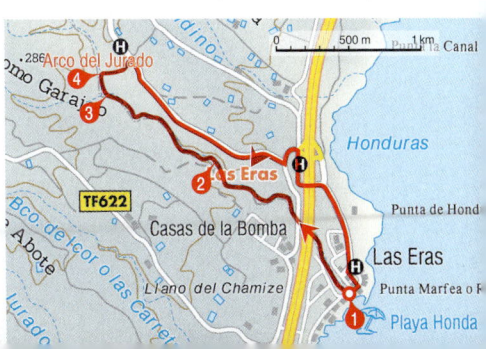

The Anaga mountains
Rugged mountain formations and an evergreen primeval laurisilva forest

The deeply cleft Anaga massif in the north-east was declared a UNESCO Biosphere Reserve in 2015. Geologically, it is the oldest part of the island. Dramatic steep coastlines, sharp ridges and chasm-like gorges characterise this mountain range which reaches an elevation of about 1000m on the main ridge. While the southern slopes are mostly barren and uninviting, the northern slopes, from the middle elevations to the ridges, are covered in dense laurisilva forest – trade winds regularly bring in clouds from the Atlantic which then disperse on the other side of the ridge.

The Anaga high mountain road opens up the main ridge, access roads descend into gentle valleys and idyllic villages – a paradise for walkers and nature-lovers who, in the Mercedes forest and the woods of the

Cruz del Carmen – view across the western foothills of the Anaga range of Teide.

Anaga mountains, will find rare flora including ferns of up to 2 metres as well as countless endemic plants.

Most of the villages and hamlets are also connected by ancient caminos which are sometimes cobbled.

Tourist villages are scarce on the coasts of the Anaga peninsula. Only the villages of Bajamar and Punta del Hidalgo have a tourist-based infrastructure – both villages boast seawater swimming pools. On the other hand, one of the island's most beautiful beach areas has been established on the south coast near San Andrés; the Playa de las Teresitas.

Playa de las Teresitas.

STARTING POINT FOR WALKS

Anaga mountain road
The Anaga mountain road which runs from La Laguna to Chamorga is one of the scenically most attractive and panoramic roads on the island. From the winding narrow road, access roads turn off to picturesque mountain villages.
As starting points for walks we recommend the following places:
Cruz del Carmen, 950m, viewpoint with chapel, Centro de Visitantes del Parque Rural de Anaga, bar/restaurant and cafeteria (trails, for example, to Las Mercedes, Chinamada, Batán and Punta del Hidalgo).
Pico del Inglés, 987m, a marvellous viewpoint on an overhanging pulpit rock (trail to Santa Cruz).
Bar/restaurant Casa Carlos, 930m, after the turn-off of the road to Las Carboneras (trails to Taborno and Afur).
Casas de la Cumbre, 825m, sprawling hamlet on the mountain road (trails to Santa Cruz and to Afur).
Casa Forestal de Anaga, 832m, forester's house between the Casas de la Cumbre and El Bailadero (trails to Taganana, Afur and to Valle Brosque).
El Bailadero, 682m, viewpoint with hostal and bar/restaurant (trails to Taganana, Almáciga and Chamorga).
Chamorga, 475m, beautifully located village at the end of the Anaga mountain road.

VISITOR RESTRICTIONS IN THE ANAGA MOUNTAINS

Due to conservation concerns, a permit is necessary for some trails in the Pijaral/Anaga (Walk 68, Alternative for Walk 73); an application must be made through the Centro de Servicios al Ciudadano (info: tel. +34 901 501 901, medionatural@tenerife.es).
Links to the online application form of the Cabildo de Tenerife can be found under 'Tenerife' at rother.de.

52 From Tegueste onto the Mesa de Tejina and to Bajamar

↗ 320m | ↘ 690m | 10.1km
3.35 hrs

Ancient connecting trail with a nerve-tickling peak

The highlight of the walk from Tegueste to the seaside in Bajamar is the flat-topped mountain of Mesa de Tejina – from its expansive plateau, enjoy a marvellous view of the coast at Bajamar and of the towns Tejina and Tegueste.

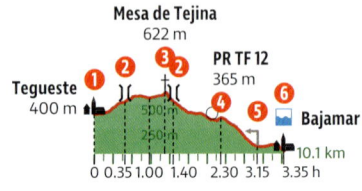

Starting point: the church square in Tegueste, 400m (bus stop for the lines 050, 052, 057, 105).
Destination: Bajamar, 20m (bus stop for lines 050, 105, 224).
Grade: consistently easy walk along mostly good caminos: only the alternative ridge trail on the Mesa de Tejina demands sure-footedness and a fair head for heights.
Refreshment: bar/restaurants in Tegueste and in Bajamar.

From the church square in **Tegueste** ❶ turn right onto the street next to the tourist office and descend (Calle Federico Fajardo, *white/yellow* waymarked). At the intersecting street turn right. 100m further on turn diagonally left (Calle Puente Palo). 50m more, leave the *white/yellow* markings behind by turning left onto the Calle Barranco Malena, so to cross over the *barranco* along

The parish church at Tegueste, in the background, the Mesa de Tejina.

The Degollada with the Mesa de Tejina. – Below: View of Bajamar.

a trail. On the other side meet up with a broad intersecting road. Cross over it and then turn diagonally left to ascend along the Calle El Sardán (SL TG 01, *white/green*). This heads directly towards the Mesa de Tejina and soon (straight ahead) becomes a camino – now opening up a lovely view of Tegueste. Directly before reaching the **Degollada de Mesa de Tejina** ❷, the trail forks – turn left here to a large threshing circle located on the saddle. Straight ahead the trail continues to Bajamar, however beforehand you really must tackle the rewarding excursion onto the Mesa de Tejina, a table mountain. So we turn left along the broad trail. At first this leads over the ridge then bears to the right along the slope, heading pleasantly out onto the high plateau of the flat-topped mountain, where a circular route opens up a fantastic view of Tegueste, Tejina, Bajamar and Punta del Hidalgo. At the left edge of the high plateau, you can sometimes see rock climbers in action. If you wish to pay a visit to the highest point of the **Mesa de Tejina** ❸, 622m, and if you enjoy a little adrenaline rush (also, you don't mind investing some more time), at the outset of the high plateau, con-

The lovely trail to the Barranco de la Goleta.

tinue directly along the ridge or for a short stretch just to the left of it, to return to the Degollada (sometimes easy scrambling). The path passes mighty natural cave-like undercuts and opens lovely views from both sides of the ridge. Back at the **Degollada de Mesa de Tejina** ❷ turn left along the camino (a meadow trail at the beginning). This veers to the right towards the slope to descend pleasantly and then leads on the level onward. 20 mins later, the trail hooks around the rim above the Barranco de la Goleta – now a view opens up to Moquinal. Just before traversing the *barranco*, the camino crosses over a threshing circle. Afterwards ascend for a short stretch, pass a tumbledown house and then merge with the PR TF 12 ❹ (*white/yellow*, see Walk 51), which we take to the left to descend to Bajamar. At a disused stone quarry the camino becomes a roadway. Soon after that reach the first finca. Because of dogs patrolling the road it can be skirted around by taking the trail to the left. After that continue along the road. 150m before reaching the main road (roundabout) the trail veers off to the right ❺, now with a view of the Roque de Izoque and the Mesa de Vargas, whilst following the track traversing the slope, crossing over to a road at the Barranco de San Juan. Turn left onto it to descend to the main village street in **Bajamar** ❻. The bus stop for line 105 (to Tegueste) is 50m to the left and, on the opposite side, you could descend to the seawater swimming pools where some bar/restaurants and cafés are awaiting.

↗ 850m | ↘ 820m | 13.5km

5.05 hrs

From Bajamar via Moquinal to Punta del Hidalgo

53

Solitary walk through the western Anaga mountains

Although this pleasant walk through the western Anaga mountains lacks in any spectacular highlight, it is nevertheless an attractive one thanks to its quiet trails and its scenery. In Punta del Hidalgo, or in Bajamar, you can enjoy marvellous bathing in the seawater swimming pools.

Starting point: Bajamar, 30m, village centre near the post office (*Correos*) on the main village street (bus stop for lines 050, 105, 224) – or (20 mins shorter) the roundabout at the village limits of Bajamar (500m from the Caja Canarias).
Destination: Punta del Hidalgo, 60m, or Bajamar, 30m (bus stop for the lines 050, 105, 224).
Grade: predominently easy walk but one that requires surefootedness and perseverance. The ascent to Moquinal is very exposed to the sun.
Refreshment: bar/restaurants in Bajamar and in Punta del Hidalgo.

At the bus stop in the village centre of **Bajamar** ❶ (near the post office/ *Correos*) the *white/yellow* waymarked PR TF 12 sets off to Cruz del Carmen (sign). Head for 30m along the main village street in the direction of Punta del Hidalgo and then, before reaching the *barranco* bridge, turn right onto the steeply ascending street Camino Isogue. A good 5 mins later, the trail forks away to the right along a roadway that leads pretty much on the level through terraces and plantations. Another good 10 mins after that, before reaching the Barranco de la Goleta, the roadway merges into an intersecting street ❷ which is ascending from the roundabout on the main road, 150m away (see starting point). Turn left to ascend along this street. 3 mins later, a path forks off to the right (large sign: 'Al Sendero') along which you can skirt around the property that follows and the 'dangerous' dogs. A few minutes later the roadway passes a disused stone quarry and then becomes a camino after that. 50m further on, the trail forks – turn left here to ascend along the waymarked camino,

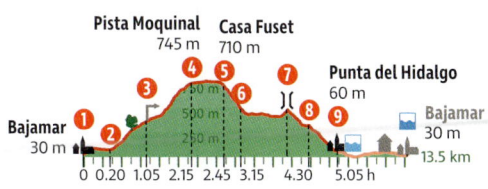

which climbs, keeping to the right, and after a few minutes crosses a water channel. Continue mostly pleasantly through the barren slope, extremely exposed to the sun, leading above the Barranco de la Goleta and heading up the valley, soon passing a solitary palm tree (good spot for a break). Not quite half an hour from the watercourse, the trail forks above a tumble-down finca ❸: diagonally right, a trail continues through the *barranco* and, on the other flank of the valley, turns right, continuing through the slope to reach the Mesa de Tejina saddle (1¼ hrs) – we, however, follow the trail diagonally to the left that ascends gently. 15 mins on the trail passes above a mighty, solitary eucalyptus tree (stone bench) and, in front of a little valley gully, ascends more steeply. Not quite 10 mins later, the trail, now somewhat stony and sometimes somewhat overgrown, changes over to the right flank of the valley but, soon after, returns again to the left flank. 10 mins more, the trail levels out noticeably and leads along a terrace wall. Afterwards the trail ascends again diagonally through the slope via a beige-coloured outcrop of rock. Some minutes more, the trail hooks left and then forks shortly after – turn left here and at the fork 50m before reaching a finca built into a rock face, turn sharp right onto the broad forestry trail ascending to the Moquinal track ❹ in 15 mins (barrier). Before continuing along this to the right, you really should bear left, then turn left passing under the transmission tower (150m on, left again) to reach the rocky ridge. A view opens up over the Mesa de Tejina to Teide.

But now follow the Moquinal track to the right, passing **Moquinal**, 795m. 15 mins later, you could turn right via the PR TF 12.1 to ramble on to Tegueste (1¾ hrs) – but we keep to the track, heading straight on. 5 mins later, leave the

On the return, pass the remote hamlet of El Peladero.

track behind (as well as the PR TF 12) by turning left onto a disused forestry trail forking away. When this ends (5 mins), descend along the camino to reach the **Casa Fuset** ❺ – unfortunately, the former villa has been destroyed and defaced by vandals. At the round terrace continue descending straight ahead – the camino descends pleasantly over a ridgeline, passing a eucalyptus forest and then opens a marvellous view of Bejía. Somewhat above El Peladero, the trail merges with the PR TF 11 ❻ (*white/yellow*) which turns left towards Punta del Hidalgo (at the fork above the first houses turn left). The lovely but narrow trail leads in a marvellous manner through the slope above the valley, in steady up-and-down walking. Afterwards it ascends somewhat steeper to a mighty intersecting ridge ❼ from which we can already spot the first houses of Punta del Hidalgo. Now continue climbing down to the right along the other side of the ridge, passing through a heather tree/brush wood. The trail crosses over a little valley notch (the watercourse trail of Walk 52 forks off to the right) and ascends once again for a short stretch to a power pylon where our camino becomes a road ❽. This road descends steeply to **Punta del Hidalgo** ❾ and, across from the church, merges into the main village street (bus stop for line 105 to Bajamar).

If you prefer to go on foot to Bajamar (1 hr), follow the main street to the left. 300m further on turn right along the street leading to the Hotel Oceano. Just afterwards, turn left at the fork. Thus, pass to the left above the hotel and the seaside promenade (with seawater swimming pools and bar/restaurants) and always continue straight ahead along the narrow road to reach the main road and take this back to **Bajamar** ❶.

TOP 54

From Punta del Hidalgo to Batán de Abajo

↗ 780m | ↘ 780m | 12.6km
5.30 hrs

Circular route to idyllic high mountain valleys

In the past, when access to the spectacular canal trails through the Barranco Seco and Barranco del Río was still permitted, the circular walk from Punta del Hidalgo to Batán counted as one of Tenerife's absolutely top walks. Unfortunately, both of the canal trails have been prohibited because of numerous accidents, so now this circular route has lost a significant part of its thrill – however, some of its highlights still remain, such as the tranquil mountain valley of Bejía, the secluded village of Batán de Abajo and, last but not least, the vertiginous path across the rock face into the Barranco del Río.

Starting point: church on the main road in the centre of Punta del Hidalgo, 60m (bus stop for the 050, 105, 224).
Grade: this is a strenuous walk. During the stretch descending from Batán, absolute surefootedness and a perfect head for heights is required (a section along a rock face, especially unpleasant when wet). Directly afterwards, the return trail crosses through a *barranco* that should be avoided at all costs during heavy rainfall.
Refreshment: bar/restaurants in Punta del Hidalgo and in Batán de Abajo.
Linking tip: with Walk 56.

From the church in **Punta del Hidalgo** ❶, walk a few steps along the main street then turn right onto the steep village road Camino El Callejón (PR TF 11, *white/yellow*). Follow the road straight on uphill (after 5 minutes, left, then right) and after a quarter of an hour, leave the last houses of the village behind. Looking back, you can now enjoy a beautiful view of Punta del Hidalgo; below to the left, you can see the Barranco Seco. 15 mins later, at the last cultivated terraces, the road becomes a gravel track at a barrier.

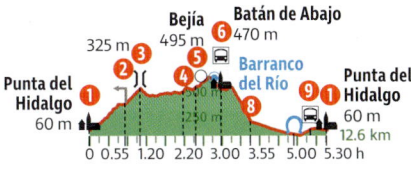

The track descends gently soon after that and becomes a path. Diagonally opposite you can already see the water canal that will dictate the onward route: first cross the little side valley and then pass above a small square water storage tank (5 mins). Directly above the reservoir, the trail forks ❷: a spectacular (but unfortunately, officially closed) canal trail forks off to the left (in its course, it leads along the rock face above the Barranco Seco and passes through some tunnels and galerías; at the end of the canal, a path ascends steeply to El Peladero). We turn left along the official walking trail PR TF 11 which ascends – sometimes stepped – through open scrub wood and, 25 minutes later, crosses over a flat mountain ridge with a view of El Peladero ❸ – do not continue along the ridge along the left or right side but instead, cross over it to descend on the opposite side and afterwards, traverse the slope, keeping steadily towards El Peladero. The high trail leads almost on the level, a very lovely stretch. Directly above **El Peladero** the trail forks ❹ – to the left, a path forks away to the valley road but we turn right along the waymarked walking trail. This climbs steeply for a short stretch and then traverses the slope (at the next fork, bear left, to head straight on) and, 10 minutes later, merge with the valley road. Follow the road for 150m and then turn left along the concrete-paved roadway ❺ but, 100 m on, bear left onto the lamp post flanked trail to leave it behind. This ascends, passing the lush gardens, little farmsteads and cave dwellings of **Bejía**. 5 minutes later, the camino forks – turn right here and shortly afterwards go right again up over the ridge – now with views of the Barranco del Río towards Chinamada. A few mins later, the trail joins the road once again. 2 mins after that, a camino

Officially prohibited: the marvellous canal trail above the Barranco Seco.

One of the most idyllic little spots on Tenerife – the hamlet of Bejia.

branches off left past a rocky knoll. It leads along the left hand side of the ridge for a short way uphill and then, with dizzying downward views, leads over onto a small col with a striking pinnacle and an electricity pylon. On the far side of the col, climb down the steep steps cut into the rock and at the junction turn left onto an intersecting trail (little picnic area and a cave with an enclosed spring) into the nearby mountain village of **Batán de Abajo** ❻ (bus stop for the 274 at the end of the tarmac road, also Mi Pueblo bar/restaurant, closed Tuesdays).

In the village, directly before (above) the community centre, the signposted descent route branches off to Punta del Hidalgo. This should only be attempted by experienced mountain walkers and only in fair weather, never when it's wet (serious accidents have occurred here). The trail leads downhill for a short distance to the cultivated terraces of the village and forks after 200m – continue uphill to the left, past a bench cut into the rock and traverse onto a faintly defined col enjoying a beautiful view of Chinamada (10 minutes, do not turn off left uphill just beforehand). On the other side of the col, immediately keep sharp left and descend – always following the main trail – steeply downhill.

After 5 minutes, the trail runs on the level across a terraced vineyard then descends steeply again and keeps left over to the next ridge ❼. The mountain path now appears more alpine in nature – leading over rocks and down a steep ridge with staggering views down into a gorge to the right. This nail-biting stretch lasts for 10 minutes, but now we have negotiated the most unpleasant sections – nevertheless, do not get over-confident just yet because the onward descent along the ridgeline of the mountain ridge is quite tricky. 20 minutes later, reach the stream bed of the **Barranco del Río** ❽ to continue the descent. Afterwards, meet up with a dam wall where a **water canal** begins. Just a few metres of walking along the canal, the path to Punta del Hidalgo forks off to the right (the canal is closed and prohibited now, in the past, accidents have occurred, some of them even fatal, especially along sections of overhanging rock; if you decide to follow it anyway: after not quite 1 hr, just past a water storage tank, leave the canal behind by picking up a roadway).

Our route usually follows the stream bed and is only distinguishable as a path when it runs off to the side of the stream bed or when it shortcuts bends. The going is very strenuous, especially when wet, because you often have to walk over solid rock or stones. In addition, you will pass numerous rock pools which are sometimes extremely slippery with algae. The plod through the *barranco* takes a good hour, then the trail joins the walking path PR TF 10, approaching from Chinamada (just before this point, pass a galería).

Subsequently, the trail leaves the *barranco* behind by turning left and, at a tumbledown building, becomes a roadway that leads to the traffic island at the end of the main road in **Punta del Hidalgo** ❾ (terminus for the 105 bus; follow the road for 10 mins to return to the church in the centre of town).

Descent into the Barranco del Río.

↗ 780m | ↘ 220m | 8.6km

55 Punta del Hidalgo – Chinamada – Las Carboneras

3.20 hrs

🚌 ✕ 🕴

Marvellous ascent passing through a bizarre craggy landscape to some cave dwellings

The walk from Punta del Hidalgo to the cave dwellings of Chinamada is one of the most popular walking routes on Tenerife – not without reason, as you soon will see!

Starting point: traffic island at the end of the main street in Punta del Hidalgo, 70m (terminus for the lines 050, 105, 224).
Destination: Las Carboneras, 630m (bus stop for the 275).
Grade: a sometimes very strenuous walk along a camino which requires sure-footedness.

Refreshment: bar/restaurants in Punta del Hidalgo, Chinamada and Las Carboneras.
Alternative: from Las Escaleras along the PR TF 10 (*white/yellow*) to Cruz del Carmen (see Walk 54, ¾ hr; bus stop for the lines 076, 077, 273–275).
Linking tip: with Walks 56 and 60.

From the traffic island at the end of the main street in **Punta del Hidalgo** ❶ head along the road leading downhill to the left from which a roadway soon branches off to the right (signpost to 'Chinamada', PR TF 10, *white/yellow*). Enjoying a view of Roque Dos Hermanos you soon come past a barrier and then a semi-derelict building to reach the floor of the Barranco del Río. At the stream bed, ascend for 50m to the right (left goes to the coarse pebbly beach of Playa de los Troches) until a broad trail ascends to the left. The camino now climbs steadily up the valley, passing between splendidly furrowed and hollowed-out rock faces whilst presenting a lovely view of the Barranco del Río. A good 20 minutes later, pass a huge rock overhang ❷ divided in the middle by a black wall of lava. Now the camino zigzags uphill through a small valley as far as a steep drop where it bears right again. After a good hour of walking you reach the ridgeline (fantastic spot to take a break and enjoy the views) and 5 minutes later,

Viewpoint on the path to Chinamada – a beautiful resting spot.

The fabulous trail to Chinamada – left of centre, the rock arch on the ridgeline.

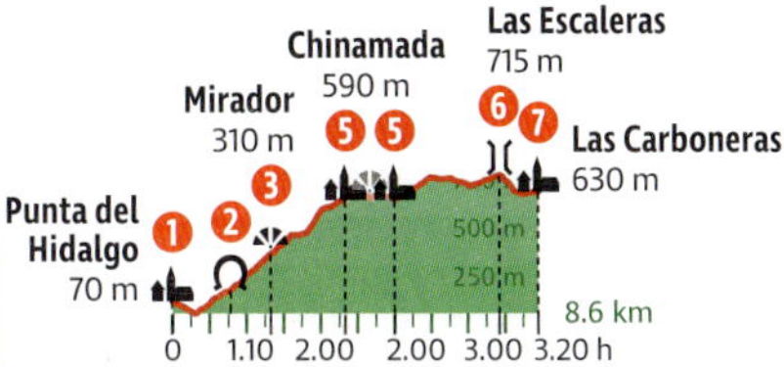

come past another marvellous resting place on the ridge with vertiginous views down to the sea ❸. Now the trail turns once again towards the slope on the *barranco* side. After 15 minutes, sometimes ascending steeply over rock outcrops, the camino levels out at an overhanging rock – a wonderful stretch! (50m on, just before going down the steps, an extremely indistinct rocky alpine path branches off to the left to descend via tiny hewn footholds, leading to a gigantic rock arch on the ridge above; a good 5 minutes, see photo above). A good 10 minutes later, the path veers towards a mountain ridge, climbs steeply uphill and then, soon after, turns towards the slope ❹ (possible ascent here to the left via a narrow, precipitous path to the already visible Mirador Aguaide, one of the most spectacular viewpoints on the island). Past cultivated terraces and cave dwellings you reach the church square in **Chinamada** ❺ (water tap; bar/restaurant La Cueva, closed Mondays/Tuesdays; a signposted detour to the Mirador Aguaide, a good 10 minutes).

Now follow the street and after 5 minutes turn diagonally right along the ridge with the PR TF 10 (the road continues to Las Carboneras, PR TF 10.1, a good ½ hr). Ferns, horn clover, woods of laurel and tree heathers surround the beautiful mountain path, passing high above the widely branching network of gorges making up the Barranco del Tomadero. Passing a few houses hidden in the wood, a good half an hour later, reach a farmstead (Casa Tamé) on a mountain col. The path leads around the house and eventually ascends to a col with an electricity pylon – **Las Escaleras** ❻. The trail forks here – straight ahead leads to Cruz del Carmen (see Alternative), but turn sharp left onto the other side of the ridgeline to continue on to Las Carboneras (PR TF 10.1, passing a cave with a bench and a water source). Soon, a marvellous view opens up towards Taborno.

In a quarter of an hour, down some steps at the end, reach the road to **Las Carboneras** ❼ which leads left in 5 minutes to the village square.

Cave dwellings in Chinamada.

↗ 980m | ↘ 980m | 13.9km

5.30 hrs

From Cruz del Carmen to Chinamada 56

Grand scale circular route through one of the loveliest Anaga valleys

An absolute treat for Anaga fans, this lengthy circular route is still widely unknown – and aside from that, offers numerous combinations with other walks.

Starting point: Cruz del Carmen, 950m, on the Anaga mountain road (bus stop for the 076, 077, 273–275).
Grade: rather long, but mostly easy walk via good trails; some stretches on the narrow trail from Chinamada to Batán, however, require surefootedness and a head for heights (somewhat precipitous steps cut into the rock).
Refreshment: bar/restaurants at Cruz del Carmen, in Chinamada and in Batán de Abajo.
Alternative: direct descent over the Lomo de los Dragos to Batán de Abajo (1¾ hrs from Cruz del Carmen): follow the trail until it meets the road to Las Carboneras (see below). Leave the road 1 min later, before the bus shelter, along the roadway branching off left uphill. It leads past some houses on the right and then becomes a camino which runs down over the mountain ridge (panoramic view of the Batán Valley). After a good 20 mins, the camino crosses the Pista de los Dragos which ends here and for 5 mins becomes a roadway. At the end of this roadway go straight on

A broad camino to Chinamada begins to the right of the bar/restaurant **Cruz del Carmen** ❶ (PR TF 10, white/yellow). Follow this, bearing right, while descending through the laurisilva forest. 20 minutes later, it crosses a forest track (Pista de las Hiedras), passes through a small *barranco* and then joins a roadway. It's a leisurely descent down

(right) down the camino keeping to the ridge (a marvellous viewpoint a good 10 mins later and, just after, lamp-posts line the way; the trail now steepens and becomes more slippery). After 25 mins, just before the valley floor, next to a drago and across from the Cueva del Lino, meet the trail from Chinamada – continue left here, over the bridge, and reach Batán de Abajo in 20 mins.
Linking tip: with Walks 54, 55 and 60.

197

The marvellous path from Las Escaleras to Chinamada.

left, past the **Casas del Río** ❷. After 10 minutes, the trail joins the road to Las Carboneras. Follow this road left (after 1 minute, you can descend left to Batán de Abajo, see Alternative) and, 2 minutes later, turn right following the waymarkers to a couple of houses. A path continues straight ahead which soon leads left again downhill to the road and crosses the road. A few minutes later, reach a trail junction at the **Degollada de Las Escaleras** ❸ – go straight on here along the PR TF 10 (on the right a possible descent down the PR TF 10.1 to Las Carboneras, see Walk 55). The camino leads along a marvellous high route traversing the slope (after a good 10 minutes passing Casa Tamé). 45 minutes later it merges into a road (3 minutes to the left on the road brings you to the church square in **Chinamada** ❹ and to the bar/restaurant La Cueva, closed on Mondays/Tuesdays).

Directly at the junction with the road, your route forks to the left towards Batán (sign). The camino leads, fairly pleasantly at first, across the slope (pass through a gate a few minutes later and shortly afterwards ignore the path forking off to the left) but then descends sometimes quite steeply. After 25 minutes you reach the most difficult stretch of the entire walk: the trail descends over a steep, somewhat exposed rock ledge with narrow steps that have only been cut a foot wide (extremely unpleasant when wet). Immediately afterwards the camino crosses the Barranco del Tomadero ❺ and ascends steeply for a short while on the other side; after 5 mins, continue to the right along a cliff face to reach a breach in the rock

on a mountain ridge. The trail now leads across the slope, then descends to the Barranco del Río ❻. Arriving at the valley floor, follow the trail that ascends up the left flank of the valley. After a good 5 mins the trail crosses over to the right flank of the valley and forks 50m further on – go left here continuing along the stream bed (to the right, another possible ascent to Batán). Shortly afterwards the trail leads a good 10m over a rocky ledge in the stream bed, then returns to the left side of the valley and a few minutes later ascends through terraced fields, passing to the

View from Batán to the Lomo de los Dragos.

right of a *drago* and a couple of houses (to the left towards Lomo de los Dragos, see Alternative; on the right side of the valley the Cueva del Lino). Past the houses cross over a bridge spanning the Barranco del Río and ascend in 20 mins – always following the lamp-post lined trail through the idyllic village – up to the *plaza* of **Batán de Abajo** ❼ (water tap). – If you don't want to go to Batán, you can ascend instead directly through the Barranco del Río: a few minutes after the *barranco* bridge, when the main trail traverses right over to the next ridge, the PR TF 11 (*white/yellow*) turns off left and, 25 mins later, next to the bridge near the tunnel, joins the trail Batán – Cruz del Carmen (see below, sometimes narrow and precipitous). At the community centre, cross over left to the road (bus stop for the 274; bar/restaurant Mi Pueblo, closed Tuesdays) and continue uphill along this road. Not quite 10 minutes later, a road forks off left. Another 15 minutes later, after passing through a roughly 150m long tunnel, the road ends at a cul-de-sac. A lamp-post lined trail continues here, leading down to the Barranco del Río. Turn left across the bridge ❽ and then continue to the right along the PR TF 11 (*white/yellow*) into the valley (in front of the first house, again to the right). Soon afterwards, reach the stream bed and bear left along this. The camino now ascends pleasantly up along the right side of the valley. Not quite half an hour later, meet up with the Pista de los Dragos ❾. 50m further on to the right, the old stone-paved trail continues sharply left. It zigzags up a wooded ridge and, a half an hour later, crosses over the Pista de las Hiedras. 20 minutes later, the wide camino merges with a forestry road. Turn sharp left (PR TF 11/12; 100m to the right, the Casa Forestal ❿). Now keeping straight ahead, return to **Cruz del Carmen** ❶ in 15 minutes.

57 From Pico del Inglés to Santa Cruz

↗ 40m | ↘ 1020m | 8.9km
2.40 hrs

Along an old mountain path from the Anaga main ridge to the capital

The Mirador Pico del Inglés is one of the loveliest viewpoints on Tenerife: vast areas of the North lie at your feet as well as the neighbouring island of Gran Canaria, that seems to lie only a stone's throw away. An old trail leads from here down to Santa Cruz – it's also worthwhile to extend the walk by adding on a stroll through the capital or a trip to the Playa de las Teresitas.

Starting point: Mirador Pico del Inglés, 987m (bus stop for the 273).
Destination: Barrio de la Alegría (Santa Cruz), 10m, on the motorway Santa Cruz – San Andrés (several bus lines).
Grade: easy walk along an old path connecting the villages.
Refreshment: in Santa Cruz.
Alternative: if you prefer a circular walk (a total of 2½ or 3¾ hrs with a detour to the Casa Santiago, a good 600 vertical metres), turn left at the 1st or the 2nd farmstead (El Chorro) onto the trail to the Degollada de las Hijas. After 15 mins, it reaches the ridgeline (houses) and now keeps straight on across the slope (the PR TF 2 leads down on the right). After 10 mins, cross a small col and a good 5 mins later, go straight on at the fork uphill across the slope (on the right, a possible descent to Catalanes). ¼ hr later, the trail enters a scrub wood and a good 5 mins after that meets the approach trail which ascends to the right in 25 mins to the Mirador Pico del Inglés.
– Half way along (just under 15 mins, 10 mins before the *mirador*), you can make a detour towards the Degollada de las Hijas: at the fork 3 mins later, turn left to cross the ridge. (The path on the right-hand side of the ridge, passing below the Roque de la Fortaleza, is unfortunately extremely overgrown and has slipped away in places.) The path descends to a narrow road which is reached near a house. If you follow this to the right, a good 5 mins later a trail forks off to the right which leads in 15 mins to the Casa Santiago on the Anaga mountain road (closed Mondays, bus stop for the 076 and 077). The return to Mirador Pico del Inglés leads left via the road. Not quite 5 minutes later, a trail crosses the road. Here, ascend sharp left beside telegraph poles and, at the fork 5 minutes later, continue sharp right for 5 minutes to the Mirador Pico del Inglés.
Linking tip: with Walk 58.

The trail begins at the end of the road on the left of the **Mirador Pico del Inglés** ❶ (sign, PR TF 2, white/yellow). It leads down through the dense laurel forest, keeping straight ahead along the mountain ridge (after a good 5 mins, ignore a trail branching off to the left to the Degollada de las Hijas, see Alternative). A quarter of an hour later, pass a stone house and just under 5 mins more, reach a trail junction – continue straight on here along the middle trail. Immediately afterwards, a small path forks off to the right to reach a hidden, beautifully-formed cluster of crags with a fabulous view in the direction of Teide). 5 mins later, you could also take a path to the left for an excursion to the **Cabeza del Viento** ❷ (2 mins; heavily overgrown, but giving a lovely view of the main ridge) – and then the main trail veers away from the ridgeline and descends in zigzags, keeping to the right. Unfortunately, you also leave the laurel forest behind you now. A good half an hour after the trail junction, reach the idyllically situated farmstead of **Los Berros** ❸ with a threshing circle and a couple of animal pens built into caves (to the right of this, there's a galería; past the uppermost house, the PR TF 2 turns off left, see Walk 58). The trail is not so well-maintained along this stretch as it continues on the right of the threshing circle and, a good 10 mins later, reaches a second farmstead (El Chorro ❹).

Backwards view from Cabezo del Viento to the Anaga main ridge with Pico del Inglés.

Directly below the house, the trail forks – continue right here downhill (left uphill goes to the Degollada de las Hijas, see Alternative).
Shortly afterwards, the final descent to the Barrio de la Alegría leads to the right, downhill to the small Barranco de Valle Luis, changes there onto the right hand flank and then continues down through the stream bed, constantly changing sides – a beautiful, tranquil descent over stepped meadows, past fig trees and overgrown terrain and, occasionally, cultivated orchards. Not quite one hour later, the paved trail joins a tarmac road at the floor of the Barranco de Tahodío ❺. The road leads left through a valley landscape which, at the end, has been hopelessly spoilt, to reach the coastal motorway Santa Cruz – San Andrés ❻ (3km, a good ½ hr).

A galería can be found at Los Berros farmstead.

↗ 950m | ↘ 440m | 10.3km

4.25 hrs
🚌 ✕

From Valleseco over the Pico del Inglés to Taborno

58

Enchanting valley walk on an old camino – from the capital into the mountains

Despite its proximity to Santa Cruz, this trail from Valleseco to the Anaga main ridge redeems itself as a wonderful old camino. It ascends leisurely through a quiet valley with solitary farmsteads and terraces. In the winter months, it is accompanied by a lively babbling stream sporting numerous cascades where sometimes donkeys are grazing. Cozy little spots on the meadows invite you to take a rest. You can finish the walk either at Pico del Inglés or at the Casa Carlos as well as combine it with Walk 57 to make a circular route.

Starting point: end of the valley road in Valleseco (Las Cuevas), 110m (bus stop for the 917, daily except Sat/Sun; 1.7km from the coastal road TF-11, turn-off a good 1km from Santa Cruz's city limits, bus stop on the TF-11 for the 910, 916, 917, 945–947).
Destination: Pico del Inglés, 987m (bus stop for the 273), Casa Carlos, 930m (076, 077, 275 bus lines), or Taborno, 620m (terminus for the 275).
Grade: easy walk along a marvellous camino, nevertheless it requires some fitness. The trail climbing down to Taborno is unpleasantly slippery when it is wet.
Refreshment: Casa Carlos; bar/restaurants in Valleseco and in Taborno.
Linking tip: combination possible with Walks 57 and 60.

At the end of the tarmac road in **Valleseco** ❶ (bus stop), a narrow concrete road continues but ends after 300m. At this point, pick up a wonderful camino (PR TF 2, *white/yellow*) that soon leaves the last houses of Valleseco behind. It ascends comfortably along the left hand side of the idyllic valley, and from then on, changes sides several times. After three quarters of an hour, pass a bridge for a water canal and, some minutes later, another one (Acueducto de Catalanes ❷) – and 5 minutes after that, a water tap. A good half an hour later the camino runs for a short stretch between a low rock wall and a terrace. The trail now moves away from the valley floor and ascends past a eucalyptus tree to then join an intersecting trail 10 minutes later by a couple of houses.

The wonderful trail in the Barranco de Vallesceso.

Right goes to Catalanes – but we turn left to cross over to the level col and then descend for 10m to reach a fork. Turning left, you could descend to Santa Cruz/Barrio de la Alegría (see Walk 57), but we turn sharp right with the PR TF 2 traversing the slope over to the finca **Los Berros** ❸ on the neighbouring mountain ridge (10 minutes). The camino now joins the trail Pico del Inglés – Barrio de la Alegría (see Walk 57).

Follow the trail to the right uphill, past two caves (on the left of the trail, a pool, with a galería behind) and after 45 mins, reach the ridge line of Cabezo del Viento ❹. Now continue an ascent through a marvellous laurisilva forest (at forks, continue straight ahead, following the main trail, PR TF 2) to the **Mirador Pico del Inglés** ❺ (bus stop for the 273) where you have another downwards view of Anaga's southern region.

Now continue for just under 10 minutes along the road, passing the Cruz de Afur, before the waymarked trail turns right again to follow a path (turn-off 5m past a right hand turn for a dead-end street). The path ascends gently through a laurisilva forest but levels out again a few minutes later next to a fence and then descends to the Anaga mountain road TF-12 (a wonderful stretch of trail, but very slippery if it's wet). Reach the road directly opposite the turn-off to Las Carboneras (bus stop for the 076, 077, 275). Follow the road to the right for 100m to the **Casa Carlos** ❻ (good bar/restaurant, very popular, closed Tuesdays) and then turn left onto the broad trail that descends pleasantly along the ridge. It runs mostly through laurisilva forest and tree heathers so you can only rarely catch views of Las Carboneras, Taborno and across to the Afur Valley.

After descending for a good half an hour (with a short ascent inbetween), ignore a trail turning right to Afur ❼, and a good 20 mins later, the camino joins the main road TF-138 at the village limits of **Taborno** ❽ (opposite the bus shelter). The road ends in Taborno. About 100m towards the village centre, you will find a bar/restaurant (closed Mon–Weds).

Taborno – the destination of the walk.

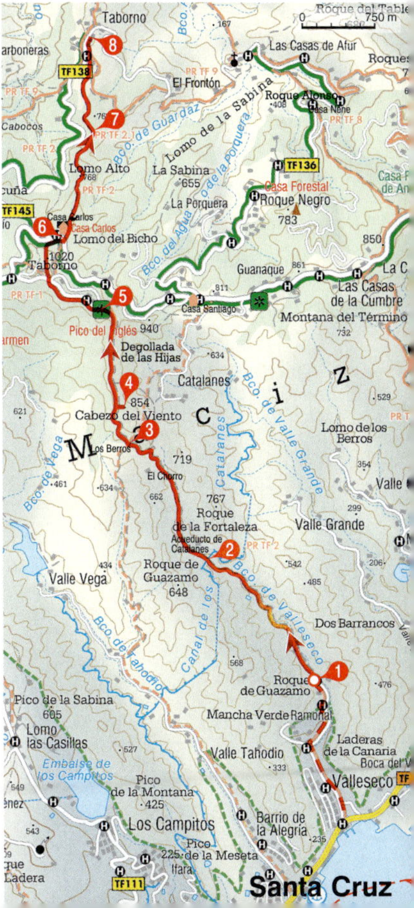

↗ 290m | ↘ 290m | 7.1km

59 Canal de Chabuco – from Valle Grande to La Galería

3.15 hrs

Thrilling canal walk along the southern side of Anaga

In the middle of the decade beginning 2010, the path along the Canal de Chabuco was made secure with steel cables nearly like a via ferrata at many narrow, dizzying stretches as well as numerous aqueducts. Since then, the canal path has evolved into a popular target for adventurous walkers. Our circular route, which sets off from Valle Grande, is limited to the central, easiest section of the canal path – it reveals the fascinating southern side of Anaga at its loveliest. Despite the partially-provided security features, absolute sure-footedness and a perfect head for heights is demanded along a couple of the more precipitous sections.

Starting point: Valle Grande, 203m (no bus service). Approach: a good 2km from Santa Cruz's city limits, a road to María Jiménez forks away from the coastal main road TF-11 that you follow up the valley. 1.5km on, past the Restaurante Dos Barrancos, a narrow road forks off to the left, crossing over a bridge and heading to Valle Grande. After 1.7km, a farm road forks away to the right that is concrete paved for the first metres (just before this point, parking is possible along the road; the tarmac ends after 600m).
Grade: along the canal (especially starting from La Galería) and for the descent to Valle Grande, absolute sure-footedness and a perfect head for heights is demanded, even more so when wet. Otherwise, the walk itself is fairly simple. A torch or a head torch as well as trekking poles are recommended! Undertake only when weather is stable and never after heavy rainfall! The canal path was recently (2023) very overgrown.
Refreshment: La Cochinera Guachinche

at the end of the valley road in Valle Grande (Weds–Sun, opens at 1pm).
Alternative: if you wish to tackle the Canal de Chabuco in its entire length from Valle Brosque all the way to Valleseco (head torch/water shoes essential!) follow Walk 65 to waypoint ❸. A few mins on, the canal crosses the camino. The outset is extremely overgrown and also further onwards the canal path is often very overgrown. Because of this, we can only recommend the stretch to Lomo de los Berros ❸ to hardened mountain walkers; to reach this point, you have to reckon 1½ hrs – from waypoint ❺ to the valley trail at Valleseco (see Walk 58) you have to add ½ hr (on the way, a tunnel with a length of 200m).

Some stretches of the canal path are narrow, precipitous and somewhat overgrown.

1.7km from the valley road in María Jiménez, from the narrow street in **Valle Grande** ❶ a farm road forks away to the right, concrete-paved for the first metres, descending to the floor of the *barranco*. Here the farm road becomes a camino. On the opposite flank it ascends whilst heading up the valley. The road passes a little rocky plateau, then it crosses a canal. 15 mins later, reach a small saddle on a ridge and, shortly after that, meet up with a fork in the trail ❷: to the right, you could descend to Valle Crispín, but we turn left along the camino ascending over the **Lomo de los Berros** enjoying a view taking in the main ridge and the mighty Fortaleza. A quarter hour later, the trail forks once again: the route to the left is easier but we continue an ascent for another 5 minutes over the ridge until the **Canal de Chabuco** ❸ crosses our trail (you can spot the canal more easily before-

View from the ascent trail to the impressive Fortaleza: the canal runs about halfway along the slope; on the left in the photo, the houses of Valle Grande.

hand than you can when you are above it since it is running underground here). Just past a breach in the rock wall with 'Coto de Caza' written there, turn left over rocks to descend for a couple of metres to the canal path that we steadily follow from this point on – now and again, it leads through a short tunnel or over a cable-secured aqueduct (a couple of mins later, by the way, the easier trail crosses ours and continues an ascent to the Anaga high mountain road; see above). 45 mins later, via the canal path, reach the houses of **La Galería** ❹, by forking off right past a water tunnel (sign).

We keep to the canal path that afterwards leads left over an aqueduct (just after, a lovely trail forks to the right to Catalanes; sign). The tunnel following after the next one, about 75m in length, is the longest one for this canal path – you could skirt around it to the left but you could also cross through without a torch. It's the same with the next tunnel (beforehand, two aqueducts). The canal path now continues directly towards Fortaleza. A few minutes past the tunnel, a distinct path forks left, traversing the right flank of the ridgeline, down the valley towards Valle Grande – this path is sometimes unpleasantly precipitous, especially when wet. Because of this, we keep to the canal path that subsequently leads directly at the foot of the Roque la Fortaleza through the steep slope (a short stretch of canal is narrow and precipitous). 10 minutes later, the canal path leads through a breach in the rock wall, some metres high. 40m after that, an alpine path forks left over the rocky ridge ❺ bearing left and descending via

rock steps, then steadily along the left flank of the marvellous rocky ridgeline, following walls of volcanic rock. Some minutes later, the rocky ridgeline levels off and we meet up with an intersecting trail; turn sharp right to follow this for 10m. Then, at the fork, turn left along a somewhat overgrown, but distinct path to descend to a fence. Follow along the fence to the right (don't cross over it!) to reach a farm road (the outset is behind a gate) and then descend along this to reach the valley road at **Valle Grande** which we meet at a farmstead (La Cochinera Guachinche). Along the road, in not quite 10 mins, return back to the starting point ❶.

Backwards view from Valle Grande of the descent trail and the Fortaleza.

↗ 370m | ↘ 370m | 6.7km

60 Roque de Taborno

2.30 hrs

Exposed circular route around the 'Matterhorn of Tenerife'

The Roque de Taborno (703m) is by no means one of the highest, but is certainly one of the most celebrated peaks on the island. From up close, the summit does not have the same appeal as it does from afar, but the bird's-eye views of the coast that open up during the often rather precipitous walk around the foot of the summit block, more than make up for it.

Starting point: Las Carboneras, 630m (bus stop for the 275).
Destination: Taborno, 620m (terminus for the 275).
Grade: surefootedness and lack of vertigo required.
Refreshment: bar/restaurants in Las Carboneras and in Taborno (closed Mon–Weds).
Alternative: from Taborno to the Casa Carlos (1 hr, PR TF 2, *white/yellow*; see Walk 58) and on to Las Carboneras (a good 1¼ hrs): the camino begins at the village limits by the bus shelter and leads for the most part through laurisilva forest up to the Casa Carlos bar/restaurant, 930m (bus stop for the 076, 077, 275). 5 mins before the Casa Carlos (100m past the first house No 66) a camino intersects – turn right onto it and continue fairly on the level through the laurisilva forest (after passing a wa-

terworks, some stretches are precipitous). ¼ hr later, pass a finca (200m on, keep to the main trail which traverses the slope). 5 mins past the finca, a trail merges from the left, coming from the TF-145, just 30m away. The path continues to the right over the ridgeline, at first ascending, then descending. It merges into the TF-145. Turn right with PR TF 10 (*white/yellow*) to reach the Degollada de Las Escaleras (¼ hr, see Walk 56) There turn right to follow the PR TF 10.1 to Las Carboneras (20 mins).
Linking tip: with Walks 55, 56, 58 and 61.

From the bus stop in the village centre of **Las Carboneras** ❶ retrace about 100m along the main road and, across from bar/restaurant Valentin, turn left onto a small road from which the old connecting path to Taborno forks off after 50m on a left-hand bend (PR TF 9, *white/yellow*). This descends for a short stretch between terraces and then traverses the slope without much change in elevation. After 5 minutes pass an electricity pylon and then a second one shortly after. Now the camino descends through terraces and scrub wood into a valley notch. Just past the Barranco de Taborno (a good ¼ hr) ignore a path forking to the left (this leads to Las Carboneras) – our trail ascends steeply to the road leading to **Taborno** ❷, here turn left and, in 10 minutes, reach the village perched on a mountain ridge with wonderful views.

Continue the walk by passing to the right of the chapel. The broad, reddish concrete trail passes numerous cave dwellings. About 5 minutes later, climb down some steps (a *mirador* straight ahead) and then descend immediately left along the concrete trail to a **col** (water tap). The trail now runs again on the right hand side of the ridge. 50m later ignore a right fork – a trail leading to Playa de Tamadite – then pass a final house and reach the ridgeline by passing through a gate for goats.

Roque de Taborno, one of the most striking elevations in the Anaga mountains.

The Taborno peak now rises up ahead. Soon afterwards a path branches off to the right but keep along the ridge (or actually a little to the left of it) and then, below a stone hut with a corrugated iron roof, reach the foot of **Roque de Taborno**.

The path continues (usually slightly descending) across the slope and then a path turns off left 5 minutes later – carry straight on here. A little later, pass a cave (splendid downwards view to the Playa de La Fajana). The path forks soon afterwards – go right up along the ridge in the direction of the summit. Just below the base of the rocky peak, a path forks off to the left and, a few minutes later, crosses over to the **Era de los Cardos** ❸, an extended rocky plateau with a stupendous view of the northern coast (not quite ½ hr from the stone hut). To the east, the view sweeps over Playa de Tamadite and Playa de San Roque to the Roques de Anaga; the Punta del Hidalgo emerges in the west.

Now ascend the mountain ridge to the base of the summit. The path bears left here towards the slope and, continuing straight ahead, passes a goat pen (cave). 15 minutes later, back at the stone hut with the corrugated iron roof, the path merges again with the approach route, leading back to the bus stop in **Taborno** ❷ (on the saddle, take the path on the right across the slope, if it has not been closed).

61 From Taborno to the Playa de Tamadite

↗ 720m | ↘ 720m | 9.6km
4.30 hrs
🚌 ✕

Enjoyable descent to the remote Tamadite beach

The Tamadite Gorge provides nature lovers with a sneak preview of the more famous Masca Gorge: here too, the walk follows along beside a small stream. The gorge is not quite as spectacular as the one at Masca, but it is nevertheless rugged and winding. At the stony beach, you will meet up with a small finca, decorated with buoys, creating a very cheerful sight. If you prefer to avoid the descent from Taborno – one of the most impressive and most scenic routes on the island – you can start the walk in Afur instead.

Starting point: church square in Taborno, 620m (terminus for the 275).
Grade: easy as far as Afur. To reach the Playa de Tamadite, some sure-footedness and a head for heights is demanded. The return route to Taborno requires absolute sure-footedness, a perfect head for heights and some orientation skills.
Refreshment: bar/restaurants in Taborno, a bar in Afur, Casa Nene on the road between Afur and Roque Negro (closed Mon/Tues).
Linking tip: with Walks 60 and 62.

There are two possible choices for the first stage of the walk: you can either start from the church square in **Taborno** ❶, following the street descending on the right and ending in El Frontón (when wet, the better choice, not quite ½ hr). Or take the prettier route: starting at the turn around area when you enter the village (bus stop), ascend the cobbled camino then, after 10m, turn left onto a lovely path (PR TF 9, *white/yellow*), that traverses the slope mostly on the level and above some terraces. A good 5 mins later, bear diagonally right at the fork, then again to the right not quite 10 mins later. Some minutes after this (shortly after a gate), reach a ridgeline ❷ (the PR TF 2.1 merges here). Now descend to the left along a wide camino to reach the end of a street in the hamlet of **El Frontón** ❸ (¼ hr). The camino

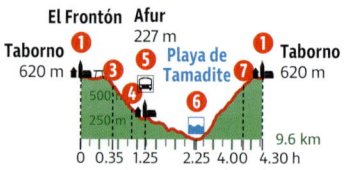

The wonderful descent path from El Frontón to Afur.

continues, descending along the ridge, and 40m further on, before reaching the house, the camino changes to the right side of the ridge (water tap), and descends again, soon passing some more houses. A good 20 mins later, the camino becomes a concrete trail by a picturesque cluster of houses partly built into the rock face (Lomo Centeno; ❹). Pass the houses to the right and descend to the Barranco de Tamadite. Continue through the *barranco* to finally reach the *plaza* in **Afur** ❺ (terminus for the 076).
To the right, past the little church, a concrete trail continues the descent and becomes a path after passing the last house in the village (PR TF 8, white/yellow). It crosses a concrete trail and a roadway after a total of 5 mins. Shortly after, pass a massive black boulder. Now continue above the valley floor around a left hand bend along the slope. 5 mins later, immediately past a low rock wall, the trail forks in front of a gigantic beige-coloured boulder – here continue sharp right (sign). The trail leads over some rock steps to the next barrier ridge and from there descends steeply down some steps to the stream (a good 10 mins). The path now changes over onto the left hand bank and ascends again past a cascade. When you reach the next barrier ridge but one (¼ hr), you can see the Playa de Tamadite ahead. The trail now runs below terraces (before the last terrace wall, another trail turns off left to Taborno, see below) down to the next little barrier ridge (small rocky plateau, a good 5 mins). The trail now leads right, almost all the way down to the stream bed, then ascends gently again, past some terraces, and follows the stream bed in the end. Shortly before reaching the beach, the path forks – to the right, the PR TF 8 crosses

Playa de Tamadite – a delightful beach.

over the stream as it branches off to Taganana (see Walk 62) but we keep to the left bank and pass a stone hut to reach the **Playa de Tamadite** ❻. Now walk back to the first major cascade (large rock pool, 5 mins; Charco de La Pasada). Here, just past a fin-like outcrop of rock that intersects the trail, a path forks off to the right (*white/yellow* 'X'). Afterwards, it traverses the rocky valley notch (cairns; do not turn right onto the path to continue) then turns right to cross over terraces. It continues climbing up the notch, now terraced (to the right, solitary little houses), and then changes back to the left flank. Soon the path crosses to the left along the rocky ridgeline and then merges onto a path heading up the valley (this forks away from the valley trail 10 mins past the waterfall and 100m after the small rocky plateau: this is an alternative route in case you have a problem finding the trail).

The path now continues steadily up the right side of the valley. Only after 10 mins, just before a giant boulder in the stream bed, does the path run through the stream bed for about 10m. Subsequently, on the left hand side of the valley, climb very steeply up stepped rock, past terraces and then left through a field up to an overhanging rock face. The main trail skirts round this to the right and then, before the next cave, bear right or left to climb over rock steps (somewhat precipitous).

Shortly afterwards climb over a small rock barrier into the side valley to the left. Here, along the edge of the little gorge, continue further up the valley. 10 mins later the path runs directly along the stream bed for 100m and then ascends to the right over rock steps. Soon pass terraces on the right to reach a fork after a short level stretch – here turn right along the main trail continuing uphill. This soon bears to the left again to the valley floor and then ascends to a fork (not quite 5 mins). Go straight on here (left) onto the left side of the valley. The path at first traverses the slope then heads right through a thin scrub wood ascending to a mountain ridge ❼; ascend along this to the ridgeline and the first houses. Here reach a wide intersecting trail (see Walk 60). Turn left onto the trail and return in 10 mins to the church square in **Taborno** ❶. At the halfway point to the bus stop, it is worthwhile to take refreshment at the French restaurant 'Historias para no dormir' (closed Mon-Weds; a reservation is recommended!).

↗ 710m | ↘ 710m | 11.6km

4.20 hrs

From Afur to Taganana

TOP 62

Spectacular panoramic circular walk for aficionados

The circular walk from Afur across the Playa de Tamadite to Taganana is one of the most varied routes in the Anaga mountains and due to its splendid views, the coastal section is especially stunning.

Starting point: Afur, 227m (terminus for the 076).
Grade: mostly a simple, but strenuous circular walk which requires an extra amount of physical fitness and, in some sections of the route, surefootedness and an absolute head for heights (precipitous and somewhat vertiginous).
Refreshment: in Afur and in Taganana bar/restaurants.

Linking tip: with Walks 61, 64 and 66.

From the car park in **Afur** ❶ continue along the track and, after 2 minutes, turn off right onto the PR TF 8 (*white/yellow*). 10m on, cross a roadway and shortly afterwards, pass a huge black boulder then continue across the slope above the valley floor. 5 minutes later, directly past a low rock face, the trail forks before a gigantic beige-coloured boulder. The main trail (sharp right) is currently closed (landslip, but for those with a head for heights problem-free). Straight ahead, a deviation through the valley avoids this perilous stretch. At the next valley barrier ridge, descend steeply via steps down to the stream.

The path now changes over onto the left hand bank and ascends again past a cascade. When you reach the next barrier ridge but one you can see the Playa de Tamadite ahead. The route now leads below terraces (above

a little house) down to the next little barrier ridge (small rocky plateau, a good 5 mins – turn right here, following the main trail almost down to the stream bed. Passing terraced fields, the trail slightly ascends again then follows along the stream bed once and for all. Shortly before reaching the beach the path forks – to the right, crossing over the stream, the onward path branches off to Taganana (PR TF 8), but before that continue heading straight on, passing a stone hut to reach the **Playa de Tamadite** ❷, only a few minutes away.

After the detour, at the fork, continue heading towards Taganana. The path ascends at first a good 20 minutes to a small col next to a rocky knoll and then runs in easy up-and-down walking across the slope above the steep coastline. The trail is always sufficiently wide so that you can enjoy a wide view of the main ridge of Anaga in all its glory and the Roque de Dentro; the beautiful shape of Roque de Taborno can be appreciated as you look back. After a good half an hour the marvellous coastal trail becomes a roadway ❸ and not quite a quarter of an hour later, passes the first houses (**El Chorro**, water tap, idyllic vineyards).

Just before Playa de Tamadite.

About 10 minutes later, the waymarked trail forks off to the right onto a camino which follows a conduit. Some minutes later, the camino merges again with a road, from which, 50m along, the Camino Lomo La Chanca forks off to the left ❹. You could descend to **Taganana** here (cross over the first road, then the second one leads to the right, crossing to the *plaza* of the pretty wine village, ¼ hr; bus stop for the 946 Taganana – Santa Cruz on the main road to San Andrés, there are no buses to Afur!).

But now follow the road, keeping right at the following fork, and continue

The impressive hiking path from Playa de Tamadite along the steep coastline to Taganana – view of Roques de Enmedio and the island of Roque de Dentro.

immediately afterwards along the concrete track heading straight on towards La Cumbrecilla. A quarter of an hour later a broad cobbled path turns off left, following power lines. 100m further on the camino to La Cumbrecilla turns off to the right ❺. This climbs quite steeply, almost parallel to the tall power line and soon leaves the terraced fields of Taganana behind. A quarter of an hour later, pass a beautiful little resting place by some boulders and then the trail enters scrub wood. 20 minutes after that, reach the top of the pass **La Cumbrecilla** ❻ – a fabulous viewpoint with views towards Roque de Dentro and Anaga's main ridge, with Roque de Anambra and Chinobre in the east, and Afur and Taborno (with the peak of the same name) in the west.

At the top of the pass, meet a fork in the trail: take the trail which veers sharp to the right and leads down the other side of the ridge (the other two trails lead to the Casa Forestal de Anaga; see Walk 64). Twenty minutes later, at a farmstead, the trail becomes a steep concrete roadway, which you leave again 5 minutes later, by turning right to a farmstead. Here a camino continues which descends to the Afur road ❼. Turn right at the road and, 10 minutes later, turn left onto the concrete trail that runs parallel to the road and, passing below an enormous rock overhang, returns in 5 minutes to **Afur** ❶.

↗ 920m | ↘ 920m | 11.1km

63 From the Casa Carlos to Afur

5.15 hrs

Along quiet trails through the dream-like Afur Valley

This circular route allows us a first-hand experience of the Afur Valley as it leads along narrow, seldom-walked trails that create a quite different impression than the one given by the classic cobbled ways. We will be especially captivated by the untamed stretch in the valley with its bizarre rock faces where numerous cascades are tumbling down after rainfall.

Starting point: the bar/restaurant Casa Carlos, 930m, on the Anaga high mountain road, TF-12, at the turn-off for the road to Las Carboneras (bus stop for lines 076, 077, 275).
Grade: a demanding walk along sometimes narrow, sometimes heavily overgrown trails; absolute sure-footedness is a requirement.
Refreshment: Casa Carlos (closed Tues), a bar in Afur and Casa Juaní in Roque Negro (closed Weds). Also, Casa Nene (recommended; closed Mon/Tues) on the Afur – Roque Negro road.
Alternative: return route via El Frontón (not quite 1½ hrs): at the fork in the Afur Valley (see below) turn left to the PR TF 9 (*white/yellow*) and climb up along it to El Frontón. Continue ascending over the ridge to reach a trail junction (20 mins) – here, straight ahead via the PR TF 2.1 to the ridgeline (20 mins; unpleasant when wet), where the PR TF 2 merges. Turn left onto it to reach Casa Carlos.
Linking tip: with Walks 62 and 66.

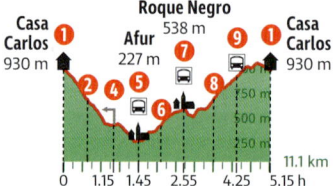

Next to the **Casa Carlos** ❶ a broad trail descends along the ridge in the direction of Taborno (PR TF 2; *white/yellow*). Just 3 mins later, a distinct path intersects; turn right onto it. The lovely ancient camino (if it is extremely overgrown, you should continue descending along the PR TF 2 and then continue along the PR TF 2.1/9) at first leads on the level through the slope then descends along a mountain ridge through scrub wood and laurisilva forest. A half hour later, the trail forks in

The northern side of the Anaga ridge is covered in evergreen laurisilva forest.

front of a tumbledown cottage ❷ – here you really should walk out a few metres onto the ridge to enjoy the view over the Afur Valley. Afterwards turn left along the camino which, shortly after, forks again along the ridge – here turn left to descend (beware: after a short descent, bear right to remain along the trail traversing the slope and do not bear left to climb down over rock). Soon a view opens up over the Afur Valley with its bizarre, moss-covered rock faces where numerous waterfalls tumble down after it rains – an especially beautiful view can be had from a small protruding rock. Shortly after, skirt around to the right of a final protruding rock (passing directly below the rock face) then the trail reaches the valley floor, changes to the other flank of the valley ❸ and continues along the slope heading down the valley (here often very overgrown; some minutes later, a trail merges from the right and, soon afterwards, a trail to El Frontón forks off diagonally to the left; see for the return route). 15 mins later, at a saddle in front of a rocky knoll, the trail merges into the PR TF 9 (*white/yellow*) ❹. Turn right to descend, passing the picturesque rock face settlement of Lomo Centeno, then reach the Barranco de Tamadite through which we reach the *plaza* of **Afur** ❺ (terminus for bus line 076).

219

Scenic rocky slopes in the Afur Valley. – Photo below: Roque Negro.

Now take the same trail back again and, directly past the first bridge spanning the valley, turn left onto the trail heading towards 'La Casa Vieja' (sign). This climbs upwards (sometimes along rock steps; at the fork turn right), passing a couple of houses, to meet up with an intersecting trail. Turn left along this trail for 15m until meeting up with a path forking off to the right. This ascends diagonally to the right through the slope and, a few minutes later, passes by an aerial for a house (on the other side of the valley, you can spot Lomo Centeno and, in front of you, the Roque Negro). Now ascend along a ridge, then the little camino veers right towards the slope (power pylons). Soon ascend again noticeably to the saddle next to the **Roque Alonso** ❻, where a couple of houses (half in ruins) have been built into the impressive rock face of the summit. If you wish, ascend to the summit – but indeed, you must negotiate a rock face, 5m in height, whilst climbing (scrambling demanded)! Our camino continues ascending along the ridgeline. 5 mins later ignore a trail forking off to the left (to Casa Nene on the main road). Afterwards, the trail changes over again to the right-hand side of the ridge and soon passes the first terraced fields and houses. Merge onto a narrow road (Pista Pedro Martín) and ascend to the left to meet up with the main road not far away. Turn right onto the main road, passing the bus stop shelter, to reach the village centre of **Roque Negro** ❼ (5 mins), then turn right to pass the chapel and descend over the *plaza* to reach the bar Casa Juaní.

Passing on the left-hand side of the Casa Juaní, now descend along a stepped trail (at forks, turn left) to reach a valley road and cross over this at the washhouse in front of the Galería de Roque Negro. A little

Backwards view from the trail to Roque Negro.

alpine path, sometimes cut into the rock, ascends to the next ridge and merges into a narrow road there. Ascend along this for 125m, then turn right onto the roadway to continue to a junction located on the other side of the valley. Turn left here, ascending, and at forks, bear left to keep following the camino which, when the roadway ends at the last houses, continues. Passing below a cave, soon reach the crest of the ridge and continue ascending along it, also at the fork, 25m on ❽ (the trail forking right heads to Lomo Bicho). About 5 mins later, another camino forks off to the right towards Lomo Bicho – but continue climbing up along the trail, now broader than before. Further up, the trail crosses over an intersecting track, only to merge with it a couple of mins later on. But only 100m further, at the lantern, continue along the ridge heading straight on. Some mins later, next to a house, our camino merges into the Anaga high mountain road **TF-12** ❾ (bus stop for lines 076/077).

To return to the Casa Carlos, turn right and follow the road for 100m, then turn left along the roadway for 30m until a camino turns off to the right to ascend to the old road. Turn right to Pico del Inglés street and, 5m on, a path forks away from it (PR TF 2, *white/yellow*). The path climbs up pleasantly through the laurisilva forest and, only a few mins later, levels out next to a fence and then drops down to the Anaga high mountain road, TF-12 (a wonderful stretch of trail but very slippery when wet!) to meet up with this directly opposite to the turn-off for the road to Las Carboneras – the **Casa Carlos** ❶ is 100m to the right.

64 Vueltas de Taganana: Casa Forestal – Taganana

↗ 730m | ↘ 730m | 9.3km
3.30 hrs

Classic tour through a laurel wood

This trail, called the 'Vueltas (bends) de Taganana', leads through one of the best preserved laurisilva forests on the island: gigantic fern fronds up to two metres high and the dense, lichen-covered laurel wood flank the defile-like camino, which descends in countless bends to Taganana.

Starting point: Casa Forestal de Anaga, 832m, on the Anaga mountain road TF-12 (bus stop for the 076, 077).
Grade: easy walk on a lovely camino, which is, however, unpleasantly slippery when wet.
Refreshment: bar/restaurants in Taganana.

Alternative: from Taganana to the Playa de San Roque (a good ½ hr): at the end of the *plaza* continue the descent by passing to the left of a chapel and, a short time later on, reach a bend in the main road. A path below the houses provides a short cut across the wide bend in the road (at the bottom, turn to the right over the bridge) then you only need to follow the main road which continues on to reach the black sand beach of Playa de San Roque and the hamlet of Roque de las Bodegas (restaurants, bus stop for the 946).
Linking tip: can be combined with Walks 62 and 66.

Left of the former **forestry house** ❶ sign: 'Policía local', amongst others) follow the trail branching off to the right (signpost 'Taganana', PR TF 8, *white/yellow*). This ascends to a walled cave (go straight on here) and then leads on the level through the laurel wood. About 10 minutes later, continue straight on as the broad trail now zigzags downhill round countless bends. After a total of 50 minutes, the alpine wood thins out. The camino crosses the Barranco de la Iglesia and then descends along the left edge of the *barranco* through terraced fields and vineyards. 5 minutes later, ignore the trail forking off left to

One of the showpieces of Tenerife – the wine village of Taganana.

Cumbrecilla (a short cut for anyone wishing to avoid the descent to Taganana). Another 10 minutes and the trail forks at the reed-blanketed notch of the stream – to the left, a camino heads towards Afur ❷ (your return route), but carry straight on to Taganana. A good 5 minutes later, reach the village limits. Passing a small palm grove, meet a road ❸ and follow this to the right. After a few minutes a set of steps leads to the left, passing a dragon tree, down to the church square of **Taganana** ❹.

Now walk back to the fork in the trail mentioned before ❷ (25 minutes) and then turn right onto the trail in the direction of Afur. 5 minutes later, it joins a track which you leave after 50m on the left along a broad cobbled trail. 100m on, a camino forks off to the right and ascends steeply, almost parallel to a large power line, to reach the panoramic crest of the **La Cumbrecilla** pass ❺ (a good ½ hr from the track).

At the fork, continue along the middle forest trail, heading downhill (the trail to the left has more appeal, but it is sometimes very steep and precipitous). Not quite 5 minutes later, the trail leads through a *barranco* and ascends (now concreted) past terraces and houses steeply up to a road. Follow this road left uphill and leave it again on the next right hand bend to the left along a forest road. Keep following the broad forest road that ascends up through laurisilva forest (after ¼ hr, bear left to keep to the broad forest road and, a few minutes later, continue along the concrete-paved road heading straight on); arrive at the **Casa Forestal de Anaga** ❶ after a good ½ hr.

The plaza of Taganana.

65 From the Casa Forestal de Anaga to Valle Brosque

3.30 hrs

A quiet circular walk on Anaga's southern side

When the northern side of the Anaga mountains is shrouded in clouds produced by the trade winds, this less spectacular route offers a leisurely and quiet circular walk on the southern side. The descent trail to Valle Bosque is rather strenuous in sections but, to compensate for this, the return route past the gigantic cave of El Majimial proves to be a marvellous camino.

Starting point: Casa Forestal de Anaga, 832m, on the Anaga mountain road TF-12 (bus stop for the 076, 077) or Valle Brosque (Los Vallitos, last stop for bus number 916).
Grade: for the most part, an easy walk but sometimes you have to negotiate narrow and steep sections.

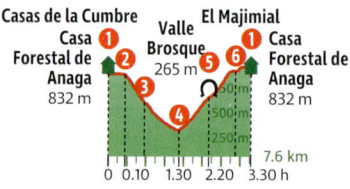

From the former **forestry house** ❶ (sign: 'Policía local', amongst others), head westwards along the Anaga high mountain road. After 700m (10 minutes) at the hamlet limits of **Casas de la Cumbre**, pass a church and, 100m after that, the PR TF 3 (*white/yellow*) turns off left into the

The hamlet of Valle Brosque with the striking El Pelotón rock (in the middle of the photo).

scrub wood diagonally opposite the school and the building of the Unidad de Montes ❷. Next to a house, it joins a roadway which you follow downhill to the right. After 100m, a trail turns off left again – it is rather steep, but it regales you with beautiful views of the south side of the Anaga mountains and towards Santa Cruz. Cross over

El Majimial cave.

the roadway twice, then the path leads down along a steep ridge. About 20 minutes from the roadway cross a small valley notch ❸ (up above, an animal pen in a cave) and 10 minutes later another one – the scrub wood is now taken over by succulents. After another 10 minutes the path changes over onto the left hand side of the valley, soon passing the first terraces. The path now runs mostly near the stream through this delightful valley – a cheerful, but sometimes somewhat wet stretch of trail! The houses of **Valle Brosque** ❹ (Caserío El Pelotón) soon appear ahead. Pass one of the first houses, cross over the Barranco de Valle Brosque and then pass more houses to reach the end of the valley road (bus stop for line 916).

Immediately after crossing the *barranco*, but before the houses, the return trail turns off left up the *barranco* (PR TF 3, white/yellow). It soon runs below a striking, mushroom-shaped rock (El Pelotón) and ascends gently along the right hand side of the Barranco de Valle Brosque. Not quite 15 minutes later, the marvellously constructed camino crosses over the small valley notch. Far above, you can see a huge cave with a dwelling built into it – **El Majimial** ❺. To get there, after a good half an hour, take the trail that branches off at a level stretch (white/yellow 'X'; 5 mins there and back).

The trail now zigzags uphill (at the fork shortly afterwards, do not go straight on), and, not quite a half an hour later, enters a fayal-brezal wood. A last lovely view back to Valle Brosque and Santa Cruz and then the trail levels out and leads gently down to the **Anaga high mountain road** ❻ (TF-12). Follow the road for a good 50m to the left until the camino continues on the right. At the fork 5 minutes later keep left (right goes to El Bailadero, see Walk 66), a few minutes later the trail descends. 5 minutes after that the trail forks again – go left here all the way down to the **Casa Forestal de Anaga** ❶.

66 From the Casa Forestal to Roque de las Bodegas

↗ 1030m | ↘ 1030m | 13.5km
5.25 hrs

Circular route from the Anaga main ridge to the Playa de San Roque

Is there really an ideal walk? This one should leave very few wishes unfulfilled: the splendid camino leads through atmospheric laurisilva forests and over panoramic ridges. You can also look forward to several cosy places for taking a rest stop as well as a beautiful sandy beach which, in calm seas, is a delightful spot for a lengthy swim. If you came by bus, then you can end the walk here if you so wish, and save yourself the strenuous ascent of 800 vertical metres to the Casa Forestal.

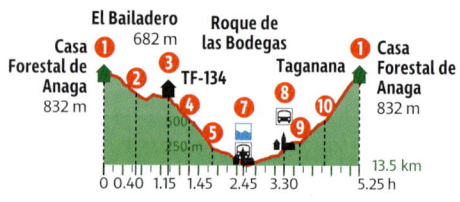

Starting point: Casa Forestal de Anaga, 832m, on the Anaga mountain road TF-12 (bus stop for the 076, 077).
Grade: easy, but rather long circular walk mostly on lovely caminos.
Refreshment: bar/restaurants in El Bailadero, Almáciga, Roque de las Bodegas and Taganana.
Alternative: the circular route Gollada Abicore – Taganana – PR TF 4 – El Bailadero – Gollada Abicore (3½ hrs; a lovely natural path via the Lomo Abicore).
Linking tip: with Walks 62 and 64.

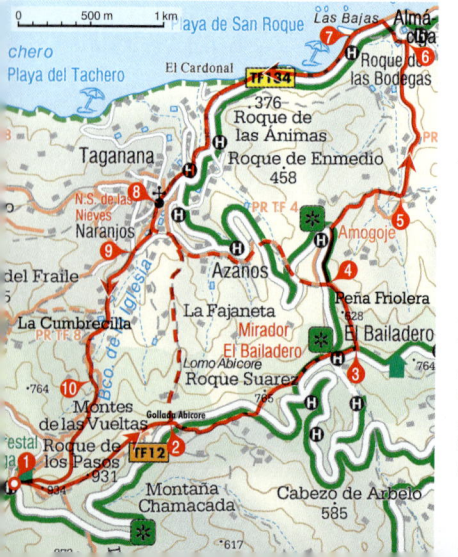

On the left of the (former) **forestry house** ❶ follow the trail turning off right (PR TF 3, *white/yellow*). It leads in a few minutes up to a walled cave next to which you turn off right. The trail climbs for another 5 minutes through the laurisilva forest and then descends gently and forks after 2 minutes – go diagonally left here slightly uphill (the PR TF 3 leads downhill on the right). Now the wonderful trail runs down a gentle slope across the steep southern face of the Roque de los Pasos. After a quarter of an hour the wood thins out abruptly next to a rocky ridge on your right (mar-

View back from the trail of Roque de los Pasos.

vellous view) – the path now zigzags downhill and 10 minutes later, on the **Gollada Abicore** ❷, meets up with the TF-12. By turning left (along the concrete trail, 30m on turning left again at the chain barrier), you could descend to Taganana along a narrow path via the Lomo Abicore (1¼ hrs, the trail leads through private property and you should not stray from it). But we turn right through the chain barrier and then follow a narrow road, only to leave it again after just under 5 mins along a camino forking off straight ahead. More or less on the level it leads across the slope and after a few minutes passes below a gigantic cave. Just afterwards, a path forks off to the left (sign 'Camino El Bailadero') and, at the upper edge of the terraced fields, turns right to traverse the slope. Some minutes later meet up again with the high mountain road. Follow this road for 15m to the right and turn sharp left onto the camino that takes a shortcut across two bends in the road and, after 10 mins, joins the mountain road again. Along this, we pass the splendid Mirador Bailadero straight away – from the crest of the ridge, we can enjoy a downwards, almost a bird's eye view of the coastline

Huge cave above the trail.

View from the Anaga ridge near El Bailadero to Taganana.

between Taganana and Almáciga. 200m further on, reach **El Bailadero** ❸ (bus stop for the 077, 947; to the right on the road, a simple bar/restaurant, 350m on: the Albergue Montes de Anaga, with a cafeteria).

At the other end of the ridge's crest, a cobbled path turns off left which soon enters a dense laurisilva forest (PR TF 4, *white/yellow*). It zigzags down across the slope of a mountain ridge and now and again affords a beautiful view of Taganana. 10 mins later, above the rock tower of Peña Friolera, the camino crosses over the crest of the mountain ridge (fabulous view of Taganana and Almáciga). A good quarter of an hour afterwards, meet the **main road TF-134** ❹ to Taganana. The PR TF 4 continues opposite downhill to Taganana, but walk down the road for 200m to the Mirador Amogoje and then leave it on the sharp left hand bend, directly in front of the rock tower on the right of the road, along the path turning off right (PR TF 4.1, *white/yellow*). The trail soon forks after a few metres – continue right, down the mountain ridge. On the left can be seen the prominent Roques de Enmedio and de las Ánimas. 20 mins later, the trail forks – keep straight ahead and 5m on, descend to the left while following the *white/yellow* waymarkers. Now the path steepens as it descends over a little ridge to reach the valley floor where it meets up with a track ❺. This leads in 20 minutes to **Almáciga** ❻ (terminus for the 946) and joins a road (the waymarkers have already veered away to the right 100m before; also there, the bar/restaurant El Drago, closed Mon). Keep left along this road and, after a few metres, turn left onto the camino (*white/yellow*) which brings you in a good 5 mins down to the hamlet of **Roque de las Bodegas** ❼ at the **Playa de San Roque**. Several fish restaurants await you and a lovely, in places sandy lava beach with a panoramic view of the rock needles of the Anaga mountains. The bay is enclosed by the rocky peninsula of Las Bajas that juts far out into the sea (underwater cave); a trail runs out along it.

Now continue along the main road until, about 25 mins later, at the village limits of **Taganana** a road forks off to the right, leading to the other side of the valley. 20m past the bridge over the *barranco* turn left along the footpath that leads uphill through the pretty village to the *plaza* with the parish church ❽ (a good 10 mins). At the back of the church continue uphill along the path (Camino Los Lirios; *white/yellow*). After a few minutes, it leads past a splendid dragon tree and 5 mins later joins a road that you follow to the right (the *white/yellow* waymarkers fork off to the left). After 5 mins it crosses a *barranco* and 50m later, in the part of the village called Los Naranjos ❾, the trail turns off left to the Casa Forestal (PR TF 8, *white/yellow*). The broad stone-paved camino leads quite purposefully up between terraces that are predominently cultivated with vines. 10 mins later ignore a camino turning off right to Afur (see Walk 64/62). A quarter of an hour later the fabulous trail enters the laurisilva forest ❿ and winds its way uphill round countless bends over the mountain ridge. After just under an hour, the trail levels out considerably – 5 mins later, pass the walled cave from the approach trail and then walk back down to return to the nearby **Casa Forestal de Anaga** ❶.

The pretty Playa de San Roque is the destination of this walk.

↗ 420m | ↘ 420m | 5.0km

67 From Benijo to El Draguillo

2.15 hrs

Classic walk for aficionados

If you are looking for a somewhat shorter and a not too strenuous walk in the Anaga mountains, we can warmly recommend this scenic circular walk: the trail regales you with fabulous views of the north side of the Anaga and in Benijo you can look forward to some inviting restaurants and a lovely sandy beach at the nearby Playa de San Roque.

Starting point: Benijo, 78m, hamlet on the TF-134, 2km east of Almáciga (terminus for the 946, from here ½ hr on foot to Benijo).
Grade: apart from a few precipitous sections of trail, this is, for the most part, a usually easy walk (along a leisurely track until you get to El Draguillo).
Refreshment: there are a number of bar/restaurants in Benijo.
Linking tip: with Walks 66 and 70.

Keep left at the junction in **Benijo** ❶, past the Restaurante El Frontón (PR TF 6.2, *white/yellow*). The road becomes a track, concrete in places, and runs predominently uphill along the heavily eroded steep coastline (do not attempt this walk in rain or stormy weather!).
After a good half an hour, reach the pretty hamlet of **El Draguillo** ❷. At the point where the road veers left downhill, two caminos turn off to the right. Take the upper camino that leads up past a dragon tree and

The walk runs along a track by the coast as far as El Draguillo.

From the trail – here from the spur – enjoy amazing views of the coast with Benijo (middle of the photo) and Almáciga.

continues through the lovely valley towards Chamorga (PR TF 6, *white/yellow*). About 25 minutes further along the way, leave the last terraces behind and a good 10 minutes after that, the camino forks just below the edge of the forest (440m).

Leave the main trail to Chamorga here and turn right onto the slightly descending trail ❸ (PR TF 6.3, *white/yellow*). This leads in 10 minutes of easy up-and-down walking over to a prominent rocky knoll and is sometimes rather precipitous. At the rear of the rocky knoll the trail descends with a marvellous view of the north side of the Anaga. 10 minutes later, you come past a rock spur ❹ (fabulous place to take a rest!) and later pass through a gate. Then the trail runs for a short time across a rock face. You are now walking along a broad mountain ridge which brings you back down to **Benijo** ❶ – a splendid, panoramic stretch of the trail!

68 Chinobre circular walk

↗ 280m | ↘ 280m | 6.5km
2.10 hrs

Beautiful ridge walk through an enchanting laurisilva forest

The mountain route between La Ensillada and Cabezo del Tejo is one of the most impressive walks you can take, not only in the Anaga mountain range, but on the entire island: hardly anywhere on Tenerife will you find a more beautiful laurisilva forest or a viewpoint taking in the Anaga mountains that compares to the one at Cabezo del Tejo – and when wisps of mist sweep over the crest, the walker will be simply whisked away into a realm of fairy tales and dreams.

Starting point: La Ensillada, 802m (bus stop for the 947) at the former picnic site situated at Km 4.8 on the Anaga mountain road TF-123 El Bailadero – Chamorga.
Grade: easy walk throughout on a lovely camino, but very slippery when wet.
Refreshment: none on the way. Bar/restaurants in Chamorga and in El Bailadero.
Alternative: from Cabezo del Tejo to Chamorga (35 mins): the camino continues at the end of the *mirador* – it leads downhill to a junction (a good 5 mins), go right here and, ¼ hr later at the fork, left down through the valley into the village (bus stop for the 947).
Linking tip: with Walks 69, 67.
Important note: for this route, you need a permit for the Pijaral that you should book well in advance (at least 16 days beforehand; see info for the Anaga mountains on page 183).

From **La Ensillada** ❶ car park, walk up the roadway that runs parallel to the road in the direction of Chamorga and after a few minutes becomes a wonderful camino. A quarter of an hour later, it reaches a knoll where a path turns off left to the summit of **Chinobre** ❷, 910m – unfortunately, the detour to the the panoramic summit is prohibited. The ridgeline trail now descends (do not turn off right after 1 minute; your return trail later on) and runs leisurely up-and-down through the impressive laurisilva forest. The

Roque de Anambro.

trees and bushes are almost entirely covered in moss. Fern fronds of up to two metres in height line the trail. 15 minutes later, pass a large boulder (view of Anambro) and, another quarter of an hour after that, pass the huge **Roque de Anambra** ❸ rising up from the ridge like a finger – a Guanche sanctum. A good 10 minutes later, next to the viewing platform of the **Cabezo del Tejo** ❹, the camino joins a roadway. Enjoy a great downwards view of the coast far below between El Draguillo and Almáciga.

Now turn right onto the roadway (this is unpleasantly slippery when wet) to reach the Anaga high mountain road **TF-123** ❺ (¾ hr). 10m past the barrier, turn right onto the ascending camino. It leads in not quite 10 minutes up to the ridge trail ❷, that brings you back left in a good 10 minutes to **La Ensillada** ❶ car park.

You can also return by walking back along the Anaga high mountain road (20 minutes).

The mountain ridge trail.

69 Montaña Tafada, 593m

↗ 320m | ↘ 320m | 5.6km
2.20 hrs
🚌 👣

Contemplative and rapt high mountain walk replete with able-bodied interludes

The surroundings of the picturesquely situated village of Chamorga is a paradise for walkers. Beautiful old paths traverse the laurisilva forests and frequently open up magnificent views of the coast – as is the case on this less spectacular, but nevertheless entertaining route. If you wish to extend the walk, we recommend taking an excursion from Montaña Tafada to the lighthouse – in early summer you may stumble upon wonderfully colourful Teide bugloss in full bloom on this stretch of the route.

Starting point: Chamorga, 475m, at the end of the Anaga mountain road (bus stop for the 947).
Grade: good trails and paths, but sometimes rather precipitous and rocky.
Refreshment: bar in Chamorga.
Alternative: descent to Faro de Anaga, 240m (¾ hr one way): from the stream at Montaña Tafada, follow the PR TF 6.1 (*white/yellow*), a fabulous trail down across the northern slopes of Montaña Tafada, soon enjoying a lovely view of the coast and the lighthouse. The path heads over to a ridge and then descends

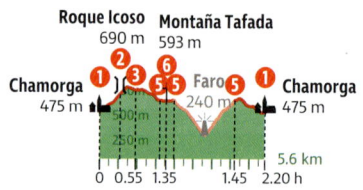

steeply to the Faro de Anaga (5 mins before the lighthouse, the PR TF 6 from El Draguillo merges from the left).
Linking tip: this walk can be combined with Walks 68 and 70.

Opposite the church of **Chamorga** ❶ follow the trail forking off sharp left, the PR TF 6 (*white/yellow*; signpost 'El Draguillo'), that ascends through an idyllic little valley. At a junction a good 10 minutes later bear right (the PR TF 5 joins from the left from La Cumbrilla). The trail now leads back to the valley floor, crosses the stream and ascends on the right side of the valley to a trail junction ❷ (658 m) on the ridgeline of the Anaga main ridge (total time ½ hr); here, bear right. At first the trail ascends steeply, often affording breathtaking views down to the coast between El Draguillo and Almáciga. Some minutes later, the trail traverses the slope to the right of the ridge for a while. At the striking rock finger of **Roque Icoso** ❸ the trail returns again to the ridgeline – far below, you can see the hamlet of Las Palmas as well as the Roques de Anaga. Afterwards, other beautiful views of Chamorga open up.

20 minutes after passing Roque Icoso, reach a col, 597m, with an abandoned house – about 75m before the house you meet the PR TF 6.1 (*white/*

View a long way down from the ridge of Las Palmas and Roque de Dentro.

yellow) approaching from Chamorga sharply to the right ❹ (this will be your return route later on). The trail forks before the house: the main trail leads to the right continuing along the ridge (after 2 mins ignore the PR TF 6.1 turning off left to Faro de Anaga, see Alternative; ❺) to the last elevation of **Montaña Tafada** ❻ (10 mins) which drops away steeply to the east. From here, enjoy a fantastic downwards view of the Roques de Anaga, Roque Bermejo and Faro de Anaga.

Now walk back to the house on the col before Montaña Tafada and, about 75m further on at the fork, follow the left-hand, less-distinct ascending trail PR TF 6.1 (*white/yellow*) ❹. 20 minutes later the beautiful high mountain trail ascends gently to a col next to a projecting rock. Before reaching this rock, the route leads sharp right downhill, sometimes over rocky terrain. At the 'Casa Alvaro' (bar) the trail merges with the village street of **Chamorga**; turn right here and head back to the starting point ❶.

TOP

70 Grand Faro de Anaga circular walk

↗ 980m | ↘ 980m | 13.2km
5.30 hrs

Spectacular circular walk in the extreme north-east of Tenerife

The walk around the north-eastern tip of Tenerife with its isolated, still mostly unspoilt villages and offshore islands – former volcanic cones – is one of the greatest walks on Tenerife. However, due to its length and the differences in elevation (which should not be taken lightly), this route can only be recommended to mountain walkers with plenty of stamina. You can also begin the walk in Roque de las Bodegas – in which case the walk time required will be lengthened to a good 7 hours!

Starting point: Chamorga, 475m, at the end of the Anaga mountain road (bus stop for the 947).
Grade: strenuous circular walk along trails that are often somewhat precipitous and vertiginous; constant up and down.
Refreshment: bar in Chamorga.
Alternative: from Roque de las Bodegas (Playa de San Roque) to El Draguillo (PR TF 6.2, *white/yellow*; 1¼ hrs): from the Playa de San Roque (bus stop for the 946) follow the coastal road to the east. Some minutes later, the village road of Almáciga branches off to the right; ¼ hr later, pass the Playa de Benijo (small sandy beach with two beach stalls; dangerous undertow). If the surf allows, you can continue walking from here directly along the coast (to El Draguillo) – otherwise, keep walking along the tarmac road that now ascends to Benijo (½ hr; bar/restaurant). 100m past the sign for the village limits, a roadway turns off to the left, passes El Frontón restaurant and then leaves Benijo behind. This leads high above the coast, at times ascending steeply, reaches El Draguillo in a good half hour ends at this point.
Tip: due to perilous passages (especially near Las Palmas), the stretch between El Draguillo – Faro has been officially closed (attempt only at your own risk).
Boat service: to Roque Bermejo www.nauticanivaria.com.
Linking tip: this walk can be combined with Walks 64–69.

Opposite the church of **Chamorga** ❶ follow the PR TF 6 sharp left (*white/yellow*, signpost 'El Draguillo'), that ascends through an idyllic little valley. A good 10 minutes later, at a junction where trails merge, bear right (the PR TF 5 joins from the left from La Cumbrilla). The trail now leads back to the valley floor, crosses over the stream and ascends the right hand side of the valley to a trail junction ❷ on the Anaga main ridge.

You could make a short, but sweat-inducing detour to the left to Cabezo del Tejo, 750m,

View from Cabezo del Tejo to the west – Almáciga on the right of the photo.

one of the most fabulous viewpoints on the island (a good 10 mins one way). However, continue from the col straight on and begin a descent on the other side of the ridge. The path leads downward in steep zigzags. 20 minutes later the laurel wood thins out (a path from Benijo merges from the left) – the picturesquely situated hamlet of **El Draguillo** ❸ can already be seen below. Descend into the hamlet between terraces; the first ones are overgrown with disuse but those further on are cultivated. Past a dragon tree reach a roadway (a left turn here would lead to Almáciga in a good hour, PR TF 6.2).

In Las Palmas – view of Roque de Dentro.

Before the junction with the roadway, your trail branches off to the right PR TF 6 (*white/yellow*; the sign has been removed – the trail is officially closed due to muddy/slippery sections – attempt only at your own risk). This immediately crosses through a *barranco* gully then ascends across the slope above the coast. Soon traverse two scree-blanketed slopes, one after the other, dropping steeply down towards the sea – then the next destination of the walk appears ahead, the isolated hamlet of Las Palmas, situated on a verdant promontory in front of the Roques de Anaga. The coastal trail initially ascends to an altitude of not quite 300m. Only shortly before reaching **Las Palmas** ❹ does it descend steeply in zigzags into an eroded *barranco* and past prickly pear cactus (Opuntias) growing over two metres high, to reach the first house of this idyllic and almost completely abandoned hamlet.

At the first house and a junction, bear right (the ancient coastal trail is extremely imperiled by slippage) to pass an abandoned farmstead with a chapel. Past the next houses, meet up again with the coastal trail (right) – opposite, the mighty, 178-metre high Roque de Dentro rises out of the sea. Our trail crosses a *barranco* and now ascends steadily. 20 mins later, pass a giant, curious-looking boulder with stone dwellings built into it as well as a wine press (Las Orobales ❺). The trail ascends steeply for a short stretch and then continues in easy up-and-down walking across the slope. Not quite ½ hr later, pass the Fuente del Junquillo ❻ at the foot of an enormous rock face (a small shrine is built into the rock). Now it takes only another 20 minutes to reach the **Faro de Anaga** ❼, 240m (5 minutes beforehand, the PR TF 6.1 joins from the right coming down from Montaña Tafada, an attractive alternative for the return, see Walk 69).

From the lighthouse continue the descent along the broad trail towards Roque Bermejo (signposted), and, 20 minutes later, reach a major trail junction with signposts ❽. To the right your route continues to Chamorga but first we recommend an excursion (straight on) to **Roque Bermejo** ❾ – the trail passes the houses and the chapel of the hamlet descending to a narrow strip of sandy beach with a few fishermen's huts and a simple bar. The port and Roque Bermejo are located in the adjoining northern bay.

Back at the junction ❽ follow the PR TF 6 in the direction of Chamorga. This ascends between orchards then over a mountain ridge to a lone, derelict house and finally ascends beside telephone lines at the edge of the impressive, chasm-like Barranco de Roque Bermejo. After a good three quarters of an hour, skirt around a rock outcrop ❿ and, a few minutes later, pass a first house. Between gardens (to the right and above you can see a small grove of dragon trees) the camino becomes a gravel track which passes the bar 'Casa Álvaro Chamorga' and then returns back to the church in **Chamorga** ❶ (you could also follow the waymarked camino to the left that merges again with the road at the Casa Álvaro).

The fishing village of Bermejo with the rocky tower of the same name beyond.

↗ 680m | ↘ 680m | 8.3km

71 From Lomo de Las Bodegas to Playa de Anosma

4.45 hrs

Quiet, less spectacular walk to the eastern tip of Tenerife

If you are looking for solitude when out walking then you should be sure to savour the descent from Lomo de Las Bodegas to the beach of Playa de Anosma – the small, stony beach is only suitable for a swim in absolutely calm seas and only a few walkers stray here since the trail is less well-known.

Starting point: Lomo de Las Bodegas, 520m. From the Anaga mountain road El Bailadero – Chamorga (TF-123) at Km 9.9 an access road turns off into the village. There is a car park at the end of the road after 500m. A bus stop for the 947 is located at the village limits.
Grade: moderately difficult walk; some sections of the trail are somewhat precipitous. Only attempt in settled weather and never during or after rain!
Note: you do not need a permit for this walk in the Ijuana nature reserve.

From the car park at the end of the street in **Lomo de Las Bodegas** ❶ walk 25m back along the road. Next to house No 1 turn right onto the stepped trail. Follow this trail left, more or less on the level, across the slope onto the opposite side of the valley (keep right slightly downhill at the two forks, one following after the other, and soon after that, diagonally right to pass through a gate) to descend between terraces. The trail soon leaves the last terraces behind and, 10 mins later, leads across the slope down into then **Barranco del Corral Viejo** ❷. Now descend for a couple of paces along the *barranco* floor, until the trail turns towards the right hand side of the valley and ascends to a barrier ridge. Keeping right, continue down across the slope (keep an eye on the trail!) and, not quite 10 minutes

The small, stony Playa de Anosma.

later, cross over a small rocky terrace before the first tall Candelabra cacti. 5 minutes later reach a mountain ridge (directly opposite, on the other side of the valley, a huge rocky outcrop). Descend along the ridge. A good 5 minutes later, cross the stream bed of the **Barranco de Anosma** ❸ and continue along the edge of the rocky, canyon-like *barranco* down the valley, immediately passing a huge boulder.

After a few minutes the trail turns again towards the right hand side of the valley to then, not quite 10 minutes later, cross through a tiny notch (on the left hand side of the valley you can see a striking rock, a mini version of the 'Finger of God'). Then the trail changes valley flanks twice more (look out for cairns!) and after a good 10 minutes runs directly along the floor of the *barranco*. 2 minutes later, it turns back to the left hand side of the valley and presently runs straight on along the sometimes narrow, precipitous course of a disused water canal (if you suffer from vertigo, you can also descend on the right into the stream bed of the *barranco* and continue there, but it's more strenuous!). Soon the sea appears ahead – the trail now returns gradually to the *barranco* floor and leads past a gorge (another short unpleasantly precipitous section) all the way down to the **Playa de Anosma** ❹.

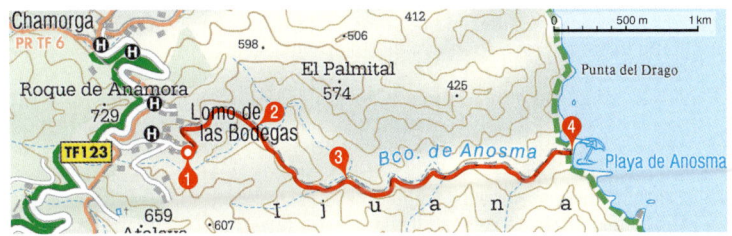

↗ 760m | ↘ 760m | 9.3km

72 From Lomo de Las Bodegas to Playa de Ijuana

6.00 hrs 🚌

Classic walk for experienced, adventurous walkers

Walkers who love to scramble and possess a fondness for narrow, nearly natural footpaths are sure to be thrilled by this walk – the route leads for long stretches along a marvellous, adventurous rock face alpine path that is, however, fairly harmless because it is never truly precipitous. Nevertheless, route-finding is not always so easy. At the end, one of the most beautiful beaches on the island awaits us – as well as one of the most remote, since the sandy beach, 250m in length, is only accessible on foot and not at all by boat!

Starting point: Lomo de Las Bodegas, 520m. From the Anaga mountain road, El Bailadero – Chamorga (TF-123) at Km 9.9, an access road forks off into the settlement; car park at the end of the road, 500m on. Bus stop for line 947 at the entrance to the village.

Grade: a very demanding rock face alpine path that requires perfect surefootedness, a vertigo-free head for heights (scrambling is often required, even using handholds) and route-finding skills (the path is sometimes barely discernible or not always distinct; mix-ups are very likely!). Start off as early as possible and avoid hot days (the trail is very exposed to the sun)! Take plenty of water with you!
Important note: the beach is only suitable for bathing when the sea is absolutely calm (dangerous rip currents)!
Note: you do not need a permit for this walk in the Ijuana nature reserve.

From the car park at the end of the street in **Lomo de Las Bodegas** ❶ return along the street for a couple of metres, then turn left onto the roadway that crosses over to the other flank of the Barranco de Anosma (here, the PR TF 5 forks off to the right). 10 mins later the roadway becomes a camino and passes solitary terraced fields and houses as it ascends to a saddle ❷. On the other side, the route continues along a path that is no longer very distinct as it traverses the slope (to the right, a view of Las Casillas), leading mostly below the ridgeline, sometimes directly along the crest of the ridge. About 15 mins from the saddle, the path veers in front of the **Mesa del**

Sabinar ❸ to the right towards the slope and hugs the sheer drop at the edge of the Barranco de Ijuana for a short stretch – a splendid rock face alpine path. About 20 mins later, cross over a saddle next to a little crag – here, the alpine path veers onto the right-hand ridgeline. At first continue along the left-hand side of the slope then directly via the ridgeline towards the sea. 10 mins later reach a small sandy **plateau** ❹; here continue along the left-hand side of the ridge towards the jagged section that the locals call 'the dolomites' (to the left, the Hoya del Sabinar). In front of the 'dolomites', the path, now indistinct, veers to the right towards the slope and then descends to the right over a hardly discernible ridge to reach a rocky plateau (a good 20 mins from the sandy plateau). Now, we find ourselves almost directly above the beach. Descend along the now steep and rocky ridge to meet up with a grassy plateau. Here pick up a distinct path which, at the end of the plateau, veers right for a short stretch then climbs down in a left-hand loop to the *barranco* and the **Playa de Ijuana** ❺ below.

One of the island's most spectacular beaches – the Playa de Ijuana.

↗ 750m | ↘ 750m | 11.6km
4.30 hrs

73 From Igueste to Las Casillas

An ascent with numerous options

The destination of this walk is the delightful mountain eyrie of Las Casillas perched on the ridgeline between the Barranco de Igueste and the Barranco de Ijuana. The hamlet is virtually abandoned; only a dragon tree and two cedars are reminders of better times. If you are a very physically fit walker, we recommend using the return route via La Cancelilla – an extensive circular walk that is rich in diversity.

Starting point: the turn-off of the road into the Barranco de Igueste in Igueste de San Andrés, 32m (bus stop for the 945). If you approach by car, you can drive all the way up to Lomo Bermejo (1.8km) and save 1 hr walking time.
Height difference: 750m (circular walk via La Cancelilla: add 200m).
Grade: Steep ascent and descent in places; possible route-finding problems in poor visibility.
Alternative: continuation of the trail from the TF-123 to Chamorga (PR TF 5): The *white/yellow* marked trail turns right along the road to the cemetery and, 20m past it, turns off left onto a camino which descends through a scrub wood to reach a cobbled road. Turn left towards Las Bodegas. At the car park (30m right) the trail continues to the left, passing above the chapel. Now ascend to La Cumbrilla and continue to the left over the ridgeline. At the last houses change over to the right-hand side of the ridge. The camino enters a laurisilva forest and forks a few mins later. Continue either to the right, descending to the road (¼ hr to Chamorga) or diagonally left on the level and 15 mins later bear right at the fork descending to Chamorga (a total of 1 hr or 1¼ hrs).
Linking tip: with Walks 68, 74 and 75.

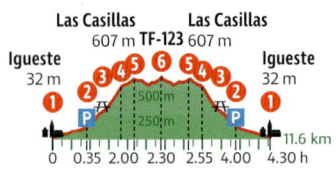

In **Igueste** ①, in the sharp bend of the main road between the two village districts, turn off onto the road which ascends the Barranco de Igueste (PR TF 5, *white/yellow*). Cross through plantations for a while and then pass below the houses of the hamlet of **Lomo Bermejo**. Half an hour later, a concrete road forks to the right ②, and then 100m on, the *white/yellow* marked trail forks away. The pretty camino leads between terraced fields,

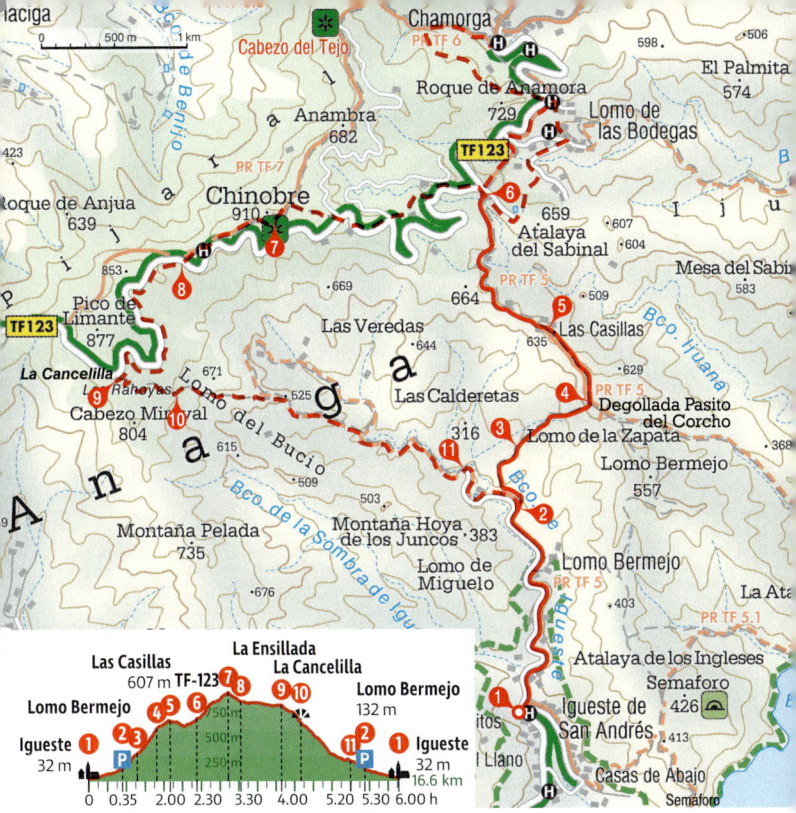

crosses a secondary *barranco*, then heads over to a mountain ridge to climb up along it. About 20 minutes from the road you reach a small col next to a little crag. The camino now skirts around to the right of a few scattered boulders on the ridgeline but soon returns (after passing a roofed bench ❸) back to the ridgeline. 200m further on, the camino bears diagonally left, heading towards the next ridgeline. Now keep steadily towards the mountain range ahead.

Just below the crest of the ridge, you can see power lines – about 50m below these, ignore a trail forking off to the right (a possible descent to Playa de Antequera, see Walk 75). The trail now ascends to the ridgeline ❹ of the mountain range (meeting it exactly at the spot where the power lines turn away from the ridgeline). Bear left and, 20 minutes later, reach the houses of **Las Casillas** ❺.

Ascent to the ridge where the houses of Las Casillas are perched.

The ridge path continues between the houses (at the fork near the power pylon, keep on the *white/yellow* marked ridge trail) and soon turns towards the valley on the right of the ridgeline. Walk across the valley to exit again on the other side and soon pass a house built into an overhanging crag. Walk through another valley notch, then the path ascends for a short stretch steeply up to the **Anaga high mountain road TF-123** ❻ (the path merges with it directly at the turn-off of an access road to the cemetery of Las Bodegas; signpost 'Igueste'; bus stop for the 947 is located on the main road; PR TF 5 continues on to Chamorga, 3.4km, see Alternative).

Return route via La Cancelilla (for the very physically fit walker, 3½ hrs): turn left on the TF-123 for 150m until a path forks off to the right. This ascends steeply and then forks past a footbridge near a fenced-in waterworks — bear right here, climbing up over outcrops of rock. Some minutes later, the trail levels out on the ridgeline and, shortly afterwards, meets up again with the road. Ascend along the road for 100m and then leave it behind again by turning diagonally right along a trail forking away which, a few minutes later, crosses over the road. Shortly after that, at the turn-off of a barrier-blocked roadway leading to the Cabezo del Tejo, merge again onto the road. Turn left, and 10m further on, a camino forks off to the right (for which, however, a permit is required — otherwise turn left onto the road). This ascends in not quite 10 mins to a ridge trail ❼ (unfortunately, the excursion to Chinobre is no longer permitted). Turn left onto the trail and in a good 10 mins descend to the car park **La Ensillada** ❽. — Until reaching the turn-off of the camino to Igueste, unfortunately, we have to make do with the road again: not quite a half hour of walking leads to the car park **La Cancelilla** ❾ — here, at a breach in the wall, the trail forks away. It forks again 20m on — turn left here and, 100m more, turn left again and then keep bearing right along the main trail. The camino leads subsequently along a little valley notch, through a marvellous laurisilva forest. Some minutes later, in front of a cataract, change over to the right flank of the valley. Now descend steeply through a brush wood. 10 mins later pass a small protruding rock ❿ — a lovely place to take a break and enjoy views of the *barrancos* at Igueste! The camino now traverses the slope and then climbs out over a mountain ridge, descending with a view of some fincas in the Barranco de Igueste (a trail from the fincas also merges here; see Walk 74). A good 15 mins later, ignore a trail forking off straight ahead (this leads to a cottage, nestled picturesquely below a dark rock face). The trail now drops down into the *barranco* and merges into an intersecting trail. Turn right onto this trail and then immediately change over to the other flank of the valley. Continue descending through the unspoiled, idyllic and labyrinthine *barranco*. 20 mins later the camino becomes a roadway and, 150m after that, merges into the TF-121 ⓫ which leads in 10 mins to the turn-off **Lomo Bermejo** ❷ then returns again to **Igueste** ❶ in another ½ hr.

↗ 310m | ↘ 310m | 4.9km
2.30 hrs

74 Barranco de Igueste

Marvellous tour into the idyllic, water-blessed Igueste Valley

The circular walk in the Barranco de Igueste is not spectacular, but it is rich in variation. The approach route meanders through the picturesque valley, always following the stream with its stunning cascades and rock pools. The return route then leads over a ridge with magnificent views.

Starting point: the end of the tarmac (car park) at the terminus of the TF-121 road into the Barranco de Igueste, 2.5km from the junction in Igueste de San Andrés, 32m (bus stop for the 945).

Grade: mostly an easy circular walk, only the ascent to the ridge is steep and somewhat overgrown. Do not attempt during or after heavy rainfall!
Linking tip: with Walk 73.

When the **tarmac ends** ❶ (car park), a road continues which shortly afterwards turns into a camino (keep straight ahead). The path steadily leads alongside the lively babbling Igueste stream, winding its way through the idyllic valley whilst forming countless cascades and pools. Just a little less than half an hour later, soon after crossing a secondary stream, ignore a path that branches off sharply to the left ❷ (our return route) and keep on the main path along the stream. It now changes sides several times, crosses a small gorge and climbs past a cave on the left to a mighty, ancient eucalyptus tree (20 mins). The path is now narrower, but continues to

From the Cancelilla trail, enjoy another view of the valley with the fincas.

be captivating and sometimes jungle-like. Soon after, the valley widens as a few houses appear. The trail forks below the second house – turn right here (passing the house on the left) and ascend. The camino then runs along the edge of meadowland terraces and forks again. At this point, stay on the trail heading straight on until reaching the next stream with a little cottage and a medlar tree ❸ – now turn left to cross the stream (straight ahead, in a few minutes, an excursion could bring you to a valley head with two houses and also a gigantic black rock face where, sometimes, a small waterfall is cascading). Our path now leaves the high valley and climbs steeply, somewhat overgrown, to the next crest of a ridge. Here, meet up with the **Cancelilla trail** ❹ (see Walk 73, a pleasant place for a break).
Enjoy another view taking in the valley, then continue left over the ridge or down the slope next to it. After a good half hour our path in the valley joins up with the approach route ❷ – follow this to the right back to the **starting point** ❶.

↗ 930m | ↘ 930m | 12.5km

75 From Igueste to Playa de Antequera

5.30 hrs

Extremely varied coastal walk to the remote Antequera beach

Stretches of this walk require some patience since the path is often indistinct; a head for heights is also necessary during the somewhat exposed traverse above the coast to Antequera beach. You will be rewarded, however, with a goodly dose of untamed adventure as well as a beautiful beach at the end of the walk.

Starting point: end of the main road in Igueste de San Andrés, 20m (terminus for the 945).
Grade: moderately difficult walk that requires some surefootedness, a head for heights and a good sense of direction. This walk should not be undertaken in rainy or stormy weather.
Boat service: nauticanivaria.com.

Linking tip: with Walk 73.

Follow the footpath continuing from the end of the main road in **Igueste** ❶ into the village (*white/yellow*). At a fork past the church take the upper trail, soon passing between two short radio masts, then head straight on towards the sea. After a total of a good 5 minutes a camino branches off to the left just before some railings (sign 'El Semáforo'; straight on leads to

Backwards view of Igueste. – Below: Descent from Atalaya de los Ingleses.

the cemetery) which ascends steeply in zigzags. A quarter of an hour later, the trail passes a rock outcrop (a small plateau as viewpoint). 20 mins later, reach the seaward side of the mountain ridge. Now keep a careful lookout: after about 15m on the seaward side, a distinct rock face path branches off to the left ❷, traverses the slope and crosses inland to ascend the ridge of the mountain range (sign; a detour straight ahead to the panoramically situated Semáforo is worthwhile, a good 10 mins; *white/yellow*). It is somewhat precipitous in places but nevertheless okay to walk along.

After a walking time of almost 1 hr, reach the ridgeline at a cairn, then continue ascending the ridge by bearing left to reach **Atalaya de los Ingleses** ❸, 429m, with an old, chapel-like stone house.

Antequera beach – an eagerly awaited destination along the giddy traverse.

The path continues to the right past the house – the approach onto the next slope is to the right of the ridgeline of the mountain ridge you are on and is clearly marked with large cairns. The path at first descends in a 15-minute traverse of the slope below the rocks, then turns to the right at a cairn onto a sometimes indistinct path that leads down into the valley. After a good 10 minutes, the cairn-marked path switches to the right side of the *barranco* then, 10 minutes later, back to the left side. The path forks 3 minutes later – bear left traversing the slope in easy up-and-down walking. Almost 10 minutes later, pass an overhanging rock ❹ (rest spot). Another 5 minutes more, just before a gully, go left at the fork (to the right a possible descent to the tiny Zapata beach) and shortly after, cross the gully. 5 minutes after crossing the gully, the narrow, precipitous path passes below a rock tower.

The most unpleasant part of the walk follows – a traverse of a good quarter of an hour to Antequera Bay, crossing high above the sea and sometimes rather exposed. As soon as you approach the rim of the Barranco de Antequera, continue along the mountain ridge, then to the right of it down across the slope to the elongated **Antequera beach** ❺ which you reach directly next to the mouth of the *barranco*.

If you do not want to return to Igueste along the same route, we recommend going back through the Barranco de Antequera: just before the end of the beach go left up the trail that leads past a couple of houses. (Directly to the left from the first house, an excursion along a path to the saddle above the house is worthwhile, with a stupendous view of Anaga's un-

tamed eastern coast and a downwards view of a little sand beach below. At the second, smaller, building a camino forks off to the right. At first the sometimes indistinct path leads to the right along the slope high above the *barranco* then, later on, always keeps in the **Barranco de Antequera** ❻ itself, changing sides several times. A good 1¼ hrs later, pass below a light-coloured, elongated rock face on the left hand side of the valley. Some minutes later you reach the ridge with the **Degollada Pasito del Corcho** ❼.

View from the mountain col to Antequera beach (above) and of the rugged Anaga eastern coastline (below).

The trail now runs for a few metres along the ridge and then turns towards the left hand side of the ridge to fork after 50m. Follow the trail leading diagonally left slightly downhill and at the next fork below a power line ascend right, up some rock steps to the next mountain ridge where you meet a camino ❽ (on the right to Las Casillas, see Walk 73). Walk along this camino in 40 mins down to the road in the Barranco de Igueste ❾ and along the road in half an hour back to **Igueste** ❶.

The Cañadas del Teide
Wide sand plains, bizarre rocks and a white sugar loaf mountain

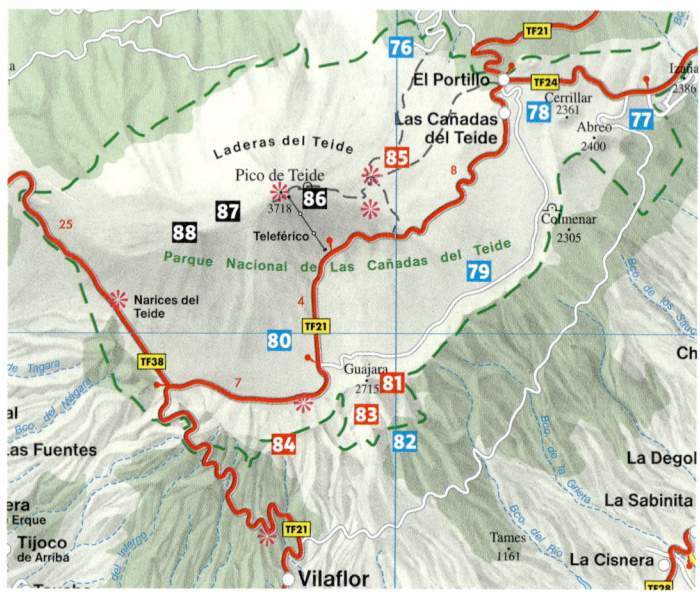

The National Park 'Parque Nacional de las Cañadas del Teide' is the main attraction of the island, drawing millions of visitors annually; a normally cloudless sky presents a weighty argument for holidaymakers sojourning in the north of the island who only seldom enjoy a break in the clouds brought in by the trade winds. The sand and lava terrain at the southern foot of Teide, with sparse vegetation and characterised by bizarre rock formations and volcanic cones, guarantees lasting impressions. In early summer (May/June) the volcanic landscape of the Cañadas is covered in a sea of rare flora. White-blossoming Teide broom, bright golden-yellow budding common broom and other varieties envelop the area with a captivating fragrance; to top it off, the candle-like floral crowns of the Teide Bugloss (Tajinaste) up to two metres high, and countless other plants, only found in the caldera, compete for the attention of bees collecting pollen. Some plants just flower for a few hours or days and then the landscape once again returns to its a desert-like character, reminiscent of a Lunar Landscape.

The caldera was formed about 300,000 years ago through the collapse of a mighty volcanic cone, out of whose floor the Pico del Teide, Pico Viejo and

Teide and Montaña Blanca, seen from Guajara. La Palma is in the background on the left.

numerous other volcanic mountains formed in subsequent eruptions. The so-called 'Sugar Loaf' (Pan de Azucár or Pitón) – the white peak of Teide above Rambleta (here the summit terminus of the Teide cable car can be found) – is of more recent volcanic origin. In this area, puffs of sulphurous gas still emerge from the depths of the mountain.

STARTING POINTS FOR WALKS

El Portillo, 2053m
Traffic junction at Km 32 on the Cañadas road, at the north-eastern edge of the Cañadas. Bar/restaurant and National Park Visitor Centre (Centro de Visitantes; with an exhibit explaining the creation of the Cañadas and trail information). Trails to Fortaleza, Montaña Blanca and the southern rim of the crater.

Teleférico del Teide, 2356m
Valley station of the Teide cable car, at Km 42.5 on the Cañadas road. Starting point for the ascent onto Teide (the actual starting point is 3km to the east).

Parador Nacional de las Cañadas, 2151m
State-owned hotel and National Park Visitor Centre at Km 46.5 on the Cañadas road. Ideal base for any walk in the Cañadas (accommodation available) and the starting point for walks to the Roques de García, to the Guajara and several other destinations.

Boca Tauce, 2055m
Road junction at Km 53 on the Cañadas road at the south-western edge of the Cañadas. This is the starting point for walks to the caldera crater rim and Pico Viejo.

TRAIL CLOSURES DUE TO MOUFLON HUNTING

Sometimes the trails are closed in the Cañadas because mouflon are being hunted. Please be sure to enquire at the national park offices!

↗ 230m | ↘ 230m | 8.8km

76 Fortaleza, 2159m

3.10 hrs

Warm up tour to the rock fortress

If you want to acquaint yourselves with the marvellous walking terrain of the Cañadas, the route to the Fortaleza (fortress) is an ideal choice. Begin with an interesting visit to the Centro des Visitantes (Visitor Centre) where a small, informative exhibition about the geology, flora and fauna of Teide National Park can be found. The walk leads through gently undulating hills of lava and sand on the northern edge of the Cañadas, broken up by sprinklings of common broom and white Teide broom, flowering in early summer. At the end of the walk, you can look forward to the reddish-brown rocky massif of Fortaleza and, near the Cruz de Frege, lovely rest spots.

Starting point: Centro de Visitantes (National Park Visitor Centre) in El Portillo, 2053m, 250m past the road junction at El Portillo bar/restaurant (bus stop for the 342 and 348).
Grade: consistently easy, leisurely walk, only the direct ascent to the Fortaleza is more demanding.
Refreshment: there is nothing available en route.
Alternative: descent from Cruz de Fregel to Icod el Alto (see Walk 15).

The trail (No 1) begins directly to the left of the **Centro de Visitantes** ❶. This passes below a small viewpoint then through a gate in the fence to continue towards Teide in steady up-and-down walking. Usually the trail is flanked with stones and, from time to time, stone benches tempt you to take a break. After a quarter of an hour, the trail forks on a small plain – continue straight on. 5 mins later, just below **Roque del Peral** ❷, ignore a trail forking off to the left. The route leads around the group of rocks and then heads towards the rocky ridge of Fortaleza in gentle up-and-down walking. Near the foot of Cabezón, the trail descends (on the way ignore trail No 22 turning off left) into an extensive, beige-coloured sandy plain, the **Cañada de los Guancheros** ❸. Cross the plain towards the west. Immediately at the outset, the ascent trail turns to the right (No 29) to the Cruz de Fregel.

However, before that, you could walk along trail No 1 across the plain (10 minutes) and continue along the path straight ahead for 15 minutes as far as the precipice to enjoy a magnificent view of the north-west-

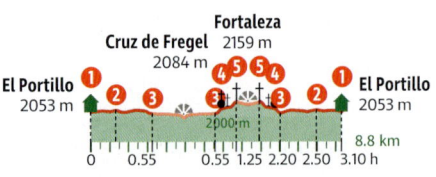

Fortaleza and on the right, the col of Degollada del Cedro.

ern coast (here, trail No 33 forks off to the left). Back at the start of the plain ❸, ascend with trail No 29 up to the **Cruz de Fregel** ❹ (small chapel) in the Degollada del Cedro ('Cedar Col', now-a-days, there are only two cedars left here).

Now follow the gently ascending track to the left. Pass a shrine and, shortly afterwards, the track ends. Turn left here onto a lovely trail, flanked by rows of stones, up to the highest point of **Fortaleza** ❺ – the view stretches from Teide to the vast forests of the Orotava Valley. If you would like to add a short circular walk, follow the trail onwards – this leads to a viewpoint and then returns back to the roadway.

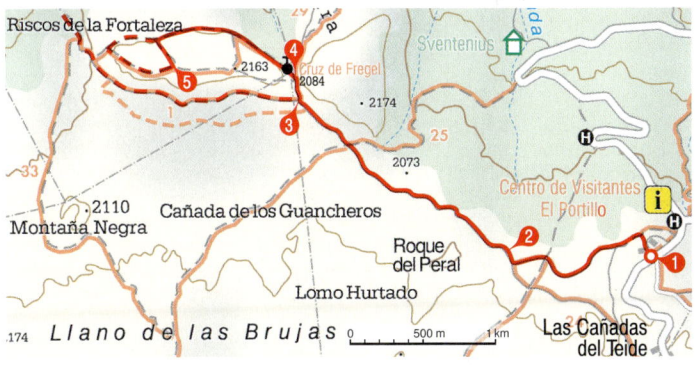

↗ 250m | ↘ 250m | 8.3km

77 Volcán de Fasnia

2.15 hrs

Pleasant circular walk within sight of the Izaña observatory

When flowers are in bloom, this usually rather drab circular walk over the gently rolling, broom-covered plateau at the edge of the Cañadas counts as a lovely ramble. In other times, the reward lies in a thoroughly pleasant stroll-like walk.

Starting point: the car park Corral del Niño, 2305m, at Km 38 of the high ridge road of the Cumbre Dorsal (TF-24 La Esperanza – El Portillo), 4.8km east of the junction El Portillo (here is the closest bus stop for the lines 342 and 348) or alternatively, 800m west of the Izaña turn-off.
Grade: throughout, an easy, pleasant circular walk.
Refreshment: nothing en route.

From the car park **Corral del Niño** ❶ follow the walking path that runs parallel to the road, heading towards Teide. A few minutes later, reach a large trail board, situated a couple of metres away from the road – here, our trail No 20 veers away from the road and ascends pleasantly through the slope, with a view opening up of the Izaña observatories and the coal-black Volcán de Fasnia. Later on, the trail levels off and keeps heading steadily towards Teide. At a fork ❷ (sign) keep straight on along trail No 20 (trail No 37 forks away to the right). Just afterwards,

The walking path opens up lovely views of Teide (above), below, the Volcán de Fasnia.

our trail veers to the left and then winds its way along, through the sandy, broom-covered plateau to reach a **saddle** ❸ and, from there, next to a beige-coloured pumice terrain, heads down the valley. Gradually, Teide appears again to our right then the trail merges into a roadway that leads eastwards. At the foothills of the Volcán de Fasnia, meet up with another roadway that is flanked by crash barriers; turn left onto it.

The road heads directly towards the observatories at Izaña whilst passing the **Volcán de Fasnia** ❹. Past the chain of black hills, a roadway forks to the right through a gate and provides for a rewarding detour to enjoy a view of the reverse side of the volcano ❺ (very photogenic; 10 mins one-way, then the roadway begins a descent). After the detour, ascend again along the roadway to reach the **Izaña road** ❻ – before the merge onto the road, the walking path forks to the left and, in 10 minutes, brings us back to the car park **Corral del Niño** ❶.

↗ 360m | ↘ 360m | 12.3km

78 Arenas Negras and Alto de Guamaso

3.30 hrs

Pleasant Cañadas circular walk from the road junction El Portillo

The Cañadas are the most popular walking area on the island – not only because of the unique terrain but also because of the location above the clouds brought in by the trade winds. Because of this, two short but pleasant circular walks are presented here which can be negotiated in just half a day.

View of Teide from the Arenas Negras circular walk. – Photo right: Alto de Guamaso.

Starting point: road junction, El Portillo, 2034m (restaurant; bus stop for line 342 and 348).
Grade: a circular route that is easy and pleasant throughout and which could also be shortened to an abbreviated walk (Arenas Negras or Guamaso).
Refreshment: nothing en route.

From the **Cruce El Portillo** ❶ follow the main road towards the Cañadas for 300m (you could also take the trail below the road instead) and across from the **Centro de Visitantes** ❷ National Park Visitor Centre), turn left onto a forestry road (barrier; trail No 2). At the fork 5 mins later bear left (the right-hand trail is our return route). A good 5 mins after that, the trail breaks away from the forestry trail at a chain barrier. It leads pleasantly through the slope with a view of the Guamaso. A good ½ hr later, reach a broad saddle ❸, 2295m, between the Montaña de las Arenas Negras and the Montaña del Cerrillal (a total of 1 hr). Now both Teide and the Guajara make up the view. Keep to the trail along the slope which descends gently and, 5 mins later, meet up with a post and an expansive sandy plain on the left-hand side ❹ (Llano de Maja). The main trail, No 2, hooks off to the right, flanked by rows of stones, and heads directly for Teide along the left edge of a delightfully coloured gully and then opens a far-reaching

260

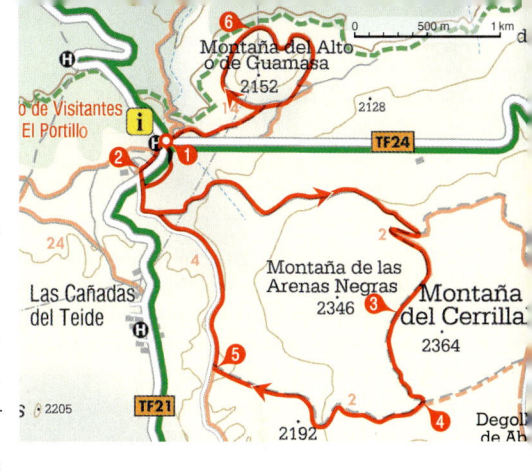

view of the Cañadas and all the way to the restaurant complex, Las Cañadas del Teide. The trail now descends in zigzags while crossing over a black slope of volcanic cinder and then continues onto the plain until it merges with the intersecting trail No 4 ❺. Turn right onto this to return to the visitor centre ❷ (25 minutes) – 30m before reaching the barrier on the main road, a footpath forks off to the right to the **Cruce El Portillo** ❶, 300m away.

If you are still keen for another short walk (or if you want to use up the time until the bus departs), we can recommend the Guamaso circular walk (trail No 14; a good hour). The trail sets off on the other side of the roundabout between the crash barriers and is marked at the outset with *white/red* waymarkings (GR 131). A few minutes onwards, the GR 131 leaves our trail behind by turning left – our trail ascends gently over to the foot of Guamaso and, a quarter of an hour later, forks. Bear left here – the trail skirts around the summit in a clockwise direction while keeping almost on the level. The Orotava Valley lies at our feet ❻ and, later on, we can enjoy a splendid view of the Cumbre Dorsal capped with observatories. About half an hour later, meet up with a broad trail on a saddle, but leave it behind again shortly afterwards by turning right along a trail flanked by rows of stones, passing over a stony platform. Shortly thereafter, reach the fork already met on the approach and turn left to return to **El Portillo** ❶.

79 Siete Cañadas – from the Parador Nacional to El Portillo

↗ 180m | ↘ 290m | 15.9km
4.30 hrs

Easy walk along the foot of the caldera rock faces

This pleasant walk leads along the edge of the Cañadas, passing between gigantic fields of lava and the impressive rock walls of the caldera rim – a tranquil ramble. Physically fit walkers could extend the route to a grand circular walk by combining this one with the Cañadas high mountain trail (see Alternative) – if this be the case, an early start is called for.

Starting point: Parador Nacional, 2151m (bus stop for the 342 and 348).
Destination: El Portillo, 2034m (bus stop for the 342 and 348).
Grade: easy, but long walk on a consistently wide roadway.
Refreshment: hotel-restaurant Parador.
Alternatives: if you find the walk to El Portillo too long, you can turn off left after almost 1 hr onto the roadway leading to the Teide cable car (No 16): this passes the Sanatorio (20 mins) on the way to the

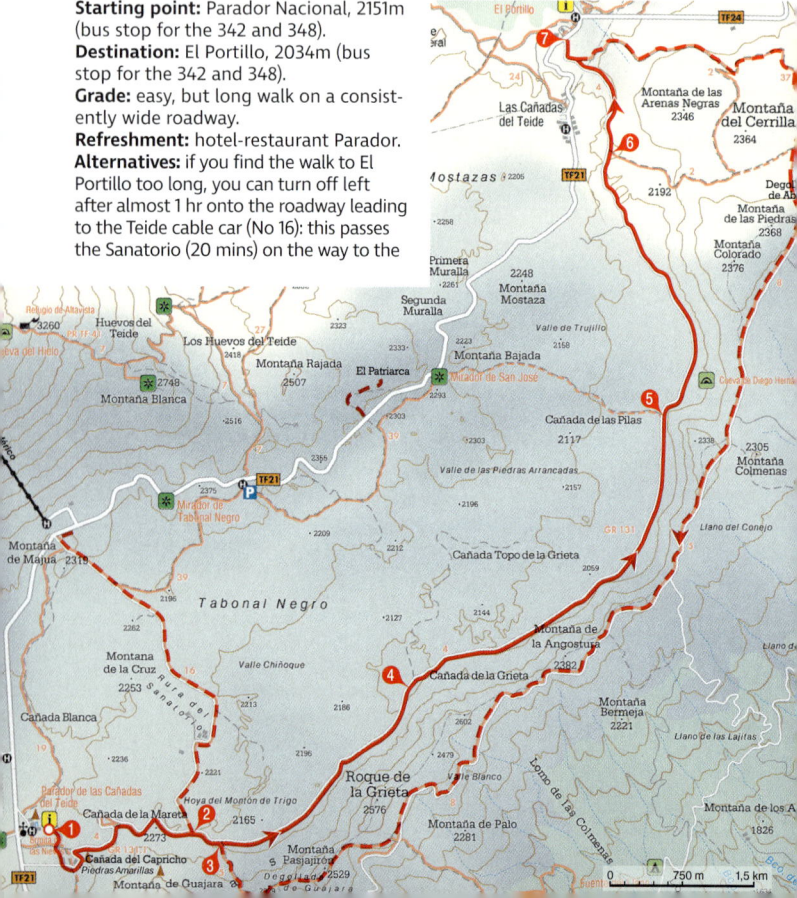

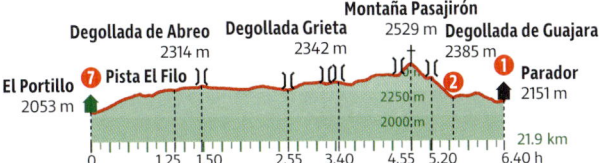

Cañadas road (1 hr); from there, 15 mins to the valley station or with trail No 19 to return to the Parador (not quite 1 hr). Grand circular walk via the Cañada high mountain trail (5¾ hrs from El Portillo to the Cañadas roadway; Notice: at the moment, the trail is closed starting from the Degollada de Abreo as a military exclusion zone – be sure to enquire at the visitor centre!): across from the Centro de Visitantes in El Portillo a forestry road (barrier) begins, then forks 5 mins later – turn left here (No 2). After another good 5 mins, at a chain barrier, the path breaks away from the forestry trail and, ½ hr after that, in a hairpin bend, forks straight on with trail No 37. This merges into a forestry road 35 mins later (No 8); turn right here. 40 mins afterwards reach the vague saddle of the Degollada de Abreo (a wooden cross). Shortly thereafter, the trail has been closed temporarily as a *Zona militar* (barrier). 1 hr later, reach another vague saddle near the rim of the drop-off for the Caldera. The roadway then veers away somewhat from the ridgeline (now also opening a view of the southern coast). Not quite ½ hr later meet a saddle with a view of the Cañadas and of Teide. Another good 1 hr more the broad trail suddenly becomes more overgrown – here, a path (No 8) forks off diagonally right following a row of stones, ascending easily along the slope. 5 mins later, this joins the PR TF 86 (*white/yellow*) and leads to the saddle in front of the Pasajirón. Via the ridge, passing a couple of rock faces, continue ascending to the summit plateau where you pass 30m away from the highest point of the Montaña Pasajirón, 2529m (½ hr from where the path forked off). Shortly afterwards, the trail sinks down to reach Guajara Pass. From here, climb for 3 mins along the ridge until, at a large info board, trail No 5 (*white/red/yellow*) descends to the Cañadas roadway (20 mins). Take this left to reach the Parador in not quite 1 hr (40 mins on, just past the barrier, turn right with trail No 4) – or turn right with the trail described below to return to El Portillo (3½ hrs.).
Linking tip: with Walk 78.

Above: The former sanatorium. – Below: Rock climber in the Cañada del Capricho.

From the roundabout directly next to the **Parador Nacional** ❶ (bus station) follow the *white/red/yellow* marked path (GR 131/No 4), which heads in an easterly direction onto Guajara. After a quarter of an hour, meet a roadway and turn left to continue the route. Immediately pass a small stone-built National Park hut and skirt round the bizarre cluster of rocks of **Cañada del Capricho** (Piedras Amarillas). A little later on, you pass another group of rocks. Not quite three quarters of an hour later, trail No 16 turns off left to the Teide cable car ❷, some minutes after that, trail No 5 turns off

to the right towards the Guajara Pass ❸. Remain on the roadway, now *white/red* marked (No 4), that subsequently passes below the Montaña Pasajirón. Pass a beautiful group of rocks then head gently downhill along the foot of Roque de la Grieta into a gully bordered on the left by a huge lava flow – scores of red bugloss grow along the sun-bathed slopes. At the foot of Topo de la Grieta the roadway descends further to a rather large alluvial plain, the **Cañada de la Grieta** ❹. Further along, the scenery becomes more and more monotonous. 45 mins later, reach a vast plain, the **Cañada de las Pilas**; on the other side of the plain (a good ½ hr)

The trail leads steadily along the foot of the mountains surrounding the Cañadas – in the background: the Topo de la Grieta.

pass between boulders and a rock tower. On the next plain enjoy the fascinating, colourful layers and formations in the rock faces.

At the end of the plain (almost ½ hr), the roadway makes a hook ❺. 25 minutes later, another small plain follows where trail No 2 joins from the right ❻. Continue along the roadway, passing a barrier 15 minutes later, shortly afterwards, reach the Centro de Visitantes in **El Portillo** ❼ on the main road (bus stop 300m to the right).

EL PATRIARCA, METHUSELAH JUNIPER IN THE NATIONAL PARK

A short but worthwhile excursion is to El Patriarca, a Canary Islands juniper tree that is over 1100 years old (just under 1km; ¼ hr one way): from the car park Minas de San José at Km 38 of the TF-21 Cañadas road, follow the trail heading towards Teide, soon bordered by rows of stones, into a sandy valley with betimes green glimmering sandy hills. The trail ascends to the right. One level further up it leads in gentle up and down walking through a magnificent and bizarre volcanic-sand terrain to reach the tree, surrounded by a wall.

↗ 155m | ↘ 155m | 3.4km

80 Roques de García

1.15 hrs
🚌 🚶

Unforgettable walk around the most bizarre crags of the Cañadas

The Roques de García in the heart of the Cañadas at the foot of Teide are the island's most beautiful natural monument. Especially Roque Cinchado, the so-called 'Finger of God', attracts swarms of tourists. It takes just a few minutes, however, for the walker to be immersed in the tranquility of the Cañadas and to discover, undisturbed, the fantastic natural wonders around this bizarre polymorphic rock massif.

Starting point: Parador Nacional de las Cañadas, 2151m (bus stop for the 342 and 348), or the car park at the Mirador de la Ruleta, at the foot of Roques de García.
Grade: easy walk.
Refreshment: Parador Nacional hotel.
Linking tip: with Walk 81.

From the roundabout at the **Mirador de la Ruleta** ❶ take trail No 3 to the right, following the enclosure and passing below the Roque Cinchado. After only a few minutes reach a small col at the end of the enclosure. About 10 minutes later, a lava flow encroaches from the right extending toward the rocks. After another 10 minutes, reach the last, solitary rock tower of the Roques de García, the Roques Blancos (just beforehand trail No 23 branches off right to Pico Viejo). Pass this to the right and reach a small **viewing plateau** ❷ at the sheer drop at the rim, facing the Llano de Ucanca plain (nice spot to take a break).

Circumventing the little group of rocks that follows, descend in the direction of the Ucanca plain, bearing left. – If you like, after the short descent, you can then ascend to the right along the lava flow; otherwise descend the small valley to the left of this. After about 20 mins, arrive at the foot of a huge, multiple-peaked rock formation. Continue at its foot

Roques de Garcia – a much-visited group of rocks.

down to the Ucanca plain, directly towards the **Catedral** (the 'Finger of God' appears again up on the crest). The roughly 100m high rock bastion displays several striking towers and looks not unlike a cathedral – from time to time you can see climbers clinging to the steep rock faces.

100m before the Catedral the trail forks ❸. Turn left here past the Catedral along the steep trail No 3 back to the **Mirador de la Ruleta** ❶ (20 mins; half way along, the detour to the sheer drop at the rim facing the Ucanca plain).

Catedral – popular with climbers.

If you want to extend the walk, go past the Catedral on the right along trail No 26 for a detour to the Mirador Llano de Ucanca (½ hr). Pass a rock formation riddled with holes then, 5 mins later, a volcanic vent on your right. 5 mins more, the waymarked trail veers to the right just before the edge of the plain (the path straight on leads past Azulejos up to the main road) and runs across the Ucanca plain over to the *mirador* on the main road (a good 10 minutes).

TOP 81

↗ 650m | ↘ 650m | 10.1km

From Parador Nacional onto Guajara, 2718m

4.20 hrs

A fabulous panoramic mountain with titillating routes

The broad-shouldered Guajara is not only the highest but also the most striking mountain formation in the wide circle of elevations along the caldera rim. Not only offering a pleasant mountain experience, it also affords the walker a magnificent panorama of Teide, the Cañadas and the neighbouring islands of Gran Canaria, El Hierro, La Gomera and La Palma. To top it all, countless red bugloss grow on its sun-bathed slopes, in early summer blooming in a luxuriant floral display. From the Parador Nacional, two routes lead up to the summit: the ascent follows the more popular route, which can be undertaken by any walker; the descent route is negotiated via a breach in the extensive Guajara rock face and via the Ucanca Pass – if you do not feel comfortable with this rather demanding route, you can return to the starting point via the ascent route (2 hrs). Experienced mountain walkers are recommended to undertake the walk in the opposite direction over the Degollada de Ucanca (see Walk 83).

Starting point: Parador Nacional de las Cañadas, 2151m (bus stop for the 342 and 348).
Grade: the ascent is easy but the descent demands sure-footedness as it leads sometimes along a rock face (danger of rockfall during rain or storm).
Refreshment: in the hotel Parador Nacional.
Linking tip: with Walks 80, 82 and 83.

From the roundabout directly next to the **Parador Nacional** ❶ (bus station) follow the path (No 4, *white/red/yellow*) which heads in an easterly direction onto Guajara. A quarter of an hour later, meet a roadway ❷ and turn left (trail No 31 continues opposite to the Degollada de Ucanca). Straight away the roadway passes a little, stone-built National Park hut and skirts round the **Cañada del Capricho** (Piedras Amarillas) – now and then you can watch climbers on the bizarre rock faces of this monumental

Guajara with the Parador. The descent route leads through the breach (in the uppermost rock face, one third of the way from the right) to Ucanca Pass.

craggy metropolis. Later pass another cluster of rocks, less spectacular in shape. On the following left hand bend, a shortcut turns off right and shortly afterwards meets the roadway again. You now find yourself at the foot of the huge Guajara. Just under half an hour from the National Park stone hut ignore a path (trail No 16) turning off left to the Teide cable car, then arrive at the edge of an elongated plateau. Here the waymarked ascent trail turns off right to the Guajara Pass ❸ (No 5/GR 131/PR TF 86). Cairns guide you along the trail that winds up between gorse bushes (always stay on the main trail). Not quite half an hour later, ignore a path forking off to the right. Not quite another 5 minutes more, reach the **Degollada de Guajara** ❹.

The *white/yellow* marked PR TF 86 turns off to the left – but follow trail No 15 and the *white/red* marked GR 131 to the right. 25m on, the trail hooks to the left (straight ahead, a more striking path continues on, but it is steeper and scree-slippery). Soon pass below a beautiful wall of pumice rock. After a short ascent of just under 10 mins, the ascent route to the summit of Guajara branches off to the right at an iron stake ❺ (No 15; straight on, a possible de-

Summit rest with a view of Teide.

scent to the Paisaje Lunar, see Walk 83).

The trail, for the most part bearing slightly to the left, ascends the slope, soon over a faintly defined ridge. A half hour later, the trail crosses a precipitous and eroded gully and ascends in a straight line. 10 minutes after that our return route later on forks off to the left – straight on, in 5 minutes, reach the highest point on the broad summit plateau of **Guajara** ❻ – stone walls offer resting places protected from the wind.

Now retrace your course along the ascent route for not quite 5 minutes until trail No 15 turns off right towards the Parador (via Degollada de Ucanca). This descends slightly through the slope and, 10 minutes later, veers off to the left of a broad gulley that leads downwards to a broad rocky notch. Our trail leads through this crevice in the rock face and then to the left, descending steadily along the foot of the rock face whilst opening up a marvellous view taking in the Ucanca plain with the Roques de García (danger of rockfall; in the winter, the trail sometimes can be icy and slippery along this stretch). At a solitary standing tree, the walking trail veers off to the right towards the slope and then descends to the **Degollada de Ucanca** ❼.

From the top of the pass ascend about 100m to the west until a distinct trail forks off to the right (No 31, cairns). This leads for a short distance westwards then bends to the right (east) leading directly along the foot of a small, extended rock face. Over the next mountain ridge heading towards the valley, descend in tight zigzags onto a light-coloured pumice col (½ hr); from here descend to the right to reach the roadway ❷ near the **Cañada del Capricho** (Piedras Amarillas). On the opposite side, take trail No 4 back to the **Parador Nacional** ❶.

↗ 710m | ↘ 710m | 13.2km

4.20 hrs

Paisaje Lunar | 82

To the enchanting minarets and towers of the Lunar Landscape

The Lunar Landscape is one of the greatest natural wonders on the island: the curious, light beige-coloured towers, formed from pumice stone and resembling minarets, protrude from the slopes on both sides of the Barranco de las Arenas, creating a stunning contrast to the bright green pine trees – a veritable fairyland!

Starting point: church square in Vilaflor, 1420m (bus stop for the 342, 474, 482). – Alternatively, you could begin the walk from the Pista Madre del Agua (not quite 2 hrs shorter): the track forks off from Km 66 on the TF-21 Vilaflor – Cañadas; 3.7km further on, just past the Barranco de las Mesas, the trail crosses over the track road (signpost).
Grade: easy walk that demands, however, some physical fitness.
Refreshment: there are bar/restaurants in Vilaflor.
Linking tip: with Walks 81 and 83.

The starting point of the walk is the lower end of the large, sloping *plaza* at the Iglesia de San Pedro in **Vilaflor** ❶. Descend along the village street (GR 131/PR TF 72, *white/red/yellow*) and then turn left onto the second street. Bear left at both of the following forks and, 25m further on, a sign-posted camino

*A dream of a destination for walkers –
the Lunar Landscape at the southern foot of Guajara.*

forks off to the right. This descends into the **Barranco del Chorrillo**, crosses a roadway and shortly afterwards, past a round water storage tank, merges with a track. Follow this track 50m to the left until a broad paved path bordered with low stone walls turns off sharp to the right. It leads doggedly uphill through an open pine wood and, a good half an hour later, passes a large farmstead with drystone-walled terraces and a grove of almond trees (**Casa Galindo** ❷).

5 minutes later the trail forks – go diagonally right here down along the camino into the **Barranco de las Mesas** (red bugloss!) and then up along the other side of the valley to reach the **Pista Madre del Agua** ❸ (10 minutes; 3.7km to the TF-21). Cross over the track and continue ascending along the camino over a mountain ridge. At the fork, 3 minutes later, keep heading straight (your later return route turns off to right here).

Not quite half an hour later, cross over a roadway (on your left are some terraces) and 2 minutes after that, cross over a track – now carry straight on along the roadway (barrier) uphill. A few minutes later, pass a derelict farmstead (Casa Marrubial ❹). 5 minutes later, the trail turns towards the slope and ascends after another 5 minutes through a mini version of the Lunar Landscape ❺ to the next ridge where you pass a few 'huevos' (volcanic bombs), 1–2m in diameter.

Just under 15 minutes later, the trail forks – straight on leads into the Valle de Ucanca ❻ (see Walk 83), but turn right onto the *white/red/yellow* marked trail. 100m on cross over an old, narrow water canal and then the trail forks again 5 minutes later (signpost). Turn right here onto

the PR TF 72 (*white/yellow*) to descend to the Paisaje Lunar (straight on, a possible detour to the Black Lunar Landscape: after 10 minutes, in the floor of the Barranco de las Arenas, go left uphill). Some minutes later, the path passes a small viewpoint (30m to the left of the path) and 5 minutes after that, arrives at another viewpoint taking in the **Paisaje Lunar** ❼ (Los Escurriales, info board).

If you wish, you could turn left along the narrow, precipitous path for an excursion into the Lunar Landscape (5 minutes) – but please do not climb around between the bizarre rock formations!

The trail now heads to the right. At the outset, it runs gently up-and-down and, after 10 minutes, gradually descends quite clearly through the pine wood. After a good half an hour, reach a trail junction (signposts: sharp left to the Madre del Agua, 2km; the PR TF 83 merges from the left ❽, from here, 5 minutes to the car park La Florida along the Pista Madre del Agua), and carry straight on, directly along a stone wall. The trail keeps to the right, parallel to the track and subsequently touches upon it again three times (15 minutes later, pass to the right of a stone house). Not quite a half an hour later, meet the ascent trail again ❸. Turn left to return to **Vilaflor** ❶.

↗ 1470m | ↘ 1470m | 22.2km

83 From Vilaflor onto Guajara, 2718m

7.30 hrs

Long summit walk on old connecting trails

From the terraces of Vilaflor, the highest situated village on Tenerife, a marvellous old camino leads through spectacular pine woods, climbing up to the cumbre which is the start of a full day's walk onto Guajara – one of the best routes on the island and one that any ambitious walker would not want to miss. If you haven't used up all of your energy at the end, you can add on a excursion to the Paisaje Lunar!

Starting point: church square in Vilaflor, 1420m (bus stop for the 342, 474, 482); or the Pista Madre del Agua (see Walk 82, not quite 2 hours shorter).
Grade: physical fitness and surefootedness are essential. The trail from the Ucanca Pass to the summit is somewhat tricky when there's snow or stormy weather. Possible route-finding problems in poor visibility.
Refreshment: bar/restaurants in Vilaflor.
Linking tip: with Walks 81 and 82.

Follow Walk 82 a good 2 hrs to the fork ❻ (refer to the walk). Go straight ahead here onto the trail, at first waymarked *red* (later, also *green*) into the Valle de Ucanca (an 'X' on a boulder). After just under a quarter of an hour, it leads on the

right past a large boulder (straight on uphill) – the Montana de las Arenas rises up to your right; on the other side of the valley, the Roque del Encaje. 20 minutes later, Guajara appears on the right above showing its huge west face. The trail now keeps left down to a disused water canal and runs parallel to this up the valley. A few minutes later, cross over the canal again to the right. A good 5 minutes later, the trail leads directly past a small waterworks ❼. The pine trees thin out now and are replaced at the side of the path by red bugloss. About 25 minutes from the waterworks, the path changes over onto the left hand side of the valley and ascends all the way to the **Degollada de Ucanca** ❽. From here, you could descend to the Parador following Walk 81 and return to Vilaflor by bus.

Now follow trail 15 to the right, climbing steeply up to the summit wall of Guajara. Some minutes later, keep to the right along the waymarked path (the trail to the north face has been discontinued) that ascends diagonally through the slope towards a solitary tree and then turns left at the foot of the rock face to climb up to a broad breach in the rock face. Soon afterwards, the path leaves the gully behind by bearing left and, 20 minutes later, merges with the Guajara popular trail. Take this to

The Degollada de Ucanca and the Guajara (right).

Leisurely stretch of the walk – the sandy ridge on the descent.

climb up to the summit of **Guajara** ❾ in 5 minutes.

Now descend via the Guajara popular trail (No 15), that is continue straight on at the fork not quite 5 minutes later ('Parador por degollada de Guajara'). The path descends in a south-easterly direction, for the most part diagonally traversing the slope. Not quite a half an hour later, at the edge of the Barranco del Río next to an iron stake ❿, merge into an intersecting trail, the GR 131 (*white/red*) – follow this to the right (left goes to the Degollada de Guajara). The distinct path leads slightly uphill onto a mountain ridge and then crosses to the right over to the neighbouring *barranco*. Continue straight ahead and cross the small *barranco* – at its edge, continue downhill, then keep to the right heading towards the black-brown coloured, shimmering cinder cone of the Montaña de las Arenas. Now the path zigzags down a mountain ridge to a broad, gently sloping, sandy terrain – after half an hour (from the iron stake), reach the sandy ridge to continue straight on, flanked by rows of stones and enjoying a fabulous view of the south coast and the Black Lunar Landscape on the right.

The trail forks just before the sand-covered slope ends and before reaching the first pine trees – turn right here through the Barranco de las Arenas ⓫

The Black Lunar Landscape.

at the *barranco* floor (to the right a short detour to the Black Lunar Landscape is worthwhile) to the next major mountain ridge. From there, the trail descends gradually across the slope and, some minutes later, reaches a small rocky plateau from where you can enjoy your first glimpse of the Lunar Landscape. 5 minutes later, reach a trail junction – here, continue straight ahead towards the Valle de Ucanca (on the left, the PR TF 72 turns off to the Paisaje Lunar, a lovely alternative for the return route; see Walk 82). A minute later, arrive at the fork with the approach trail ❻ and return along this to **Vilaflor** ❶.

↗ 450m | ↘ 450m | 7.0km

2.55 hrs

Sombrero de Chasna, 2405m — 84

Short, panoramic route on the rocky 'sombrero' above Vilaflor

The Sombrero de Chasna is one of the most striking peaks of the caldera rim. Shaped like a hat, the steep rock face rises up from the caldera's slopes, covered by sparse pine woods. As to be expected, along the vast summit plateau, the route is rich in panoramic views; a bit of scrambling is required at the end.

Location: Vilaflor, 1420m (bus stop for the 342, 474, 482).
Starting point: the trail board by two derelict stone houses, 2035m, at a left hand bend of the main road TF-21 Vilaflor – Cañadas, at Km 59.7 (8.5km from Vilaflor and 1.2km below Las Lajas picnic area, on the bus line 342). Very little parking available, therefore it is better to begin the walk at the picnic area Las Lajas (see Alternative).
Grade: a distinct path, but sometimes crossing rather confusing terrain. The summit ascent requires a short section of scrambling (I).
Refreshment: bar/restaurants in Vilaflor.
Alternative: from the picnic area Las Lajas to the starting point (25 mins): from the information centre at the car park, a trail flanked by rows of stones heads toward the WC. This leads to the left past the toilets descending (now waymarked *green*) over the ridge. Afterwards, in somewhat toilsome up-and-down, parallel to the TF-21, head steadily straight on. Then pass through a cobbled underpass over to the other side of the road. Turn right to ascend to the starting point on the road ❶.

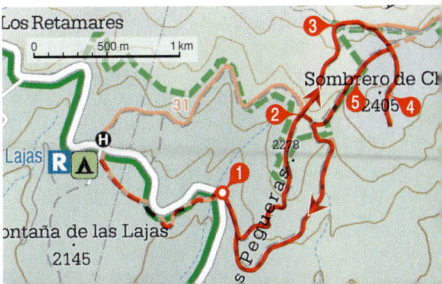

From the rim of the caldera, an awesome view opens up, taking in the Cañadas and Teide.

From the trail board ❶ a distinct path, marked with cairns (sometimes with rows of stones; *white/green/blue*) ascends to the right, passing the lower stone house. This traverses the slope almost on the level and then forks, 5 mins later – turn left along the waymarked path to continue ascending. Some minutes more and the path merges again with the *green* waymarked main trail and then ascends pleasantly over the ridgeline. The open pine wood provides an almost unlimited view of the southern coast. After walking for half an hour, the Sombrero de Chasna appears ahead. The path continues along the mountain ridge – on the right accompanied by the Barranco de la Magdalena. Soon pass a pine tree with long, spreading branches and enclosed by a stone wall. A few minutes later, meet up with the National Park trail No 31 ❷, ascending from the Las Lajas picnic area. The park trail continues climbing up the ridge to reach the ridgeline of the Caldera rim mountains ❸, where a breathtaking view of the Cañadas and Teide opens up (30m on, ignore a path forking off to the right).

Trail No 31 now leads to the right, close to the rim of the crater. In the following saddle (a ring of stones) leave the trail behind by turning right onto a path forking away; this descends diagonally through the slope, then turns left at the fork near a boulder to reach the foot of Sombrero. Here, reach an intersecting trail at a large cairn; turn left onto it to continue on to Sombrero (our return trail heads to the right). A few minutes later, ascend over outcrops of rock to the summit plateau of the **Sombrero de Chasna** ❹ (easy scrambling). Do not miss walking along to the southern edge of the summit plateau, following the waymarkers – the view of the south coast and Vilaflor is magnificent and the islands of Gran Canaria, El Hierro and La Gomera are also visible in the distance.

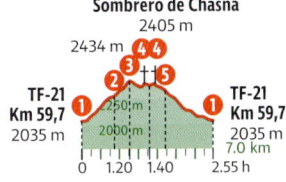

Now return to the fork near the large cairn and keep to the path along the foot of Sombrero. This path descends pleasantly along the Barranco de la Magdalena, soon passing a striking, bizarrely-formed boulder that almost looks like a miniature edition of the 'Finger of God' rock formation ❺. 15 minutes later, the trail forks – here continue along the *blue*-waymarked path traversing the slope. The trail gradually leaves the valley behind and, usually descending easily, crosses over to a high mountain ridge (always bear right at junctions whenever in doubt). After another 5-minute traverse, reach the approach trail and return along this in a few minutes to the road ❶.

View back of Sombrero de Chasna from the descent.

↗ 760m | ↘ 760m | 18.5km

85 Huevos del Teide and Montaña Blanca, 2748m

5.30 hrs

To the mighty volcanic bombs at the foot of Teide

The origin of the 'Eggs of Teide', giant spheroids of lava with a diameter of up to five metres, has not yet been satisfactorily determined. The most likely theory is that they separated from a flowing lava mass and formed into spherical shapes as they rolled downhill. The shining black 'huevos' lie scattered across the light-coloured pumice slope as if strewn there by the hand of Goliath.

Starting point: Centro de Visitantes (National Park Visitor Centre) in El Portillo, 2053m, 250m past the road junction at the bar/restaurant El Portillo (bus stop for the 342 and 348).
Grade: this is a simple but a strenuous walk.
Refreshment: nothing en route.
Alternative: possible descent on the Teide roadway to the Cañadas road, Km 40.5 (a good 1 hr from Montaña Blanca; bus stop for the 342 and 348).
Linking tip: this walk can be combined with Walks 76 and 86.

The trail (No 1) begins directly to the left of the **Centro de Visitantes** ❶. It passes beneath a small viewpoint, leads through a gate in a fence and then heads straight towards Teide in a constant up-and-down (always continue straight on). After a good quarter of an hour ignore a trail turning off right and one minute later turn left onto trail No 6 ❷ which ascends gently across a light beige terrain of pumice. 5 minutes more, next to a stone bench, cross over an intersecting trail (No 24) and con-

280

A strange contrast – the jet-black Huevos and the beige-coloured pumice.

tinue in a direct line up towards Teide. After half an hour, pass a striking dark hillock of lava sand to the right of the path, the **Montaña de los Tomillos** ❸. Not quite ¼ hr later, the trail ascends rather more steeply through a valley notch that is soon flanked on your right by rocks. At a small col (¼ hr) the trail levels out again and forks (trail No 27 forks off left). Trail No 6 leads slightly right as it heads towards the col between Teide and Montaña Blanca and, after a good quarter of an hour, begins to climb more steeply again across the pumice slopes.

After a 10-minute ascent, distinct traces of a path cross the trail (30m further on, the descent route for the way back, turns off right, trail No 22). Some minutes later, by two metal posts, the path merges with the Teide roadway ❹, ascending from the left from the Cañadas road ('Sendero 7'). Climbing the roadway in wide bends, pass the **Huevos del Teide** ❺ – along the trail's edge, you may also find some extremely rare Teide violets as well

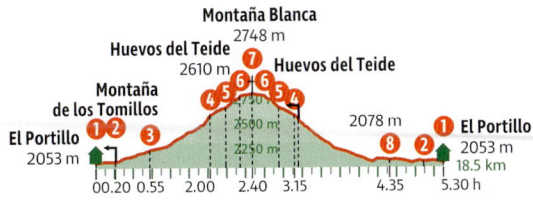

as blue Teide bugloss (echium auberianum).

After half an hour the sign-posted ascent trail to the Teide summit branches off to the right ❻ but stay left along the path that leads past a huevo, as high as a house, to the summit plateau of **Montaña Blanca** ❼ 10 minutes). From there enjoy a sweeping panoramic view of the Cañadas and the Teide ascent trail.

Now walk back for a good half an hour along the ascent trail until trail No 22 turns off left to the Cañada de los Guancheros ❹ (*white/yellow*, just under 5 mins from the Teide roadway). It heads directly towards the Fortaleza and after 150m leads immediately left past two Teide 'eggs'. Some minutes later, the path

Descent towards Fortaleza.

keeps left through a few crags and descends immediately afterwards to the right into a valley where it continues downhill. Three quarters of an hour later, ignore trail No 33 forking off to the left. A good 10 minutes after that, the path forks just before the **Cañada de los Guancheros** – continue right here along trail No 22.

Teide violets beside the trail.

The path leads to the edge of the plain and 3 minutes later ascends to a plateau (a good 5 minutes). It keeps to the left across the plateau and after a good 10 minutes merges with an intersecting trail ❽ (No 1). You could make a detour on the left to the Fortaleza (½ hr, see Walk 76), but turn right and, not quite a half an hour later, pass the **Roque del Peral** (afterwards, left at a fork), to return to **El Portillo** ❶.

↗ 1400m | ↘ 1400m | 18.7km

7.00 hrs

Pico del Teide, 3718m

TOP 86

Ascent to the highest mountain in Spain

The brightly gleaming, in winter sometimes snow-covered, Pan de Azúcar ('sugar loaf'), combined with the first-hand experience of a still active, sulphur vapour-whisped volcano, and last but not least, the thrill of being on the highest mountain in the Canary Islands, in fact, the highest in Spain – all this adds up to the fascination of this marvellous summit – but one thing certainly takes the prize: the almost unlimited panorama over Tenerife and, in good visibility, over the entire Canarian archipelago as far as Africa. It is therefore no wonder that the ascent of Teide is a dream pursued by many Tenerife holidaymakers. To get the absolute maximum out of the summit experience, walkers bent on conquering the peak would do well to divide the four-hour Teide ascent into a two-day trek: on the afternoon of the first day, negotiate the strenuous ascent to the Altavista hut. On the following day, begin before daybreak so as to arrive at the summit before sunrise – an unforgettable natural spectacle: within a few minutes, degree by degree, the rising sun bathes the entire island in a deep-red light – at first, Teide, then the caldera rim mountains and finally the Cañadas and the Anaga range – now Teide's shadow is cast all the way to the neighbouring island of La Gomera, 50km away – sensational!

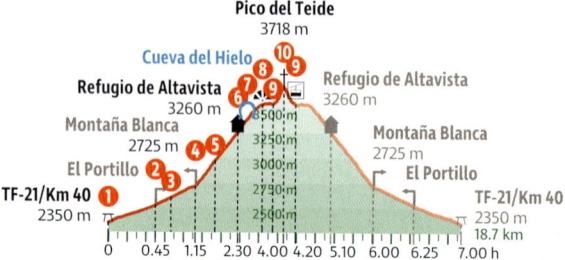

Starting point: Cañadas road TF-21 at Km 40.5, 2350m (between El Portillo, 8km, and the Teleférico, 2.5km; or 1 hr via trail No 39), at the junction of the roadway, towards Teide (signpost). Bus stop for the 342, 348.
Height difference: 1400m (a good 900m to the Refugio de Altavista).
Grade: as far as Montaña Blanca, a pleasant ascent along a roadway then a frequently steep scree trail; the final summit approach should definitely not be undertaken in stormy weather (some stretches are precipitous). In the winter months, expect frequent snow and sheets of ice as well, frozen rock-solid, making the ascent much more difficult and even requiring special equipment like crampons and an ice axe. In inclement weather (fog, snow, ice, storm), we strongly recommend that you do not attempt the Teide ascent. Also, do not take altitude sickness lightly: if, during the ascent, you experience headache, nausea and dizziness, take a rest break – if the symptoms persist, we recommend that you turn back.
Refreshment and Accommodation: Refugio de Altavista, 3260m. The hut was established in 1893 and **is closed until further notice** (tel. +34 922 010 440 or +34 922 533 720, 60 beds, linen/ woollen blankets are available; cooking facilities, dishes, beverage and coffee vending machine, internet access (WiFi); now and again no water). Reserving well in advance is an absolute must (!) at www.volcanoteide.com (especially crowded from June–November).
Cable car: the Teleférico (first summit ascent at 9 am, last return to the valley at 5 pm) is closed during storms and when the peak is covered with snow and/or ice – before starting, be sure to inquire if the cable car is running if you intend to use it to return (tel. +34 922 010 445 or +34 922 533 720).
Important notes: the trail from the cable car summit station to the peak (Telesforo Bravo) is closed due to conservation concerns. All walkers not wanting to forego the summit must apply in advance for a special permit (be sure to reserve many weeks or even months in advance!) at www.reservasparquesnacionales.es or at the Oficina del Parque Nacional, C/ Sixto Perera González nº 25, 38300 El Mayorazgo / La Orotava (Mon–Fri 9am–2pm; PassKopien mitbringen; bring copies of passports); if snowy/icy conditions, tel. +34 922 29 01 29/83 to enquire beforehand.
If you are staying overnight at the Altavista hut, you do not need a permit, however, you must quit the summit trail no later than 9 am. Warm clothing, wind and rain gear, gloves and hat (even in summer) as well as a good sunscreen, are essential. Sufficient food and drink must be taken along since the Refugio de Altavista is not catered. For an early morning ascent from the hut to the summit, a simple torch or a head torch is required.
Linking tip: with Walks 85 and 87.

A sign of bad weather – Teide summit covered in cloud.
Below: View back from Estancia de los Alemanes to Montaña Blanca.

The signposted roadway leading to Teide (No 7; after 100m, a barrier) begins at Km 40.5 on the **Cañadas road** ❶ (parking, do not leave valuables in your car!). The roadway ascends pleasantly across slopes of light beige-coloured pumice sand. 15 mins later, ignore a roadway forking off to the right (No 27), and 25 mins after that, by two metal posts, trail No 6/PR TF 41 (*white/yellow*) merges sharply from the right, coming from El Portillo ❷ (see Walk 85). The roadway now ascends in wide bends across the bright pumice slopes of Montaña Blanca and, after a few bends, passes the **Huevos del Teide** ❸ ('Eggs of Teide'). After a total of 1¼ hrs, at an elevation of about 2700m and not far from the summit of **Montaña Blanca** (10 mins from the turn-off), the signposted path (No 7) to Refugio de Altavista branches off to the right ❹.

The path ascends in steep zigzags across an ochre-coloured scree slope. About half an hour later, you have left the steepest part behind and reach a small level area on the slope with gigantic, round boulders, the Estancia de los Ingleses ('Abode of the English') — and a few minutes later, yet another, the Estancia de los Alemanes ❺ ('Abode of the Germans'). Subsequently, the trail leads through a vast field of broom, which you leave to the left after 15 mins of walking. Continue uphill in zigzags to then ascend rather more steeply and reach the **Refugio de Altavista** ❻, 3260m (½ hr), which appears at the last moment (only a metal stake near the hut can be seen before that).

To the left of the hut, the broad, in places stone-paved trail continues to the summit, ascending at times steeply and leading across a lava flow. Not quite 20 mins later, immediately after a sharp left hand bend, a path branches off to the right, through lava boulders to the nearby **Cueva del Hielo** ❼ (1 min; the entrance is closed — in the 'Cave of Ice' icicles hang

View down into Las Cañadas – Roques de García in the middle.

On the summit – view of the neighbouring islands of La Gomera, El Hierro and La Palma.

from the walls and snow can be found almost all year round). The passages of the extensive lava tube are at least 50m long.

Returning back from the cave, continue ascending the main trail. The Pan de Azúcar ('Sugar Loaf'), the brightly gleaming summit cap of Pico del Teide, now comes into view. Not quite a half an hour later, reach a level stretch on the slope, the Rambleta, and here meet up with an intersecting panoramic trail (No 11), along which you can find numerous fumaroles. 50m on the right, you can reach the **Mirador de la Fortaleza** ❽ which offers a beautiful view of the eastern island and especially of the Orotava Valley. Heading in the other direction, you will come to the **mountain station** ❾ for the Teide cable car, 3555m (a good ¼ hr) and further on to the Mirador de Pico Viejo (No 12, 15 minutes).

The final ascent to the summit.

50m before the mountain station, a steep trail (No 10) branches off right leading up to the summit. This is also stone-paved in places and, in the uppermost stretch, somewhat exposed. Bearing right at the rim of the light-coloured crater, filled with hot sulphur vapours, arrive at the summit of **Pico del Teide** ❿ to relish a nearly boundless view of Tenerife and the outlying islands.

↗ 70m | ↘ 1480m | 10.6km

87 From Teide via Pico Viejo, 3135m, to the Parador

4.30 hrs

Long descent over scree-covered lava flows and soft pumice paths

Without exaggeration, Pico Viejo, the western secondary peak of Teide and, at 3135m, the second highest summit on the island, can be called one of Tenerife's greatest. With a diameter of 800m, the massive crater is not only by far the largest on the island – it also offers a unique volcanic symphony of colour: in it's depths, the palette spans from the deepest black to red and ochre and even turquoise. The descent route described here leads in the upper section across volcanic terrain of rock and scree. From Pico Viejo, you can then look forward to a wonderful path of sandy pumice that runs for the most part gently downhill to the Roques de García. In order to enhance the experience, we strongly recommend combining this walk with the Teide ascent (see Walk 86) and staying overnight at the Refugio de Altavista.

Starting point: mountain station of the Teide cable car, 3555m (Teleférico valley terminus, 2356m, at Km 42.5 on the Cañadas road; first service to the summit at 9 am, last return trip to the valley at 5 pm, expect a long wait). No service during storms or when the peak is covered in snow and/or ice – therefore, check in advance if the cable car is running (tel. +34 922 010 445 or +34 922 533 720).

Destination: Parador Nacional de las Cañadas, 2151m (bus stop for the 342 and 348).

Grade: up to Pico Viejo a demanding walk on a sometimes indistinct path over lava and scree slopes. The path requires absolute surefootedness and, especially during periods of poor visibility, a good sense of orientation. A predominently leisurely walk from Pico Viejo. During the winter months expect snow and/or ice which make the descent considerably more difficult. During unfavourable weather conditions (fog, snow, storm), we strongly advise you not to attempt this mountain walk.

Refreshment/accommodation: along the way no opportunity for food or accommodation – in combination with the Teide ascent (2-day walk), accommodation possible in the Refugio de Altavista, 3260m (2024 closed, see Walk 86).

Important notes: warm clothing, wind and rain gear, gloves, a hat (even in summer) and a good sunscreen are recommended. Bring sufficient provisions and enough to drink, especially when staying overnight in the Refugio de Altavista.

Tip: if you arrive by rental car, it is best to park at the Parador Nacional (good overnight accommodation available here) and take the 342 bus to the Teleférico or to the turn-off for the Teide ascent path (when combined with Walk 86).

Linking tip: with Walks 86 and 88.

From the **mountain station** ❷ of the Teide cable car follow the left hand (west) branch of the stone-paved Rambleta trail (No 12) and after 15 mins, reach the **Mirador de Pico Viejo** ❸. The trail ends here and a path (distinct at the outset; No 9, cairns) begins to the left, descending across lava flows. Initially, this leads along the wall of a lava flow and then, 20 mins later, descends to the right into a volcanic valley. Subsequently, the route continues to descend over a wall of lava. 15 mins later, the path descends to the right. A good half an hour after that, meet up with a gentle, downward sloping, pumice flank for a pleasant descent. 10 minutes later, reach the saddle between the Pico Viejo and Teide ❹ – here, an excursion to the right along an (almost) traceless route is worthwhile onto the main summit of th **Pico Viejo** ❺, 3135m (¼ hr; a marvellous view of the crater and of Teide). 5 minutes later, at the foot of the Pico Viejo, reach a distinct fork in the trail with rows of stones on a pumice terrain. Here, you could turn right onto trail No 9 for an excursion to the edge of Pico Viejo's crater (10 minutes; the trail runs left across the dark volcanic scree slope; after a few minutes, ascend to the right at the fork).

Back at the trail junction, continue the descent down along trail No 23 turning off diagonally left. It leads comfortably downhill across the pumice slope, strewn with rocks, into a little gorse-filled valley and is sometimes edged with stones. A good 10 mins later, cross over a lava wall to the left and descend the little neighbouring valley over pumice sand and through gorse bushes. Another 5 mins later, a rocky lava field is crossed to the left, heading straight for a huge lava 'bomb', as high as a house, which you pass to the right ❻ (be careful: at the fork just before the vulcanic bomb turn left; do not keep straight on along the wall of brown lava). Soon after cross over a little pumice valley and another lava wall, behind which the path descends again to the right. 25m on, go left through a small valley that leads downhill in the direction of Roques de García. This is the pattern you now follow: again and again, the trail crosses left over a ridge of lava to descend ever lower down through the little valley that follows – always keep slightly left towards the Roques de García. At the end, the trail runs across marvellous lava formations. After a total of 2 hrs, the trail merges with the Roques de García circular trail ❼ (No 3; 50m on the right, the Roques Blancos). Turn left along this trail beside the fabulous cluster of crags to the **Mirador de la Ruleta** ❽ (a good 20 mins) and across the road to the **Parador Nacional** ❾ (a good 5 mins). If you need to get back to your car: it's 4km along the main road to the cable car station or 6.5km to the turn-off of the Teide roadway (a more pleasant but also longer alternative is to take trail No 19 and – from Teleférico – No 39, away from the road).

Long descent over scree-covered lava flows and soft pumice paths.

↗ 1180m | ↘ 1180m | 14.0km

6.15 hrs

From the Mirador de Chío onto Pico Viejo, 3135m

88

Fabulous, but rather demanding route onto Teide's neighbour

What is to be done when the ascent to Teide is closed due to snow and ice? The route across the western flank onto the 600m lower secondary peak quickly becomes snow-free and is also an attractive alternative, not least due to the view across the massive lava flows of the Teno mountains! The trail descends close to the Narices del Teide (Noses of Teide), enormous secondary volcanoes on the southern slopes of Pico Viejo.

Starting point: Mirador de Chío (also: Mirador Narices del Teide), 2090m, at Km 3.3 on the Boca Tauce – Chío road (TF-38; no bus connection, nearest bus stop for the 342 at Boca Tauce, 2055m, at Km 53 on the Cañadas road, 35 mins).
Grade: long, strenuous alpine walk that demands surefootedness and a certain degree of route-finding skill (the path is not always that clear). Trekking poles would be useful. Only recommended in good visibility and stable weather conditions.
Alternative: from den Narices del Teide to the Boca Tauce (2 hrs): at the Narices (see below), turn right onto the trail and descend to the rim of the crater, from which, 30m on, a distinct path turns off to the left. It initially runs across the slope, then descends more steeply across the scree-blanketed slope, 10 minutes later, crossing a trail coming from Narices. The path continues downhill in a relatively straight line. 10 minutes later, you can see some vulcanic 'bombs' in the neighbouring cleft on your right hand side (there are also some solitary ones along the path). A good ½ hr from the Narices crater, merge with a roadway (about 2300m) which you could already make out from further above. It leads gently downhill – go right at a junction after a good 15 mins and, almost 10 minutes later, take a shortcut across two bends in the road. 20 minutes later, a roadway joins from sharp left – then, after a total of 1¼ hrs, the roadway merges with the Cañadas road from Chío. It's another 5 mins left to the junction at the Boca Tauce, while to the right it's 2.7km (½ hr) to the Mirador de Chío.
Linking tip: with Walk 87.

A trail starts at the **Mirador de Chío** ❶, sometimes flanked by stones (No 9), and runs parallel to the road in the direction of Chío. 20 mins later, cross a final lava field, then join a roadway coming from the left (5 mins from Km 4.8 on the TF-38) and enter an open pine wood. 3 mins afterwards, almost at the edge of the little wood, a distinct trail branches off right (No 9) in the direction of Pico Viejo ❷. Ascend comfortably across lava sand uphill and, 10 mins later, keep left to cross a high terrain with stone walls. Here trail No 38 to the Cuevas Negras forks off to the left ❸ (see Walk 19) – we, however, keep to trail No 9. Now, climb up through a valley notch between two ridges of lava (on the right above, a lava tube) and then leave this a good 15 mins later to the left to traverse over to the next small notch. Shortly afterwards, arrive at a wide, flat valley landscape which runs up to the foot of Pico Viejo. On the right, you can clearly see the Narices del Teide. Keeping left, the trail leads uphill through some valley grooves (ignore two minor turn-offs to the left) and after about 20 mins passes a small crater on your left. Immediately after that, the trail forks: trail No 9 branches off right ❹ – an alternative for walkers who prefer to give the summit a miss and shorten the walk. Otherwise stay on the path that continues straight ahead. Pass a few small volcanic vents, keep left up to a ridge, the **Lomo de Chío**, and then pass another deep crater, **El Calderón** ❺ (do not go too close to the edge!).

The trail now steepens as it climbs in a straight line up the scree ridge and, after a quarter of an hour, passes just to the right of a beige-coloured rocky outcrop. In the following rather confusing terrain keep a good lookout for the trail (cairns)! A half an hour later, keeping slightly to the right and next to some gorse bushes, reach a beige-coloured sand and scree ridge. The route of the trail is now clear again: first in a direct line, then keeping slightly right uphill continue on the right past a volcanic vent. A good 5 minutes later pass a small, reddish-ochre coloured volcanic vent, then keep left, steeply ascending over sand and scree to a striking light beige **rib of rock** ❻ at a height of about 3000m. From here, climb up left through the small field of gorse then ascend over scree to the western rim of the crater of **Pico Viejo** ❼, 3014m (10 mins, breathtaking view across the huge crater and the main summit of Pico Viejo to Teide, see photo above).

Back at the light beige rib of rock ❻ turn eastwards towards the slope and ascend in a steady diagonal traverse through the slope (the final metres require easy scrambling) to the rim of the crater up above and to the summit plateau at **Pico Sur** ❽, 3106m (½ hr; a cairn at the highest point). At the western end of the plateau, a stunning view awaits: down below, you can see the deepest point of the Pico Viejo crater, a drop of 200 vertical metres from here. On the other side of the crater, take in the splendid colours of the Narices del Teide. Practically the whole of the western island lies at your feet – in the west, the Teno mountains, also extensive parts of the south-west coast and the Cañadas, furrowed with extremely vivid, three-dimensional lava flows, and all the way to the Roques de García. From the summit cairn continue another 30m further and turn right between two large cairns along a distinct path, waymarked with more

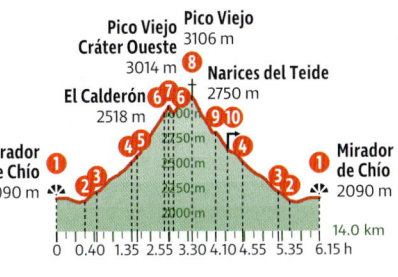

cairns (in places also *green* waymarkers) that leads down the lava slope keeping slightly right, always heading towards the Narices del Teide. The path soon runs close to the left edge of a longish field of gorse, then turns right to cross over it. Now continue downhill over volcanic scree and sand. Above the largest (about 100m in diameter) and uppermost crater of the **Narices del Teide** ❾ the trail forks: straight ahead, trail No 28 descends to the rim of the crater (see Alternative) however, we follow trail No 9 to the right. The trail traverses the slope above the crater and then continues descending. 15 minutes later, the path forks directly in front of a black, volcanic cone ❿. Bear to the right here via trail 9 which, 25 mins later, merges with the ascent trail ❹. Follow this back to the starting point ❶ (1¼ hrs). Hardy hikers can also turn left at the fork ❿ to descend through the steep

Indisputable proportions of height – Pico Viejo's summit (left) and Teide, from Pico Sur.

flank of the volcanic cone and reach the Mirador de Chío (1¼ hrs; initially a distinct path, but later, almost no path at all!): After a good 10 minutes the path, waymarked with cairns, turns towards the broad valley next to the scree-covered ridge but soon after, the path returns back to the scree-blanketed slope. A few minutes later, the downhill 'scree-run' comes to an end. The path now leads on the right past a group of rocks and descends into the valley, heading directly towards the Mirador de Chío. After a good 10 mins, reach the edge of a jet-black lava flow. 20m on, a barely perceptable path branches off to the left (you could also descend along the lava flow, but this is reserved for bravehearts!), crosses over the lava flow and continues downhill in a little valley notch between two lava flows. 20 mins later, the path is no longer very distinct as it passes a 5-metre circle enclosed by stones – the nearby **Mirador de Chío** ❶ cannot be missed (10 mins).

INDEX

0.4.0 68

A
Abache 102
Acantilado de Los Gigantes 82, 130
Adeje 138
Afur 213, 215, 219
Aguamansa 36, 38, 40, 44, 46, 49
Aldea Blanca 165
Almáciga 228, 230, 236
Amarillo Golf 158
Anaga 182
Arafo 52
Araya 62
Arco del Jurado 181
Arco de Tajao 178
Arenas Negras 260
Arguayo 116
Arico Nuevo 173
Arico Viejo 177
Aripe 133
Arona 145, 147, 150
Atalaya de los Ingleses 251

B
Bajamar 184, 186, 187
Baracán 96
Barranco Achacay 63
Barranco de Anosma 241
Barranco de Antequera 253
Barranco de Bijagua 179
Barranco de Bucarón 85
Barranco de Cuevas Negras 86
Barranco de Igueste 244, 248, 253
Barranco de Ijuana 244
Barranco de la Goleta 186, 187
Barranco de la Linde 180
Barranco de la Magdalena 279
Barranco de las Arenas 276
Barranco de las Cuevas 100
Barranco de las Goteras 152
Barranco de las Mesas 272
Barranco de la Sobaquera 100
Barranco de la Torre 97
Barranco del Chorrillo 272
Barranco del Infierno 142
Barranco del Monte 97
Barranco de los Cochinos 85
Barranco del Rey 140, 145, 148, 152
Barranco del Río 193, 199, 276
Barranco del Tomadero 198
Barranco de Masca 109
Barranco de Ruíz 33, 72
Barranco de Santiago 117, 129
Barranco de Santos 29
Barranco de Taborno 211
Barranco de Tahodío 202
Barranco de Tamadite 213, 219
Barranco Las Goteras 64
Barranco Madre del Agua 37, 38, 41
Barranco Seco 109, 126, 129, 191
Barrio de la Alegría 200
Batán de Abajo 192, 199
Bejía 191
Benijo 230, 236
Boca del Paso 137, 142
Boca Tauce 291
Buenavista del Norte 90, 97

C
Cabeza del Viento 201
Cabezo del Tejo 233
Café Vista Paraíso 32
Caleta del Sordo 179
Camino de Candelaria 43, 45, 50
Camino de la Costa 30, 33
Camino de Las Lecheras 26
Camino de los Guanches 46
Camino Suárez 145
Campamento Madre del Agua 169
Cañada de la Grieta 264
Cañada de las Pilas 264
Cañada del Capricho 264, 268
Cañada de los Guancheros 69, 256, 282
Cañadas del Teide 254
Canal de Chabuco 206, 207
Casa Arenas de Tenesco 175
Casa Carlos 203, 205, 210, 218, 221
Casa de Suárez 146, 153
Casa Forestal de Anaga 222, 224, 226
Casa Fuset 189
Casa Galindo 272
Casa Santiago 200
Casas de Araza 104
Casas de la Cumbre 200, 224
Casas del Contador 176
Casas de Tamadaya 174
Caserío de La Hoya 164
Caserío Las Casas 101
Catalanes 200
Catedral 267
Chamorga 232, 234, 236, 244
Chanajiga 67, 68
Chinamada 196, 198
Chinobre 232, 247
Chinyero 79
Chirche 133
Choza Bermeja 45
Choza Chimoche 44, 48, 50
Choza El Topo 37, 41

Choza Enrique Talg 67
Choza Pedro Gil 36, 38, 41, 45, 50
Choza Piedra de los Pastores 69, 71
Choza Viera y Clavijo 69, 71
Conde 149
Corral del Niño 258
Corral Quemado 69, 71
Costa del Silencio 157
Cruz de Fregel 69, 70, 257
Cruz de Gala 89, 93
Cruz de Hilda 93, 114
Cruz del Carmen 197
Cruz de Misioneros 122
Cruz de Tea 166
Cuesta de la Villa 32
Cueva del Hielo 286
Cueva del Lino 199
Cueva Roja 29
Cuevas Negras 80
Cumbre de Baracán 95
Cumbre de Bolico 93, 114
Cumbre del Carrizal 92, 114
Cumbre Dorsal 24, 51, 55

D
Degollada de Abreo 263
Degollada de Cherfé 104
Degollada de Guajara 263, 269, 276
Degollada de la Mesa 89, 113
Degollada de las Hijas 200
Degollada del Cedro 70, 257
Degollada de los Frailitos 145, 147
Degollada de los Horneros 28
Degollada de Mesa de Tejina 185
Degollada de Tejera 123
Degollada de Ucanca 270, 275
Degollada Pasito del Corcho 253

E
El Bailadero 228
El Chorro 216
El Contador 176
El Draguillo 230, 237
El Frontón 212
El Majimial 225
El Médano 160
El Molledo 117, 124
El Palmar 92, 94
El Patriarca 265
El Peladero 191
El Pelotón 225
El Pinar 167
El Portillo 69, 256, 258, 260, 262, 263, 280
El Puertito 135
El Refugio 140, 146
El Rincón 32
El Seco 172
El Socorro 61
Embarcadero de Bijagua 179
Erjos 86, 88
Ermita de Los Baldíos 120
Estancia de los Ingleses 286

F
Faro de Anaga 234, 238
Faro de Punta Rasca 156
Finca de Guergue 106
Finca Ramallo 132
Fortaleza 71, 257
Fuente de El Chorrillo 144
Fuente de las Pilas 146
Fuente del Til 66
Fuente de Tamaide 163
Fuente Pedro 69
Fuga de Los Cuatro Reales 59

G
Galería Chimoche 44
Galería de la Junquera 126, 130
Galería de la Puente 50
Galería La Paloma 56
Galería Union de la Zarza 69
Garachico 76
Golf del Sur 158

GR 131 145, 150, 271, 276
Guajara 270, 276
Guamaso 261
Guaza 155
Guergue path 104
Guía de Isora 132
Güímar 56
Güímar Valley 24

H
Huevos del Teide 281, 285

I
Icod el Alto 69, 72
Ifonche 140, 143, 152
Iguaste de San Andrés 244, 248, 250
Izaña 259

L
La Caldera 36, 38, 40, 44, 46
La Caleta 134
La Cancelilla 247
La Cumbrecilla 217, 223
La Cumbrilla 234, 236, 244
Ladera de Güímar 56
Ladera de Tigaiga 68
La Ensillada 232, 247
La Galería 208
La Laguna 27
La Montañeta 78
La Orotava 32
La Quinta 136
La Rambla 33, 74
Las Aguas 74
Las Américas 83
Las Arenas Negras 78
Las Bodegas 244
Las Carboneras 194, 198, 210
Las Casillas 245, 253
Las Cuevas Negras 86
Las Eras 180
Las Escaleras 196, 198, 210
Las Galletas 155, 157
Las Lagunetas 92
Las Manchas 116
Las Moradas 85
Las Palmas 238
Las Portelas 84, 92
Las Vegas 170

Some more enjoyable walks …

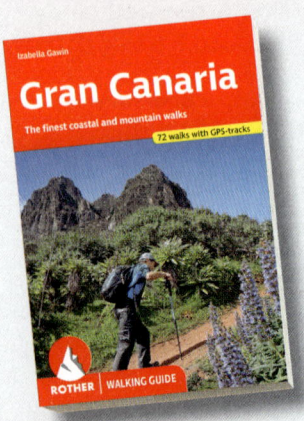
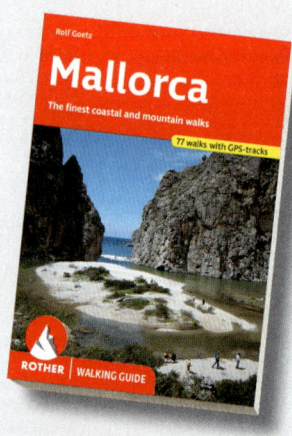
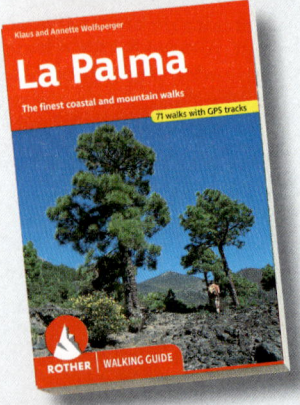
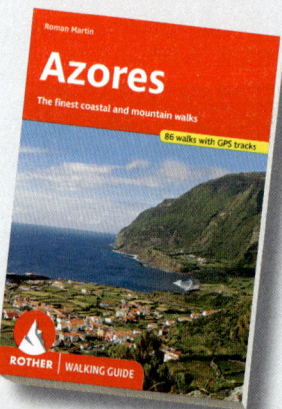

WWW.ROTHER.DE

La Vica 93, 114
Llano de Maja 260
Lomo Bermejo 244
Lomo de la Resbala 42
Lomo de Las Bodegas 240, 242, 244
Lomo de los Dragos 197
Lomo de Tablada 106
Loro Parque 33
Los Abrigos 157
Los Azulejos 267
Los Brezos 63
Los Carrizales 102
Los Cristianos 83
Los Escurriales 273
Los Gigantes 83, 131
Los Órganos 36, 38, 41
Los Silos 84

M

María Jiménez 206
Masca 90, 104, 112
Masca Gorge 108
Mesa de Tejina 185
Minas de San José 265
Mirador Aguaide 196
Mirador Bailadero 227
Mirador de Chío 291
Mirador de La Centinela 164
Mirador de La Crucita 51, 55
Mirador de la Fortaleza 287
Mirador de la Paz 31
Mirador de la Ruleta 266, 290
Mirador de Masca 104
Mirador de Pico Viejo 289
Mirador de San Pedro 33, 35
Mirador El Asomadero 67, 69
Mirador El Lance 69
Mirador El Mazapé 73
Mirador La Corona 69
Mirador Pico del Inglés 200, 203, 205
Montaña Amarilla 157
Montaña Bilma 119

Montaña Blanca 282, 285
Montaña Carrasco 144
Montaña de Guama 123
Montaña de Guaza 155
Montaña de la Botija 81
Montaña de La Crucita 51, 55
Montaña de la Hoya 116
Montaña del Ángel 116
Montaña de las Arenas 55, 276
Montaña del Limón 48
Montaña de los Tomillos 281
Montaña de Malpasito 159
Montaña Grande 61
Montaña Pasajirón 263
Montaña Pelada 160
Montaña Reventada 81
Montaña Roja 161
Montaña Samara 80, 81
Montaña Tafada 235
Monte del Agua 84
Moquinal 188
Morra del Corcho 61
Morro de la Galera 90

N

Narices del Teide 294
Nariz de García 144

O

Órganos high mountain trail 42
Orotava Valley 24
Ortiz 176

P

Paisaje Lunar 168, 273
Palm-Mar 156
Palo Blanco 66
Parador Nacional 262, 266, 268, 275, 289
Parque Nacional de las Cañadas del Teide 254
Peña Friolera 228
Pico del Inglés 200, 203, 205
Pico del Teide 68, 254, 287
Pico Verde 89, 113
Pico Viejo 289, 292

Piedras Amarillas 264, 268
Pino del Guirre 170
Pista de las Hiedras 199
Pista de los Dragos 197, 199
Playa Colmenares 158
Playa de Anosma 241
Playa de Antequera 252
Playa de Barranco Seco 127
Playa de Benijo 236
Playa de Ijuana 243
Playa de la Entrada 61
Playa de La Fajana 34
Playa del Ancón 32
Playa de la Tejita 161
Playa del Bollullo 32
Playa de Los Guios 131
Playa de los Troches 194
Playa del Socorro 33, 68
Playa de Martiánez 30
Playa de Masca 110
Playa de San Blas 158
Playa de San Roque 222, 229, 236
Playa de Tamadite 214, 216
Playa Diego Hernández 135
Playa Paraíso 135
PR TF 02 201, 203, 210
PR TF 03 224
PR TF 04 228
PR TF 04.1 228
PR TF 05 244
PR TF 06 231, 234, 236
PR TF 06.1 234, 238
PR TF 06.2 230, 236
PR TF 06.3 231
PR TF 08 213, 215, 222, 229
PR TF 09 210, 212
PR TF 10 194, 197
PR TF 10.1 196
PR TF 11 189, 190, 199
PR TF 12 187
PR TF 12.1 188
PR TF 35 38, 41, 44
PR TF 35.2 38

PR TF 40 65
PR TF 40.1 65
PR TF 41 68, 69
PR TF 43 77
PR TF 51 89, 95, 100, 114
PR TF 52 84, 86
PR TF 52.2 92
PR TF 53 86
PR TF 53.1 87
PR TF 54 84
PR TF 56 92, 113
PR TF 57 95
PR TF 58 97
PR TF 59 92, 114
PR TF 65 115, 117, 121, 123, 131
PR TF 65.1 117
PR TF 65.2 121
PR TF 65.3 117, 125
PR TF 65.4 118
PR TF 65.5 116
PR TF 70 133
PR TF 70.1 133
PR TF 71 137, 142
PR TF 71.1 136
PR TF 71.2 137, 141, 143
PR TF 72 271
PR TF 83 166
PR TF 83.1 171
PR TF 83.3 170
PR TF 83.4 171
PR TF 86 176, 263
PR TF 86.1 176
PR TF 86.2 174
PR TF 86.3 175
Puertito de Güímar 60
Puerto de Erjos 89
Puerto de la Cruz 24, 30, 33
Puerto de Santiago 83
Punta Brava 33
Punta del Hidalgo 189, 190, 194
Punta de Teno 101

R
Rambleta 287, 289
Realejo Alto 65
Refugio de Altavista 284, 286
Refugio de Las Arenas 53

Risco Blanco 117, 124
Risco de la Vera 63
Risco del Muerto 170
Risco Miguel 67
Risco path 97
Roque Alonso 220
Roque Bermejo 239
Roque Chiñaco 101
Roque de Anambra 233
Roque de Dentro 238
Roque de Enmedio 228
Roque de la Fortaleza 200
Roque de las Ánimas 228
Roque de las Bodegas 222, 229, 236
Roque de los Brezos 140, 146
Roque del Peral 256, 282
Roque de Taborno 211
Roque Dos Hermanos 194
Roque El Toscón 98
Roque Icoso 234
Roque Imoque 140, 146
Roque La Fortaleza 90
Roque Negro 220
Roques de Anaga 238

S
Salto de las Yedras 176
San Juan de La Rambla 33, 74
San Juan del Reparo 77
San Miguel 162
San Miguel de Tajao 178
San Miguel Marina 158
Santa Cruz 27, 200, 203, 206
Santiago del Teide 104, 112, 117, 118, 120
SL TF 206 132
SL TF 218 148
SL TF 231 162
SL TF 231.1 165
SL TF 294 62
SL TG 01 185
Sombrero de Chasna 278

T
Tabaiba Pass 96
Taborno 203, 210, 212
Taganana 216, 223, 229

Tahodío 202
Tajao 178
Tamaimo 115, 121, 128
Taucho 136
Tegueste 187
Teide 68, 254, 287
Teide cable car 262, 284, 287, 289
Teleférico del Teide 262, 284, 287, 289
Teno 82
Teno Alto 95, 99, 100
Teno Bajo 101
Tigaiga 68
Til de Los Pavos 66

V
Valle Brosque 225
Valle Crispín 207
Valle de La Orotava 24
Valle Grande 206
Valle Jiménez 29
Valleseco 203
Ventanas de Güímar 56
Vento 147
Vilaflor 150, 271, 274, 277
Villa de Arico 177
Volcán de Fasnia 259
Volcán Garachico 79
Vueltas de Taganana 222

Cover photo: Roques de García – Roque Cinchado with Teide in the background.
Frontispiece (page 1): Descending through volcanic cinder to the Paisaje Lunar – one of the classic routes on the island.
Page 22: Roque Imoque near Arona: one of the south's most striking peaks.
All 311 photos by the authors, except for the photo on page 234 (Jan Kostura).

Cartography:
Small walking maps to a scale of 1:50,000 / 1:75,000 and overview maps to a scale of 1:400,000 © Freytag & Berndt, Vienna.

Translation: Tom Krupp and Gill Round

Serial number: 4809

The descriptions of all the walks given in this guide are conscientiously made according to the best knowledge of the authors. The use of this guide is at one's own risk. As far as is legally permitted, no responsibility will be accepted for possible accidents, damage or injuries of any kind.

8th, completely revised edition 2024
© Bergverlag Rother GmbH, Munich
ISBN 978-3-7633-4844-2

We heartly welcome any suggestion for amendment to this walking guide! Please send an email to: bergverlag@rother.de

ROTHER BERGVERLAG · Keltenring 17 · D-82041 Oberhaching
tel. +49 89 608669-0 · rother.de